University of Pennsylvania School of Design
Department of Architecture
212 Meyerson Hall
210 S. 34th Street
Philadelphia, PA 19104-6311
215.898.5728

www.design.upenn.edu/architecture/graduate/work

INTRODUCTION
by Winka Dubbeldam, Chair

125 YEARS

Last year the Department of Architecture celebrated its 125th year! With over a century of experience in innovation, we continue this tradition by pushing our identity as a laboratory for ideas, expertise and innovations, a think tank for exchanges and debates across disciplinary boundaries, and a broadcast center engaging a growing audience and international network. We promote collaborations among our various programs, with other departments, and the University at large. We invite experts from the outside to dialogue with our students and faculty. We aim to prepare the next generation of leaders, ready to evolve the discipline and renew its capacity to be an important player in the complex set of problems we face today.

DIALOGUES 2016-17

Apart from our packed lecture series, we hosted two important Symposia. *"Under Pressure, an Urban Housing symposium"* initiated by Hina Jamelle, was held in October 2016. A group of 15 speakers, ranging from architects, developers, and cityplanners, dealt with subjects such as: *Super-Hot, New Domesticities*, and *Speculation*, the panels were moderated by Barry Bergdoll, Cliff Pearson, and Nader Tehrani.

The Spring featured the second symposium: the *"PennDESIGN Women in Architecture Symposium,"* organized by our women students. This was an in depth discussion on the role and input of women in architecture. The Keynote was by professor and architect Marion Weiss, and the panels were moderated by Joan Ockman, Daniela Fabricius, and Franca Trubiano, all at the Department of Architecture, PennDesign. This Symposium was featured in a Newsweek article relating to Women in Architecture. Our students received a special mention,"*The University of Pennsylvania's School of Design planned a Women in Architecture symposium specifically to address the subject, saying in a statement, that though "women comprise nearly half of architecture graduate programs in the United States, only 22 percent of licensed architects in the field are women and only 17 percent partners/ principals in architecture firms." It said it would launch a mentorship and networking scheme to increase incidence and visibility of women architects and "[cultivate] the next generation of leaders in the industry."*

RESEARCH

Architecture is experiencing an extraordinary renaissance in it's practice, fueled by many different sources: new technologies and materials; information technology; advances in engineering and manufacturing; globalization of culture, education and practice; crossovers with the sciences, visual arts and other design fields; a growing audience for design culture in general, and ecological architecture in particular; and a focus on creativity and innovation in leading schools around the world. At PennDesign we actively promote research, as we believe that education leads practice.

We founded an Advanced Research and Innovation Lab [ARI], that is at the forefront of advanced digital research & design; one that focuses on new design methodologies and future manufacturing through the interlinked intelligence of digital design, scripting, and robotics. We recently opened a brand new Robotic Lab with ABB.

We initiated a new Master of Science in Design [MSD] program, with a MSD-AAD [Advanced Architectural Design], an MSD-EBD [Environmental Building Design], and aim to open an MSD in Robotics in the next year. While the focus of this expansion is to deepen the pedagogical effectiveness of the program, it will also increase the offerings within Penn Design focused on design excellence, and rigorous research.

PRESSING MATTERS

At the same time, society faces many challenges, including global warming and environmental change, pollution and waste, transition to new energy and resource economies, the redistribution and reorganization of political and economic power worldwide; globalization of the construction and development industries; population growth, shrinkage and migration; urban intensification and attrition; privatization of public sector activities; and the transformation of cultural identities and social institutions. We seek to bring the expansion of expertise and creativity in architecture to bear on these challenges.

We will focus on social awareness and responsibility, and be a think tank for critical exchanges and advanced debates within and across disciplinary boundaries. We are a connective device through linking experts to students and faculty in dialogues, lectures, and publications, we engage a growing international audience in an increasing network of experts.

TO CONCLUDE

The primary mission of the Architecture Department is to educate architects through the development of the advanced design education combined with disciplinary skills, technological knowledge, and methods of inquiry into the professional practice of architecture. The Department of Architecture offers an Undergraduate major, a professionally accredited Master's degree, two post-professional Master's programs [MSS-AAD and the MSD-EBD], and a research-based Master of Science and Doctoral program. The Department is situated within a multi-disciplinary School of Design and a strong research University. This allows for many kinds of connections and specialized studies, including undergraduate minors, certificate studies at the Master's level, and dual degrees in a host of disciplines.

To further our expertise we have appointed and welcome three new tenure track faculty members: Robert Stuart Smith, Assistant professor in Architecture, Masoud Akbarzedah, Assistant professor in Architecture Structures, and Sophie Hochhäusl, Assistant professor in Architecture -History & Theory. They, together with our Standing and Associated Faculty, will be leading the Architecture Department towards a better and more responsive future.

Winka Dubbeldam, Assoc. AIA
Professor and Chair Department of Architecture
winka@design.upenn.edu

AUGUST 2016

Digiblast II and AAD Digital Workshop Orientations

Summer 2016 MSD AAD Digital Design Workshop taught by Ezio Blasetti and Danielle Willems - Mandatory Orientation Agenda

SEPTEMBER 2016

To Cairo with Amore
PennDesign Students at the Venice Biennale 2016.

Kolatan's Egyptian partners in the project included Eng. Ibrahim Mehlib, Former Prime Minister and Presidential Advisor, and Dr. Laila Iskandar. Formerly Minister of State for Urban Renewal and Informal Settlements in Egypt, and Minister of State for Environmental Affairs, Dr. Iskandar served as students' guide to the settlements and introduced them to other architects. "She has been an activist for the betterment of informal settlements for decades and was running the Maspero competition," explains Kolatan. The project was further supported by Architecture student Aly Abouzeid and his father, Medhat Abouzeid.
Faculty member Ferda Kolatan with students from his Cairo studio and Architecture Chair Winka Dubbeldam in Venice. Joining

SEPTEMBER 12TH, 2016
RECENT WORK

Minsuk Cho, Principal, Mass Studies, Seoul, South Korea
The Young Kyoon Jeong Lecture

Pixel House, Heyri Art Valley, Paju, Gyeonggi, Korea, 2003. Photography by Yong-Kwan Kim

SEPTEMBER 14TH, 2016
SUBPOP OR, STILL KEEPING IT ON THE DOWNLOW

Jason Payne, Principal, Hirsuta, Laurel Canyon, CA

'Rawhide', Joshua White; courtesy of SCI-Arc

them were Architecture student Aly Abouzeid, his father, Medhat Abouzeid, and Dr. Laila Iskandar.

cial space of tourism and its resulting hotels, its swimming pools, its lobbies, and the entrances to these things. This city is pretty dusty, and its also quite hot out. We spend a lot of time here walking around and visiting the main hotels of Havana, and then sometimes getting asked to leave those hotels, while other times being shown some indifference to our presence. When not being shooed out, we navigated the colonial courtyards, mezzanines and rooftops of these temporary tourist homes.

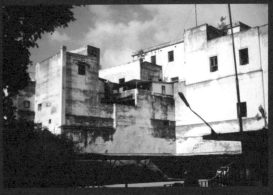

OCTOBER 2016

Francis Kere Lecture at PennDesign

Francis Kere lectured at PennDesign last week, and showed his impressive recent work. Chair Winka Dubbeldam, and Chair Richard Wesley, are shown here with Kere at the reception after. It was at the Philadelphia Museum of Art, which featured Kere's work.

Updates From The Chair

Winka Dubbeldam joined an international jury for the UIA award in X'ian, China last week. They judged over 300 proposals in one very long day. Winka gave a lecture afterwards at the University of X'ian for a packed audience on the Smart City.

700 Travel Studio Update

Havana, Cuba - Notes from Paul Preissner:

"We are in Havana, Cuba. We have come here to do a few things, but the most important thing was for us to be able to visit this city of 2million residents in the years before the start of mass tourism. Our studio is here studying the so-

Amir Shakib Arslan mosque, Moukhtarah Lebanon (photo Ieva Saudargaite)

Flip House, Shimlen , Lebanon (photo Ieva Saudargaite)

SEPTEMBER 21TH, 2016
GROUNDPLAY

Makram el Kadi, Partner, L.E.FT architects, Beirut Lebanon and NYC USA

PennDesign at AA Masterclass

The Chair joined PennDesign professor Homa Farjadi and students for their midterm at the Architectural Association in London, England. PennDesign has an ongoing exchange with the AA, where students study a full semester each Fall.

NOVEMBER 2016

PennDesign exchange with SNU of Seoul

John Hong and his students from Seoul, South Korea, are collaborating with the Design Studio of Simon Kim. They are visiting today and sharing a review. On the jury: John Hong, Simon Kim, Abigail Coover Hume, Winka Dubbeldam, Chair

DECEMBER 2016

Winka speaks at panel at Institute for Public knowledge, NYC

From the Institute for Public Knowledge: "Fast forward to the year 2100. New York, along with Phoenix, Beijing, Sao Paulo, Manila, and many more of the world's most populated cities, is irrevocably changed. Much of the earth's great middle swath is subject to droughts, wildfires, and desertification, while increasingly frequent super storms plague coastal areas, destroying precious agricultural lands by bringing seawater far inland. Where in the world shall we live, and what will

our built environments be like? The Institute for Public Knowledge's working group on Cities, Cultures, and Climate Change invites you to join us for a discussion with architect Vanessa Keith in celebration of the release of her new book, 2100: A Dystopian Utopia / The City After Climate Change. The author will be in discussion with ecologist Eric Sanderson and architect Winka Dubbeldam.

urbanNext

"The new normal is no longer new. It's where we are."
Winka Dubbeldam, Professor and Chair of the Department of Architecture, is the latest architect to sit down for an interview with the online platform urbanNext. She talks about tracking digital design to move beyond it, straddling critical theory and urbanism, and bridging the mass-produced and the virtual. With a stated mission of "expanding architecture to rethink cities," urbanNext has a deep library of videos that includes Reinier de Graaf, Mohsen Mostafavi and Saskia Sassen.

Winka Dubbeldam
The New Normal

SEPTEMBER 26TH, 2016
RECENT WORK

Francis Kéré, Principal and founder, Kéré Architecture
The Warren W. Cunningham Lecture

Gando School Library, Burkina Faso

Reuse, the house in Hasua Architecture is in constant growth. In a state of *is* becoming.

house=block=farm

House=Block=Farm

[AN] AFFORDACITY TOWARDS A FUTURE AFRICAN CITY

James George, Design Head, HTL/TAO, Lagos Nigeria and Johannesburg SA

OCTOBER 28TH, 2016
UNDER PRESSURE: URBAN HOUSING SYMPOSIUM

Existing between formal and informal systems and ranging widely in quality, typology, and audience, urban housing is a bellwether for economic, social, and political change. Housing's complexity and flexibility offers unique and exciting opportunities for architects, however, its source in private equity and public agencies often challenges its ambitions. Three panel discussions at PennDesign will focus on pressure points affecting urban housing: Super-Hot: high-pressure economic markets, New Domesticities: the changing nature of living and domesticity, and Speculation: new tools and technologies for design and fabrication. The symposium functions as a think tank for current topics under these influences by bringing together thought leaders working and writing in these arenas.

SYMPOSIUM CONVENED BY:

Hina Jamelle
Director. Contemporary
Architecture Practice
Director of Urban Housing.
University of Pennsylvania

Kutan Ayata
Partner/ Young & Ayata
Lecturer/ University
of Pennsylvania

Brian Phillips
Principal. ISA
Lecturer / University
of Pennsylvania

Graduate Assistants:
**Katie McBride,
Caleb White, Miguel Abaunza,
Alex Tahinos, Mark Chalhoub,
Insung Hwang, Jiateng Wang,
Adrian Emmanuel Subagyo,
David Harrop,
and Ricardo Hernandez-Perez.**

Panel 1 - SUPER HOT

As a major component in the global real estate market, urban housing is acutely subject to market speculations, consumer preferences, and financial crashes that characterize risk-based investment. In the world's fastest growing and highest value markets, housing takes on the characteristics of luxury brands, high-end amenities, super density, and new business models. There are also echo-effects that challenge expectations of supply, affordability, access, and urban patterns. As urban, financial, and political forces apply pressure on the entire spectrum of city dwellers, how do, can, and might architects re-act?

Introduction by **Hina Jamelle**
Barry Bergdoll (Moderator)
Martha Kelley

Patrik Schumacher
Mark Willis
Chris Sharples

Panel 2 - NEW DOMESTICITIES

Housing has become an insufficient concept to frame the complexities of twenty-first century domestic life. Private living space, once simply a retreat from the public sphere and work environment, has been radically transformed by the conflation of live and work, new family structures, and economic factors that are pushing toward new typologies and hybrids. Given these changing trends, how can and should architects help shape new possibilities for housing?

Introduction by **Brian Phillips**
Michael Bell
Mimi Hoang

Chad Ludeman
Clifford Pearson (Moderator)
Simone Tarantino

Panel 3 - SPECULATION

The discipline of architecture, especially through modernism, always produced new visions of the city through comprehensive concepts of urban housing. The shift to market economies relocated these efforts away from speculation on vast urban land to speculation on architectural objects. New lifestyles, technologies, and design tools are radicalizing the possibilities of urban housing. Fresh considerations of program, scale, material, fabrication, and form are redefining present and future visions. What are these new possibilities and how can they be deployed in ways that apply their own pressures to the emergence of new urban housing models?

Introduction by **Kutan Ayata**
Marcelo Spina
Neil Denari

Nader Tehrani (Moderator)
Laia Mogas
Kai-Uwe Bergmann

FO
DA
ON

UN
TI

FOUNDATION 501

The 501 Studio is the introductory course in the Master of Architecture Design Studio sequence. In contemporary pedagogy, design studio is the primary course in the preparation of the professional architect. Exercises and projects are designed to train the student so that the methodology gained will sustain the practitioner through the challenges of practice. More importantly, this methodology provides a framework of values and criticality to elevate the output of this practice to its highest expression.

The studio sequence involves carefully developed projects to introduce students to the first principles of material and its properties, shaped and formed in particular geometries, to produce space and enclosure that imparts meaning. Furthermore, the studio imparts the irreducible basics of architectural design media, its notations of communication, and their spaces of design.

Production requires learning of both techniques and strategies introduced through a series of design procedures. The design processes, in turn, requires the fluent use of both analog and computational tools -including those of digital modeling and fabrication. These techniques and strategies are gained through the studio's progression of projects and the lectures and readings that accom-pany each project. Each project's requirements include the appropriate 2D and 3D documents, a short writing requirement and physical models. In addition, assignments of the Visual Studies (ARCH 521) course reinforce essential skill sets integral to the objectives and deliverables of the 501 studio.

DESCRIPTIONS OF THE STUDIO PROJECTS:

There are two projects that successively build upon one another.

PROJECT01 / PAVILION

During the first stage, students engage descriptive geometry and generative analysis of a cultural artifact, working through disciplined and explicit modeling and fabrication. Once documented, a container is designed and fabricated for the partial display of that object. The container curates by hiding and revealing precise traits as well as negotiating prescribed nor-mative boundary conditions. Based on the concepts developed in the container project, generative drawing and modeling techniques are introduced to interrogate the artifact and amplify its effects. The generative exercise motivates the construction of aggregations and part-to-whole relationships by developing new objects through a series of transformations.

For the second stage, students are divided into three groups per section based on common tactics from the initial exercise. The groups proceed to design and develop full-scale (non representational) pavilions demonstrating the architectural consequences of part-to-whole relationships. Pavilions accomplishing structural span, component variation, durable construction and reaffirmation of prescribed normative boundaries for the formation of differentiated and habitable space.

PROJECT 02

For the second project, students are challenged to evolve concepts from their pavilion in the design of a larger architectural intervention within an architecturally and culturally significant context. The project utilizes skills and analytical concepts from Project 01 to fully engage architectural criteria including, enclosure, program, circulation, lighting, materiality, space and form.

Andrew Saunders, Coordinator

EUCLIDIAN TOPOLOGIES

CRITIC: **Andrew Saunders**

- Principal of Andrew Saunders Architecture + Design (2004)
- Received an M.Arch from Harvard GSD with Distinction
  for work of clearly exceptional merit. (2004)
- B.Arch from Fay Jones School of Architecture, University
  of Arkansas (1998)
- Winner of The Robert S. Brown '52 Fellows Program (2013)

With the goal of producing "Frankensteins" or monstrous child from Russel Wright's American Modern ceramic collection, students analyze the original pieces by identifying and mining specific Euclidian geometry and topological signatures. The traits are modeled, extracted, and eventually merged with characteristics from different Russel Wright pieces. The new combinations do not retain any functional relationship to the original piece, but do reference a genetic topological relationship with the parent pieces. Put simply, geometry innate to the American Modern collection is used to generate new hybrids.

    The sibling pieces are often surprising, bizarre and weird but clearly possess traits from the parent American Modern geometry. The genetic variations are something that Russel Wright never designed, but could have. Free from the original functionality of the mid-century domestic vessels, the new hybrids are developed to generate unique consequences both tectonically and spatially as architectural components.

    Transcending mere geometric transpositions, students work in teams to develop, fabricate and assemble half-scale pavilions to explore the basic architectural consequences of part-to-whole. The material and fabrication research coupled with the initial generative analysis phase culminate in a gallery proposal for the former rock quarry site of Russel Wright's home and studio at Manitoga.

PROTOMORPHS: EMERGENT ONTOLOGICAL FORMATIONS

CRITIC: **Danielle Willems**
TA: **Jasmine Gao**

- Co-Founder of Mæta Design (2008)
- Visiting Professor at Pratt University, Brooklyn NY
- Earned a MArch from Columbia University, GSAPP (2007)

CONCEPTUAL FRAMEWORK:
Protomorphs' perceives the architectural production as part of a larger, self-organizing, material process. While engaging in the production of protomorphic architectural environments through the generative capacities of algorithmic /diagrammatic logics, our primary focus will be the relationship between city and architecture. Finding the constitutive difference between the two in time, more so than in form. Protomorph is an investigation into the processes of becoming, and as such, it fuses the two modes of thought into a unified phase space. One of the challenges in the studio will be to re-invention of the means of assessment, the development of notations and techniques that will document the forces and the production of 'difference' in the spatial manifestations of the generative systems. With the introduction of a secondary scale of time in the design process, borrowing a concept from biology, symbiogenesis will be the primary force in the evolution of the projects.

PROTOMORPHS METHODOLOGY:
The studio methodology consists of three feedback layers: generative diagram, prototyping model and video. The generative diagram is the assembly machine to forms. The physical model should be a method of rapid prototyping the limits of the generative diagram in order to make specific spaces/scapes and formal behaviors in relationship to the projects spatial/temporal thesis.

SPATIAL TRANSPLANTS OF OTHER NARRATIVES

CRITIC: **Eduardo Rega**

- Editor, & Art Director of the Editorial Project and Investigation system "From Spam to Maps"
- Master of Science in Advanced Architectural Design at Columbia University
- MArch from Polytechnic University of Madrid, ETSAM
- BArch, University of Las Palmas, Spain

The design studio proposes the use of fictional narratives as efficient environments for typologic investigation. Architecture and cinema are contrasted as two areas of knowledge with a difference of potential ready to provoke productive shocks: architectural autonomy is juxtaposed to architectural agency: timeless spatial strategies are contaminated by ready made-fictions; typology is disturbed by human & non-human relations; architectural tropes reorganize networks that address Native American histories found in the following movies: Little Big Man, Atanarjuat and the very polemic Pocahontas. Design projects are constituted as accidents, failures and unprecedented anomalies that may advance the field of Architecture. The design studio provokes clashes between non-directional spaces and schizophrenia, poche and revolution, served-and-service spaces and murder.

MANITOGA

CRITIC: **Michael Loverich**
TA: **Zakariya Al-Haffar**

- Co-founded Bittertang (2008)
- Master of Architecture (MArch I) from the University of California Los Angeles; Dept. of Architecture and Urban Design (2007)
- Received the Architectural League Prize for Young Designers: Resource (2010)
- AIA New Practices New York Award (2014)

Manitoga, means 'Place of Great Spirit' in Algonquin. Russel Wright had a reverence for the site that he built his home on, reflected in his manipulation of topography and landscape and his experimental approach to architecture and its materials. He sought to combine these elements to create a holistic environment, one where he could create products, test out new material ideas and enjoy the site. His approach to part to whole is reflected in this studio's emphasis on creating new spaces defined by various elements; landscape, weather, lighting, building skins etc. Where all parts work toward not just creating gallery space for Russel Wright artifacts but in creating a whole new environment and experience throughout the entire site intervention. This sometimes involved creating a new landscape that gallery spaces could nestle into or the gardens and lighting conditions that introduce and set the mood for the visitor to the project. The studio emphasized an exploration of soft and tactile materials as a way to bridge between the lushness of Manitoga, architecture and the human body. By engaging with the sensorial each project establishes a contemporary approach for a new 'great spirit' at Manitoga.

ARCHITECTURE('S) PROBLEMS

CRITIC: **Miroslava Brooks**

- holds a Master of Architecture from Yale University (2012), where
  she was awarded the William Wirt Winchester Travelling Fellowship –
  school's most prestigious prize
- graduated Summa Cum Laude from The Ohio State University with a
  Bachelor of Science in Architecture (2008)
- has taught design studios and seminars at Yale School of Architecture
- worked as Project Designer and Research Assistant
  at Eisenman Architects

Architecture has continuously been preoccupied by specific problems, be it the plan problem, the corner problem, etc. Mobilizing discursive elements of three particular problems – the part-to-whole problem, the ground problem, and the nature-culture problem – the students were encouraged to develop their own critical position within a larger architectural discourse.

The entire 501 studio investigated the part-to whole relationship through the design and construction of a pavilion and then through the development of a design proposal for a small gallery space located at Manitoga in upstate New York.

In addition to the part-to-whole problem, of particular interest in our section was the building's relationship to the ground and the surrounding nature. Manitoga is a place of extremely challenging topography, with precisely choreographed views and site circulation winding through the seductively picturesque landscape. Although seemingly natural, the site was meticulously designed and re-constructed by Russel Wright – the industrial designer, former owner, and creator of the estate. As such, Manitoga and Russell Wright's own design work provided a rich context for the students to explore and challenge the seemingly opposing relationship between nature and architecture, a common misconception that still prevails today. How can nature be constructed? Can architecture be the ground? Drawings and physical models were the primary modes of operation, understanding them as generative rather than documentation tools.

501 [MARCH]

FOUNDATION

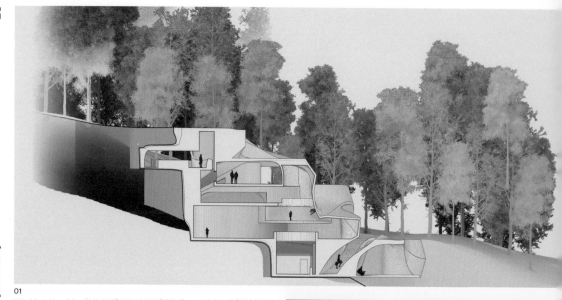

01

FOUNDATION

02

03

ANDREW SAUNDERS

STUDENT:
Ariel Cooke-Zamora   Images: 01 02 03

CRITIC:
Andrew Saunders

...blurring lines between the inside and the outside, continuity is wrought through a sculptural form that inverts into itself, creating an interweaving of interior and exterior spaces...providing two contrasting experiences.

4

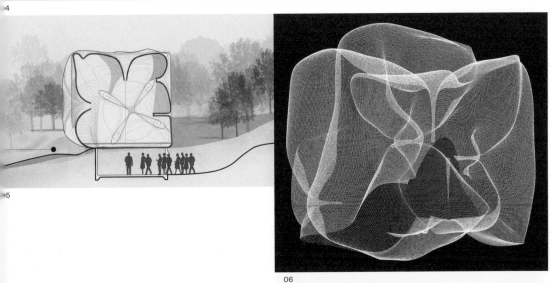

5

06

07

STUDENT:
Nicole Bronola   Images: 04 05 06 07

CRITIC:
Andrew Saunders

The formation of each seam originates from the kaleidoscope aggregations of pavilion pieces... creating a language between the galleries, and the site allowing for different light conditions to illuminate the space.

FOUNDATION

DANIELLE WILLEMS

01

02

03

04

STUDENT:
Andrew Matia   Images: 01 02 03 04

CRITIC:
Danielle Willems

...seeks to establish a new, perhaps sickening spatial sensation by evolving limited yet specific interference into a new modality for architectural expression. Corruption, for fundamental understanding of space.

#5

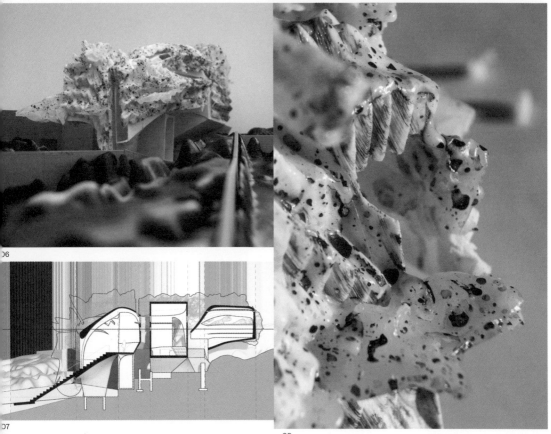

06

07

08

STUDENT:
Kurt Nelson   Images: 05 06 07 08

CRITIC:
Danielle Willems

...questions the consideration of time in architecture and the
weathering that comes with it, creating different levels of resilience
and aesthetic thresholds.

FOUNDATION

EDUARDO REGA

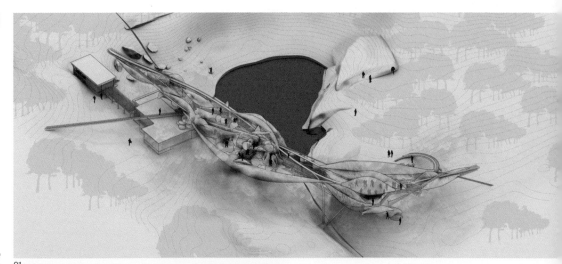

01

02

03

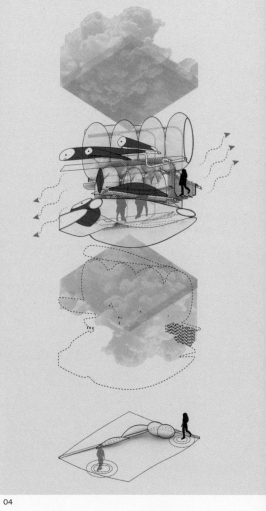

04

STUDENT:
Ian Pangburn

Images: 01 02 03 04

CRITIC:
Eduardo Rega

Using a system of pipes as a structural framework, Inflatable Intimacy is able to act as a flexible megastructure which houses events that have been studied...directly linked to the erotic exchanges.

5

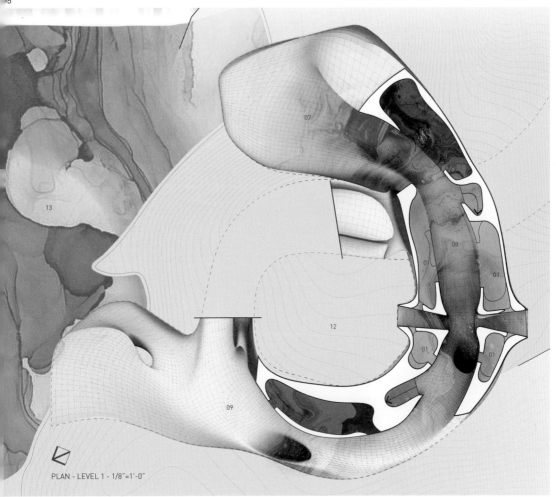

PLAN - LEVEL 1 - 1/8"=1'-0"

06

STUDENT:
Shih-Kai Lin   Images: 05 06

CRITIC:
Eduardo Rega

...open space created between poche mediates the segregated activities
that are happening in the poche. The "between-poche" spaces
and "in-poche" spaces are connected through a series of tunnels.

01

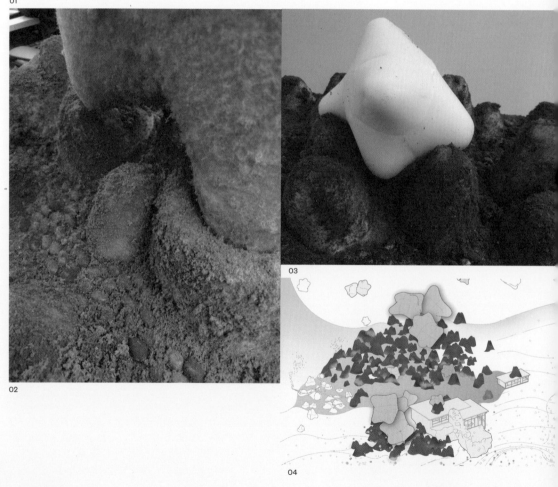

02

03

04

STUDENT:
Daniel Silverman   Images: 01 02 03 04

CRITIC:
Michael Loverich

...a collection of rooms immediately off the original entrance to Manitoga – intended to stop and distract you – potentially imbue you in a state of such timelessness that you will lose the bus. You are lured in by its bizarre quality.

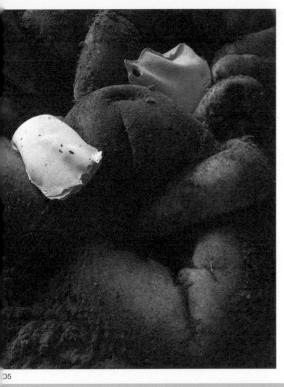

05

06

07

08

STUDENT:
Katherine Lanski   Images: 05 06 07

CRITIC:
Michael Loverich

Shyness is revealed throughout the interior spaces. Slumped interior folds act as pockets that display gallery pieces. In some cases, the overlapping folds fully conceal the object, compelling the visitor to peel open the folds.

01

02

03

STUDENT:
Elizabeth Heldridge   Images: 01 02 03

CRITIC:
Miroslava Brooks

The building dislocates one from the picturesque scenery that Russel Wright
so meticulously planned, only to reintroduce the visitor back to it, having
gained a better understanding of Wright's work and design philosophy.

04

05

06

STUDENT:
Yitian Zheng   Images: 04 05 06

CRITIC:
Miroslava Brooks

...organic curvilinear geometry create a natural & fluid environment. Visitors are led inside the space through the crack, which separates the building into two galleries, creating an ambiguity between gallery and surrounding nature.

PAVILION

FOUNDATION

501 PAVILLION REVIEW, FALL 2016 WINNING PAVILLION GETS TO BE BUILT REAL-SCALE AT THE RUSSEL WRIGHT CENTER IN MANITOGA, NY

This semester the Department of Architecture at PennDesign concluded a two-year partnership with Manitoga, the House, Studio and 75-acre Woodland garden of famed mid-century American designer Russel Wright. Under guidance of Associate Professor Andrew Saunders and the ARCH 501 faculty, 65 first-year students worked in 15 teams to construct full-scale prototypes for a new pavilion at Manitoga to be featured as their artist in residency program. In mid-October, they presented their pavilions to a jury of faculty members and Executive Director of Manitoga Allison Cross.

PARTICIPANTS

Adamski Alexandra Mae
Ai Lihan
Ali Mohamed
Bloomfield Kevin
Bonilla-Huaroc
Carla Liliana
Bronola Nicole
Castro Dyan
Chen Sirui
Chen Yifei
Cooke-Zamora Ariel Nicolas
Cueva Christian Brian
Dashiell Caitlin
Duan Xiaoyu
Gan Yu
Han Xuanhao
Hao Yunzhuo
Heim Riwan Augustin Julien
Heldridge Elizabeth Anne
Henriksen Ryan Thomas
Hernandez Mariela
Hillier Jordan Rebecca

Homick Andrew Michael
Huang Justine
Huang Yanlong
Ijaz Uroosa
Jia Weizhen
Kalantzopoulos Nikolaos Fillipos
Kane Keaton Peter
Kayyali Samia
Kim Gwan Sook
Lam Cheuk Wai
Langley Prince Alexander
Lanski Katherine Anne
Lee Jongwon
Lee Tae Hyung
Lin Shih-Kai
Liu Lichao
Liu Yuchen
Lopez-Font Isabel Cristina
Lu Yi
Matia Andrew
Nelson Kurt Alexander
Ogunmoyero Ayotunde Oreoluwa

Oh Jinah Nicole
Pangburn Ian Walter
Qi Zehua
Shoemaker Kimberly Jane
Silverman Daniel
Sinha Anya
Soejanto Grace
Su Ting
Sun Xuezhu
Teng Lingxiao
Vannoy Calvin Sheldon
Wang Ailin
Wang Bingyu
Weaver Logan Bradley
Yamba Moise Tshilonde
Zha Yili
Zhang Yefan
Zhang Yi
Zheng Yitian
Zhou Xieyang
Zhu Yi
Zhu Zheng Yang

Jonathan Scelsa and Winka Dubbeldam review student work.

Jordan Hillier and Gwan Sook Kim

501 WINNING PAVILLION IS BUILT : STUDENTS ARE ARTIST IN RESIDENCE AT MANITOGA
A construction course with Professor AlKhayer helps realize the design/build process

Master of Architecture Students at the University of Pennsylvania School of Design have designed, built and installed a full-scale, site-specific pavilion at Manitoga inspired by Russel Wright's design legacy.

The winning design concepts from 2016 - *Hereafter and Devour(ing) the Dark* - were developed by graduate students as one pavilion structure for Manitoga in the seminar Techniques, Morphology and Detailing of a Pavilion, led by Lecturer Mohamad Al Khayer, who also supervised the production and installation of the pavilion at Manitoga. Says Department Chair Winka Dubbeldam, "the pavilion installation at Manitoga is a unique design build experience. Students have the opportunity to take what they are learning at PennDesign and move it beyond our walls to engage a rich cultural context with an immediate impact.

2017 Artist Residency Program
Penndesign Pavilion

WINNING PROJECTS :
Devour[ing] the Dark by Katherine Lanski, Justine Huang, Ayotunde Ogunmoyero, Daniel Silverman, Lingxiao Teng, and Xieyang Zhou (Instructor: Michael Loverich); and Hereafter by Grace Soejanto, Mohamed Ali, Ailin Wang (Instructor: Michael Loverich).

STUDENT TEAM FOR DESIGN-BUILD:
Sookwan Ahn
Zakariya Yaseen Al-Haffar
Mohamed Ali
Musab Mohammad Badahdah
Xiaonan Chen
Justine Huang
Bosung Jeon
Hewen Jiang
Yunhwan Jung
Katherine Anne Lanski
Dongliang Li
Siyang Lv
Jia Lyu
Xiaoyu Ma
Ayotunde Oreoluwa Ogunmoyero
Taeseo Park
Daniel Silverman
Grace Soejanto
Ali Tabatabaie Ghomi
Lingxiao Teng
Ailin Wang
Yijia Wang
Ge Yang
Yunlong Zhang
Yuchen Zhao
Jianbo Zhong
Xieyang Zhou

Pavilion on site

Pavilion on site

The site at the Russel Wright Foundation at Manitoga

The first location at the University of Pennsylvania

FOUNDATION

FAIR GROUNDS
Written in collaboration with **Eduardo Rega** and **Danielle Willems**.

Since the rise of postmodernism, the field's dissociation from social or political responsibilities to enter the boudoir and the advent of the star-architecture machine, many have argued for architecture's crisis. The state in which the field finds itself today is one of deep questioning and redefinition both in how it draws its disciplinary boundaries and in how it can affect the socio-spatial realm. As a microcosm and accelerator of this debates, the various 502 studio sections this year offered a diversity of agendas, methodologies and possibilities about what architecture could be and its role as a tool in neighborhood struggles and urban activism.

The studio's traditional curricular orientation toward urbanism, in this second semester of the student's education, fully embraced this year this disciplinary challenge as essential to its pedagogy. Latent in the studio's work was a deep analysis of conventional urban attributes: infrastructure and transportation, natural resources and the environment, urban morphologies and typologies, and cultural, socio-economic and political patterns. As a fundamental corollary, however, these were tied to the circumstances and agencies of a particular West Philadelphia neighborhood known as East Parkside, a neighborhood under considerable socio-economic and morphological demand but also currently mobilizing agency from within the neighborhood's resources, a vital process. East Parkside was our partner throughout the semester, giving the studio its particular voice through a number of different interactions, a deep collaboration that will continue into the future.

The program of a community library served as a vehicle to galvanize all of these interests. Presently in the spotlight of a substantial initiative of municipal funding, the library, as both academic and realizable project, is dynamic. As a historical typological figure, the upheaval in the nature of accessing and archiving information through digital means has posed a fundamental challenge: is a physical entity even needed? Politically and socially, however, the converse reality has interestingly emerged. In recent work, it is the physical library that has manifested as a central typology fluid to community needs and desires, emerging pragmatically as multi-programmed community center and symbolically as representation of the community-in-flux. This timely reading of the library is equally colored by the possibility that, due to current discussions in Philadelphia, there might be a facility actually built, giving another dimension to the studio's work that is not simply tangential.

There are thus multiple ambitions at play in the studio: What happens when design, in full speculative dimension, and buttressed by the institutional muscle of a major university, gives agency to interaction between academia, neighborhood, and city? What impression does it leave on students' sense of what they do and why? Conversely, what impact on neighborhood and city can visionary design emerging from the institution actually have?

Annette Fierro, Coordinator

RESIDUE

CRITIC: **Annette Fierro**

- MArch from Rice University (1984)
- BS in Civil Engineering from Rice University (1980)
- Author of The Glass State: The Technology of the Spectacle/Paris 1981-1998 (MIT Press, 2003)

The US Environmental Protection Agency has estimated that every year construction and demolition processes produce 350 million tons of waste debris. Most of this leftover material is recyclable.

While the ethical dimension of sustainability demands that these materials be examined for reuse in contemporary architecture, this studio embraces the multiple connotations of such reuse. Materials, whether new or used have associated economies of resources, manufacture, and those thrown away, of neglect for various reasons often associated with the larger societal changes. By associated economies, these materials trace histories of interactions between commerce and labor, between natural resource and its subsequent evolution through manmade intervention. Manufactured material artifacts carry histories of society and culture. They are its residue.

By investigating libraries that emerged from residue—material, land, labor, and their narrative histories—and mobilized through interaction with the neighborhood itself, the studio attempted to address consequences of gentrification as well. Could old shreds of economies prompt new ones? Could scraps of material inspire spatial and formal orders which were not only historical but also speculative? Could an intrinsic tie to production and to neighborhood agency cultivate a form and process of building which was projective as well as resistant?

Narrative was used as a tool to analyze, synthesize, and project. We collected and wrote deep narratives on the community and on the site, we speculated on materials and reuse by writing new narratives: on history, on lives of people and on lives of material. As a generative tool narrative became wedded intrinsically to formal attributes of the things we designed. Nothing was left to that which one sees, but was elaborated upon by that which it connoted.

SYNTHETIC DOMAINS

CRITIC: **Joshua Freese**

- Partner of Sp[a]de (2012)
- Graduated with a Bachelor of Design in Architectural Studies from Florid International University and an MArch from Penn's School of Design

The agenda for our studio is to define a set of relationships between the physical form of the city, the cultural and social content of the neighborhood, and the programmatic extent and capacity of the library and market. These relationships seek to challenge conventional understandings of order, hierarchy, form, permanence, and speculation. The approach takes both a critical and optimistic stance on the nature of civic institutions and public space to play a greater role in serving a community.

The city of Philadelphia is a prime example of a synthetic domain. The imposition of a symmetric grid across the asymmetric topography of the site defined the extent and domain of public space, private space, and other typological constraints for commercial streets and residential lots.

The library is a collection of unique categories of spaces, information and media. The categories apply to both the orderly categorical arrangement of content and to the arrangement of spaces for collective gatherings, individual study, and institutional storage. The range of spatial typologies is flexible, and varies based largely on demand, diversity, scale, context and economy.

A community and neighborhood are defined by the physical domain that they occupy, but also by the cultural, demographic and socioeconomic traits of its residents.

Our studio will investigate patterns at a variety of scales (surface, building, city) through a series of analytical and generative studies. The objective is to reinterpret systems and relationships; between the various layers of material components, structures and environments, and people and spaces. Our understanding of the site, city, and program will be integrated into patterns, both generated and studied, to produce rules and operational ordering systems that can define relationships between the site and the city.

ONTOLOGICAL FORMATIONS · GENERATIVE METHODS OF RESILIENCE AND RESISTANT

CRITIC: **Danielle Willems**

Co-Founder of Mæta Design (2008)
Visiting Professor at Pratt University, Brooklyn NY
Earned a MArch from Columbia University, GSAPP (2007)

CONCEPTUAL FRAMEWORK:

'Ontological Formations' perceives the architectural production as part of a larger, self-organizing, material process. While engaging in the production of Ontological-architectural axioms through the generative capacities of algorithmic / diagrammatic logics, our primary focus will be the relationship between time and architecture. Finding the constitutive difference between the two in time, more so than in form. Ontological Formation is an investigation in the processes of becoming, and as such, it fuses the two scapes into a unified phase space.

ONTOLOGICAL METHODOLOGY:

The studio methodology consists of three feedback layers: generative diagram, prototyping model and video. The generative diagram is the assembly machine to forms. The physical model should be a method of rapid prototyping the limits of the generative diagram in order to make specific spaces of resistance /resilience and formal behaviors in relationship to the projects spatial/temporal thesis. The video component will be used as a different method of exploring, experimenting, generating spatial sequences, creating immersive environments, and building a narrative inside or through the architectural forms.

The studio thesis will venture into an investigation that is embodied within a novel approach, to the relationship between the emerging narrations of two modes of time/architecture. (typologies of time)

TEMPORARY AUTONOMOUS NETWORKS: THE ARCHITECTURE OF REAL UTOPIA

CRITIC: **Eduardo Rega**

- Editor, & Art Director of the Editorial Project and Investigation system "From Spam to Maps"
- Master of Science in Advanced Architectural Design at Columbia University
- MArch from Polytechnic University of Madrid, ETSAM
- BArch, University of Las Palmas, Spain

In this studio, existing Temporary Autonomous Zones, tactics that erode capitalism through local community enhancement and cooperativism, justice and defense of civil rights are architecturalized. The studio investigates key Philadelphian agents that are currently active in the city eroding capitalism, representing the excluded, enhancing communities through art and culture, broadcasting people's narratives, amplifying and defending their rights to their city, demystifying class hierarchy, sexual repression and patriarchy, questioning the status quo and inhabiting its cracks to transform it. In this urban design & architecture oriented semester, students generated a collective archive/intelligence through audiovisual, mapped and diagrammed descriptions of activist organizations, and, on the other hand, a set of manuals of architectural/urban tactics that were extracted from the Detroit Thinkgrid by Cedric Price.

The research on Philadelphian actors/activists /cooperatives/community groups, developed up until the midterm was used to project their mission, goals, visions, activities, strategies and relations on Parkside, our studio site. On the second half of the semester, students developed iterations of urban projects done in groups that hybridized spatial tactics to respond to specific struggles and polemics on the site.

IS THE EDGE A SITE OF RESISTANCE OR A SITE OF NEGOTIATION?

CRITIC: **Miroslava Brooks**

- holds a Master of Architecture from Yale University, where she was awarded the William Wirt Winchester Travelling Fellowship – school's most prestigious prize
- graduated Summa Cum Laude from The Ohio State University with a Bachelor of Science in Architecture
- has taught design studios and seminars at Yale School of Architecture
- worked as Project Designer and Research Assistant at Eisenman Architects

Our site – the Parkside neighborhood – is currently an urban enclave with clearly delineated edges, bounded by the expansive Fairmount Park to the north and railroad tracks to the east, west, and south. Therefore, our studio section began with a close study of edge conditions, analyzing specific precedents and the existing edges of the given site. Is the edge a site of resistance or a site of negotiation?

The first part of the semester was dedicated to the study of urban enclaves and urban edges, focusing on projective and speculative analysis. The second part focused on the design of a library – a knowledge enclave undergoing continual transformation within the contemporary culture of media and technology. Ultimately, the library, although a singular architectural intervention, was seen as part of a larger project on the city.

Using diagrams and drawings as conceptual and generative tools, students analyzed precedents from painting and architecture, and together created a catalogue of edge conditions (of an image, a building, or a city), which acted as a collective knowledge base. The goal was to gain a deeper understanding of an edge – both its physicality and as a conceptual device. An edge can separate or connect, it can act as a threshold, a zone, an area with a thickness, or simply a physical or visual limit (of an image or a neighborhood).

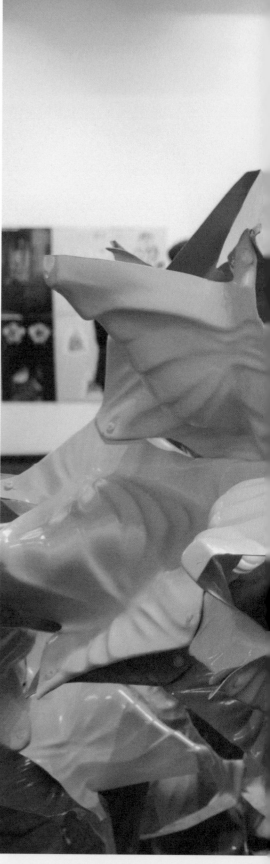

FOUNDATION

ANNETTE FIERRO

01

02

04

03

STUDENT:
Christian Cueva   Images: 01 02 03 04

CRITIC:
Annette Fierro

I oversee and establish an urban and cultural remit, acting through flexible, accessible, and welcoming communal spaces. I reveal Parkside's story while engaging through pedestrians and their past reminisce.

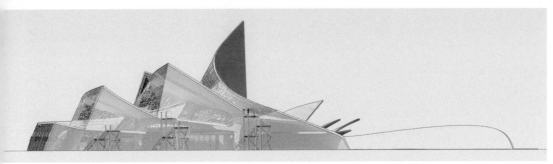

05

06

07

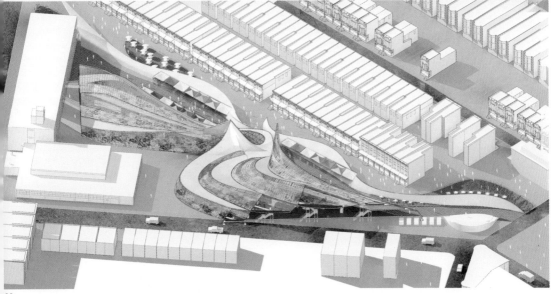

08

STUDENT:
Rachel (Yi) Lu   Images: 05 06 07 08

CRITIC:
Annette Fierro

What used to be the street, now is also part of the library as a public walk way, with road-side landscapes growing on newspapers. Bookshelves are part of the wall system, they are either structured with light weight concrete.

FOUNDATION

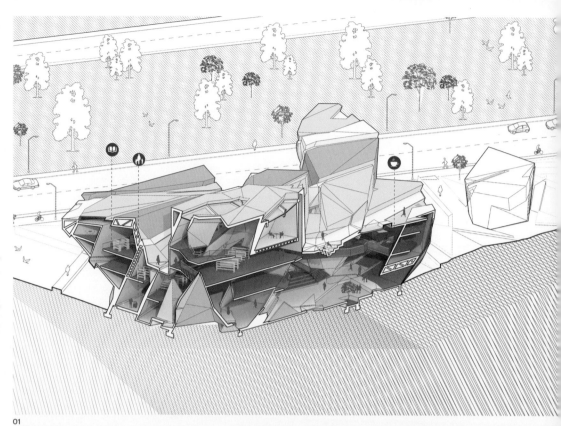

01

02

03

04

STUDENT:
Alexandra Adamski   Images: 01 02 03 04

CRITIC:
Joshua Freese

The cellular pattern structure subdivides the site; the channels, striations, and fractured cells becoming elements such as programmable hardscape, circulation, and green space and inform hierarchies of tonality and program...

5

06

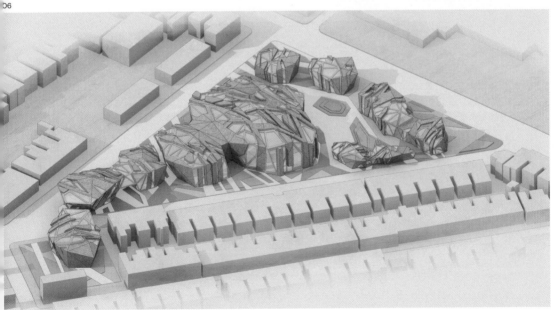

07

STUDENT:
Yefan Zhang   Images: 05 06 07

CRITIC:
Joshua Freese

...the 'directionality' and 'fragmentation' in the patterns are emphasized to form different scales and functions of buildings, connected or separated, but as a synthetic domain in a community context.

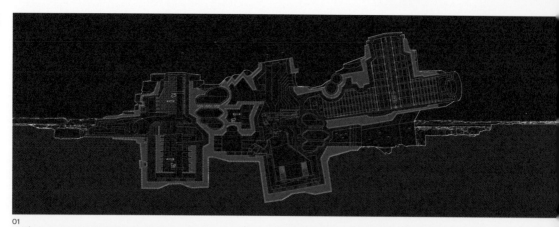

01

02

03

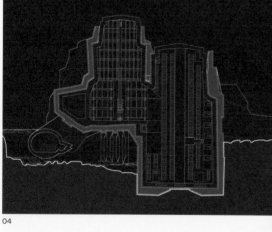

04

05

STUDENT:
Andrew Homick   Images: 01 02 03 04 05

CRITIC:
Danielle Willems

...challenges the role of the librarian, offering a new possibility of robotic agents to inhabit responsibilities, not only having the ability to track info, and literature over the course of its lifespan but also how it performs over time.

6

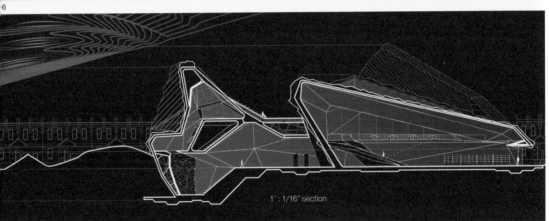

1' : 1/16" section

7

09

08

STUDENT:
Yi Zhug   Images: 06 07 08 09

CRITIC:
Danielle Willems

A boundless internet and its effortless accessibility raises an insurmountable challenge to the library: if books are becoming increasingly redundant, what then is the new purpose of the library?

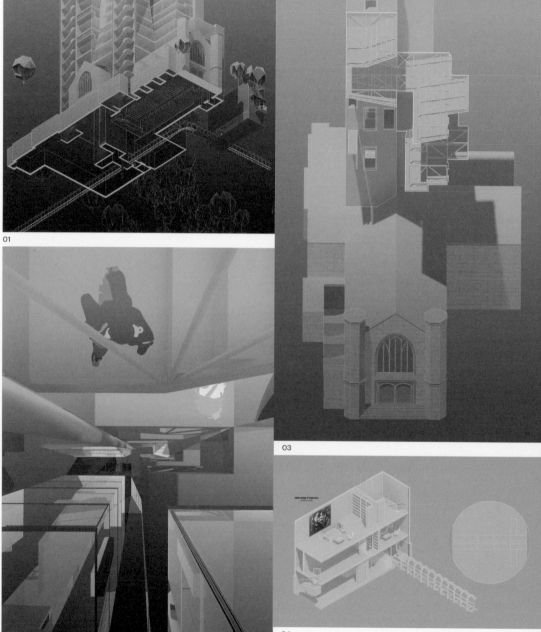

01

02

03

04

STUDENT:
Kurt Nelson

Images: 01 02 03 04

CRITIC:
Eduardo Rega

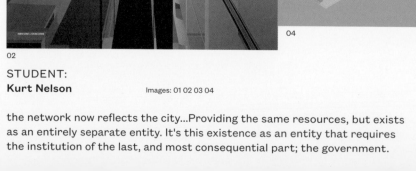

the network now reflects the city...Providing the same resources, but exists
as an entirely separate entity. It's this existence as an entity that requires
the institution of the last, and most consequential part; the government.

05

06

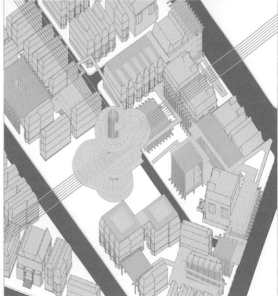

07

STUDENT:
Zheng Yang Zhu   Images: 05 06 07

CRITIC:
Eduardo Rega

By effectively leveraging the existing structure of the vacant houses,
detachable libraries can be spread throughout the entire neighborhood
based on the availability of existing vacant houses similar to acupuncture.

FOUNDATION

MIROSLAVA BROOKS

01

02

03

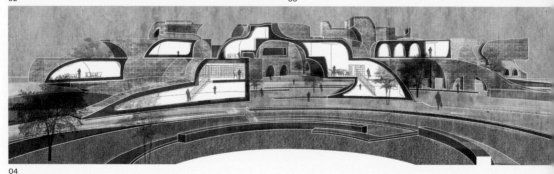

04

STUDENT:
Yi Zhang

Images: 01 02 03 04

CRITIC:
Miroslava Brooks

various curvilinear walls are generated by the combing force field of three
attracting points defined on the site, and a series of bands are formed in
between. Various programs are distributed on the bands across the site...

5

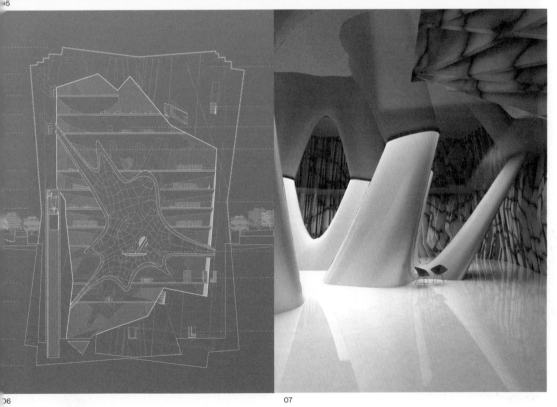

06   07

STUDENT:
Matia Andrew   Images: 05 06 07

CRITIC:
Miroslava Brooks

This architecture sees the library as an enduring physical log of human
thoughts, happenings, dreams and experiences; a constructed diary;
a megalith for eternity.

FOUNDATION

GALLERY

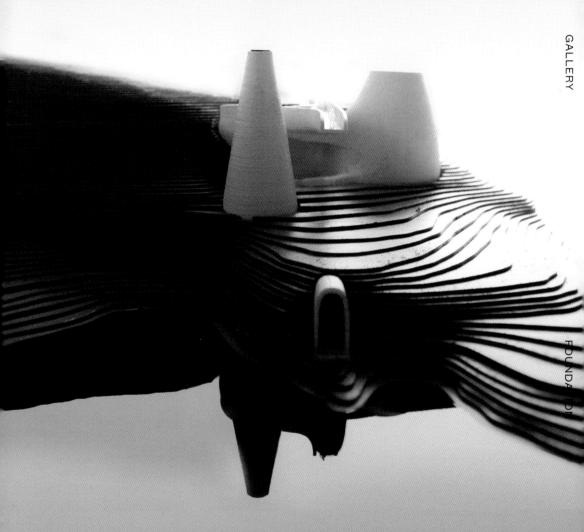

STUDENT:
Elizabeth Heldridge

Reference. page 36

CRITIC:
Miroslava Brooks

FOUNDATION

STUDENT:
Yefan Zhang

CRITIC:
Miroslava Brooks

Reference. page 51

GALLERY

FOUNDATION

STUDENT:
Andrew Homick

Reference. page 52

CRITIC:
Danielle Willems

GALLERY

FOUNDATION

STUDENT:
Daniel Silverman

Reference. page 34

CRITIC:
Michael Loverich

GALLERY

FOUNDATION

STUDENT:
Daniel Silverman

CRITIC:
Eduardo Calvo Rega

Phase III becomes an exercise of utopic speculation building upon the
establishment of a human network in Phase I and the beginning of a physical/
material infrastructure in Phase II.

RE

CORE

In 2011-12, we re-structured the ARCH 601 Design Studio to become an Urban Housing Studio that moves beyond the traditional programmatic housing studio approach to propose contemporary modes of living in an urban environment. Hybrid forms of housing/dwelling including a commercial or cultural program that can co-exist with housing is the topic explored during this semester.

Due to the difference in scale between housing and a cultural program, an inherent curricular goal is to develop formal arrangements in accumulation and scalar variation that develop a speculative, comprehensive solution for a 50,000 sq. ft. building located in an urban environment.

The use of digital techniques is a given for this semester's projects, but the goal is to use these technologies in an opportunistic fashion for the generation of growth and the evaluation of patterns in the development of the overall form. In particular, each studio examines part-to-whole organizations and their potential for architecture by offering the tools to create effects that exceed the sum of their parts.

Most part-to-whole organizations share common characteristics, including structure: defined by parts and their composition; and the interconnectivity of the various parts that have functional, structural, and spatial relationships with each other. During this semester, a primacy is given to formations that are varied, accumulative, and subject to change that may shift spatial experiences, scale, and material aspects. In addition, buildings are to incorporate program, spatiality, structure, and enclosure into a singular formation that incorporates a range of experiences and formal variations of gradated intensities and patterns.

An exceptionally sophisticated part-to-whole relationship is one which goes a step further and resolves the integration of materials, structure, scale, and spatiality to allow for the overall formation to appear suspended, or possessed of a particular lightness. In terms of formal appearance, this lightness includes qualities of fineness and daintiness, determined within the multiple individual elements and parts that constitute the building design. The scale of the part to the whole [unit to building] is attenuated, adjusted with precision and refinement, in order to produce the desired effect. If the scale of the part is too diminutive in relation to the whole, or if the whole is constituted of too many smaller building components, then the occupant of the space may be overwhelmed. When the relation of part [housing unit] to whole [building] is attuned, unique living environments and innovative housing solutions can be achieved.

The form of the building impacts the selected urban environment. Each instructor provides their own site for exploration within a city of the instructor's choice. Each building's goals contribute to and impact the city in which the building is located. The highly formed object incorporates a detailed façade and its relationship to the massing, plans, and sections, with an understanding of vertical and horizontal pedestrian circulation that maximizes their impact on the urban environment.

We brought these curricular topics to life this year by hosting an international Urban Housing Symposium titled UNDER PRESSURE in October 2016. The three panel discussions focused on pressure points affecting Urban Housing: SUPER HOT, NEW DOMESTICITIES and SPECULATION. We brought together Architects [Patrik Schumacher, Chris Sharples, Mimi Hoang, Neil Denari, Marcelo Spina, Kai-Uwe Bergmann and Nader Tehrani], Economists/ Developers [Martha Kelley from Goldman Sachs, Mark Willis from the Furman Center] in addition to Curators/ Historians , Speculators [Barry Bergdoll, MoMA, Laia Mogas and Cliff Pearson] to share their experience and insights into the unique and challenging topics of Urban Housing.

Hina Jamelle, Coordinator
Director of Urban Housing. Penn Design

SHIFTING HYBRIDS:
Transformations for a Residential Building + WE WORK/WELIVE in TriBeCa. NYC.

CRITIC: **Hina Jamelle**

- Architect and Director, Contemporary Architecture Practice, NY (2003)
- Graduated with an MArch from University of Michigan Taubman College, where she received the Dr. Martin Luther King, Jr., Leadership Award.

This studio will examine emergence and its relation to the formulation of architecture by using digital techniques in an opportunistic fashion for the generation of growth and evaluation of patterns in the development of form. In particular, this studio will examine part to whole organizations and its potential for architecture by offering the tools to create effects that exceed the sum of their parts.

In this studio we will give primacy to formations that are in variation, accumulative and subject to changes that may shift in spatial experiences, scale and materials. In addition, projects using digital techniques incorporate program, space, structure, and enclosure into a singular formation that incorporates a range of experiences and formal variations of gradated intensities and patterns.

An exceptionally sophisticated part to whole relationship is one which goes a step further and resolves the integration of materials, structure, scale, and spatiality to allow for the overall formation to appear suspended, or possessed of a particular lightness and elegance. In terms of formal appearance, this lightness includes qualities of fineness and daintiness, determined within the multiple individual elements and parts that constitute the building design. The scale of the part to the whole will be attenuated, adjusted with precision and refinement, in order to produce the desired effect.

The intended result is a project exhibiting innovative architectural organizations and strategies using topological surfaces, unit arrangements and patterns scaling from an individual room to the entire building with different spatial and material qualities contributing to the development of architecture.

HOUSING TOWER

CRITIC: **Jonas Coersmeier**

- Founded Büro NY, NY (2004)
- Received a Master's degree from Columbia University GSAPP (2000)
- Received an engineering degree from TU-Darmstadt (1998) & MIT Architecture (1996)
- Teaches studios & research seminars at Pratt & serves as guest critic at Princeton and Columbia GSAPP

The architectural design studio Housing Tower invents a combinatory logic for ultra-luxury and affordable housing, and proposes a prototype for new residential towers along the High Line urban park in New York City. It simultaneously focuses on the two primary growth markets of New York City's real estate: Luxury condominiums and subsidized housing. We study these two extreme segments in context, probe into their interaction and systematically work out areas of synergy in order to add value for all stake holders and to the community at large. We find great potential in bringing together these two housing domains, far greater than what is currently realized in the industry's practice.

The studio encourages the discussion of socio-economic and political forces in urban housing, and how they relate to architectural responsibilities and opportunities. It takes a pragmatic, opportunistic position as it focuses on core architectural expertise, granting architecture the status of an autonomous discipline. Finally, the studio takes the hopeful position that architecture holds the potential for improving human coexistence. In a series of spatial exercises the design studio develops new systems of vertical agglomeration for living quarters and work spaces. The spatial organization is well informed by circulatory and infrastructural, as well as by structural considerations. A slim housing tower reaches into the sky and redefines mixed urban housing developments by synthesizing luxury condominiums with minimal apartments.

THE IHOPE SANCTUARY (International House Opposing Partisan Extremism)

CRITIC: **Scott Erdy**

- Founding partner of Erdy McHenry Architecture, PA (1998)
- Received MArch, Syracuse University (1990)
- Received BSc Architecture, Ohio State University (1987)
- Received the AIA Philadelphia Gold Medal (2001) and the AIA Philadelphia Silver Medal (2004)

In the wake of the recent election the response has been twofold; a call to action, but also a call for refuge from an inhospitable and intolerant political climate. Though shocking in our generation, this is not the first time Americans have been forced to flee conflict within their own borders. Native Americans have long been victims of political oppression through forced relocation, disease, and genocide.

This studio explored how independence can be found amid a tumult of unrest and instability. With popular nationalists favoring deportation and relocation, students were challenged to invert this discriminatory policy by proposing an autonomous, sovereign, and self-governed nation hypothetically repatriated from Philadelphia's dense urban mélange by the Powhatan Renape Tribe.

Insulated from the political and economic conditions of its surrounding context and designed to allow its residents to live in peace and harmony, this reestablished nation state — known as the iHope Sanctuary— is foremost intended as an attractive alternative for both dissatisfied "Immigrants" as well as true Native Americans.

MEGA-BLOCK REDUX

CRITIC: **Kutan Ayata**

- Co-founded New York-based architecture firm, Young & Ayata (2008)
- Young & Ayata are winners of The Architectural League Prize (2014)
- Received a MArch from Princeton University (2004)
- Bachelor of Fine Arts in Architecture from Massachusetts College of Art in Boston (1999)

Middle of the 20th century has seen an unprecedented development of new housing projects in urban centers. The ambitions of modernity in the form of large scale housing blocks altered many city fabrics resulting in isolated mega-blocks. The ill effects of these projects are well documented and successful precedents are a handful... while the lack of urban density and mix use are the chronic short comings for these projects, no series attempt of rehabilitation beyond face-lifts have been performed. Ironically the very motivation of their initial implementation (tabula-rasa) has been the only comprehensive method to accelerate their slow death. This studio speculated on alternative paths for their future.

The studio collectively worked to transform the entire character and experience of Stuyvesant Town in New York City, a whole neighborhood consisting of 18 city blocks and 33 buildings. Unlike the modernist strategy of tabula-rasa to remedy a failed modernist urban strategy, we fully embraced the permanence of the physical context and accepted all that it has as a 3-dimensional site to operate on. Each student operated on a self-similar yet specific portion of the complex with their self-generated housing agenda to create a heterogeneous urban assembly by adding, altering, transforming the existing buildings and courtyards. Ultimately, the collective effort of the class attempted to define a prototypical urban densification strategy for this Mega-Block.

BLOCKED

CRITIC: **Brian Phillips**

- Founder of Interface Studio Architects (ISA), PA (2004)
- Received MArch from the University of Pennsylvania (1996)
- Received BSEd from University of Oklahoma (1994)
- Winner of the 2011 Pew Fellowship in the Arts
- ISA has received multiple AIA Pennsylvania Merit & Honor Awards

Housing has been at the theoretical and spiritual heart of architecture and urbanism for the last century. It has been fetishized by architects, intensely personalized by homeowners, delivered dispassionately by governments, and treated as pure commodity by private developers. Its small and flexible program, as well as its tendency to change ownership often, encourages it to be driven by financial, site and construction considerations in profound ways, in many cases resulting in highly inefficient, low performance, diminished long-term value buildings.

This studio encourages a pro-active role for the architect, positioning design as an entrepreneurial, innovative, and deeply intelligent engagement of the problem at hand. Our approach acknowledged the changing playing field for architecture among a series of rapidly evolving global, cultural, economic and environmental trends. The language of architecture acts as a proving ground for urban influence, and as a change agent across a diverse set of stakeholders beyond the confines of architecture proper.

Projects were encouraged to engage within a set of complex, sometimes contradictory, forces require the architectural proposals themselves to engage with the unfolding, and very current, cross-disciplinary dialogue around urbanism and buildings.

The site allowed for an investigation of a particular site condition, but also as a case study for urban development in general. Specifically, the work began with investigations of the basic residential building unit of Philadelphia, the rowhouse, and then expanded and distorted that unit into a block scaled ensemble that provides variety in size, user type, programs and architectural character. The final projects proposed new urban block typologies for living.

LAYER CAKE

CRITIC: **Abigail Coover Hume**

- Partner at Hume Coover Studio (2008)
- Editor & Founder of suckerPUNCH (2008)
- Graduated with a MArch from Yale University (2006)
- Earned a Bachelor of Science in Architecture from University of Virginia (2001)

Conventional urban housing typologies consist of mats, layers and stacks, both vertical and horizontal. These are layers of both living and building including apartments, floor plates, building systems and structure. Within the mat housing typology, anomalies and disruptions conventionally exist ranging from exterior space, material changes, and circulation. As stated by Stan Allen, these anomalies within the field are typically internal. By cracking open a typical mat housing block and shifting and reorganizing its inherent layers, unexpected relationships between interior and exterior, space and poche, and material and form can emerge. A delamination of thickened layers allows the typical internal anomalies to become extroverted and rethought in terms of both form and program.

This studio questioned the typical relationship of layering within urban housing. Students began with a quick analysis of mat housing typologies and with a series of layered material experiments in order to study the interaction of various materials in a stacked condition. Through the overlap of these two exercises, a series of both organizational relationships and ways to question those relationships was studied. Materials were mined for latent potentials and behaviors. Students posed questions such as: what is the impact on a heavy material over a lightweight material? how does a soft material act when wedged between two hard materials? what happens when a series of typical layers are sheared and reconnected? The friction between pragmatism and process fostered new potentials within the urban housing block. Layered forms of representation primarily concentrated on large scale 2D and 3D sections was used as a generative tool throughout the semester.

CO/HABITATION

CRITIC: **Benjamin Krone**

Founded Gradient Design Studio, NYC (2006)
Bachelor of Architecture from the University of Florida (1999)
MArch degree from Columbia University's Graduate School of
Architecture, GSAPP (2004)
Won the McKim Prize for Excellence in Design & the Sol Kaplan
Traveling Fellowship.

In the last two decades, bicycle culture has made a significant resurgence. The development of new technologies in cycle frames and components making them lighter, faster, more mobile and nimble has had a significant impact in all aspects of the sport. This is true from high speed racing to endurance to mountain bike riding. Likely the greatest change though, at least in terms of wide spread interest, is based in the commuting culture of biking. A combination of carbon footprint awareness, overcrowding of public transportation in big cities, and a new generation of people who see cars as a threat to public safety and health, has propelled the culture of bike riding to new levels. It is not difficult to understand the significant impact this is having in cities, from bike shares to complete re-designs of city master plans centered on reorienting bicycles as the primary form of transportation.

This studio will be charged with gaining a high level understanding for the culture of bicycle riding, racing, and bicycle recreation, as it currently exists as well as a historical understanding of the sport. This research will form the foundation of each teams conceptual approach toward programming, and ultimately will be the basis for redefining the typology of the sporting event venue as a hybrid between bicycle recreation center, community center, and a competitive sport complex.

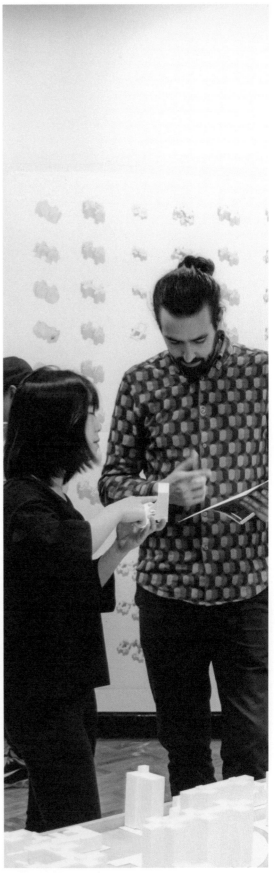

STUDENT:
Adam G Schroth

CRITIC:
Hina Jamelle

This proposal sets a new standard in which living and working are interlaced. Allowing units to cross one another to provide shared access, the work-life separation unravels, forcing a hybridization where users can access a work environment and private living space directly. The proposal provides 35 rental units, ranging from 350 to 750 SF, and 20 work units, ranging in area from 650 to 900 SF. While hybridization occurs within the private realm, it also bears a public dimension formalized in exhibition and break out space, providing tenants opportunities to present work in multiple ways.

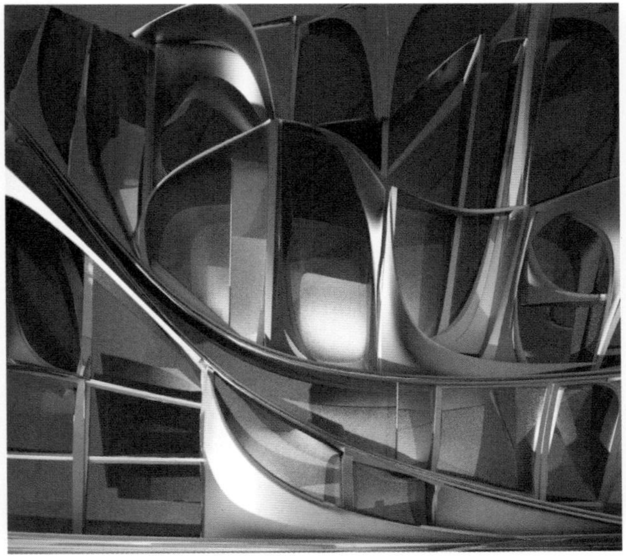

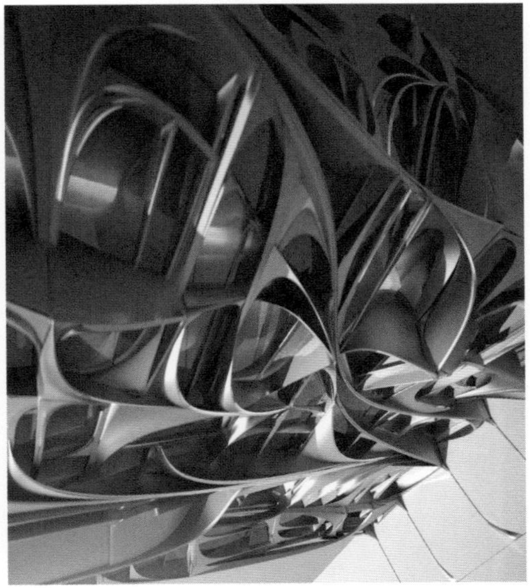

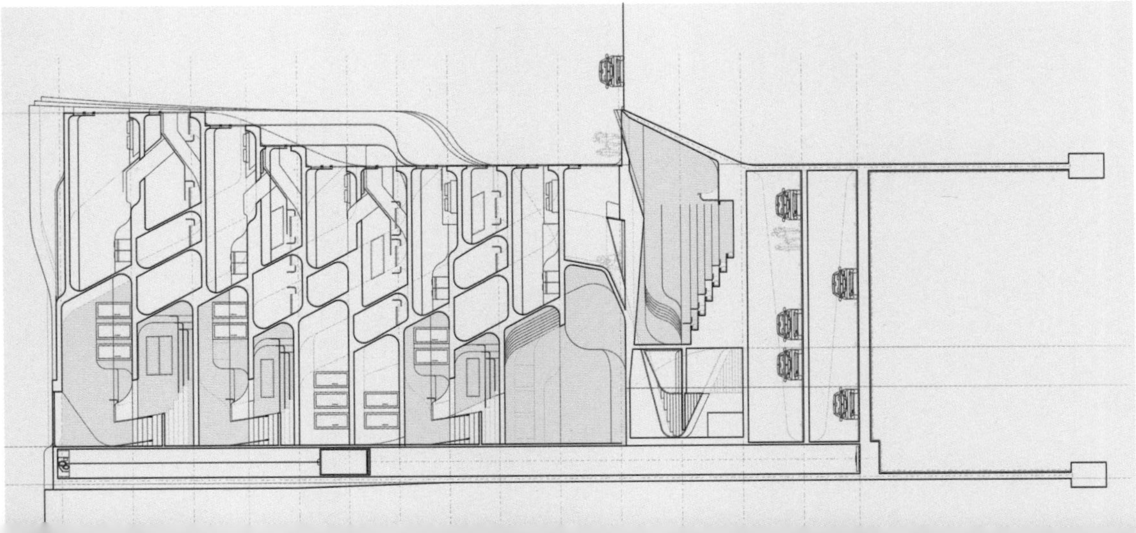

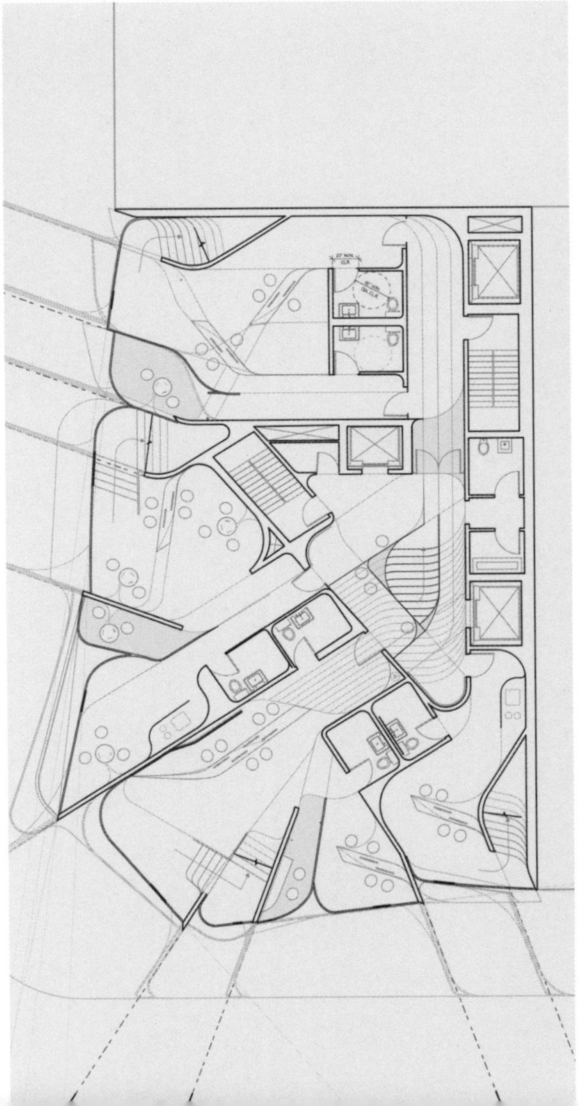

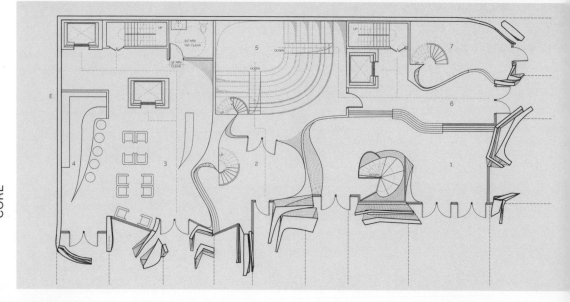

STUDENT:
Andre Stiles

CRITIC:
Hina Jamelle

Neighborhoods represent an evolutionary process. Their population diversifies and shifts based upon economic, environmental, institutional and social progress, addressing new and more complex problems as they strive to achieve a "neighborhood wholeness."

Much as the TriBeCa neighborhood has established itself into a subdivision of historic districts, with each cluster designated because of its individual association with events, people, construction methods, etc. that have made a significant contribution to the broad patterns of our history, its wholeness

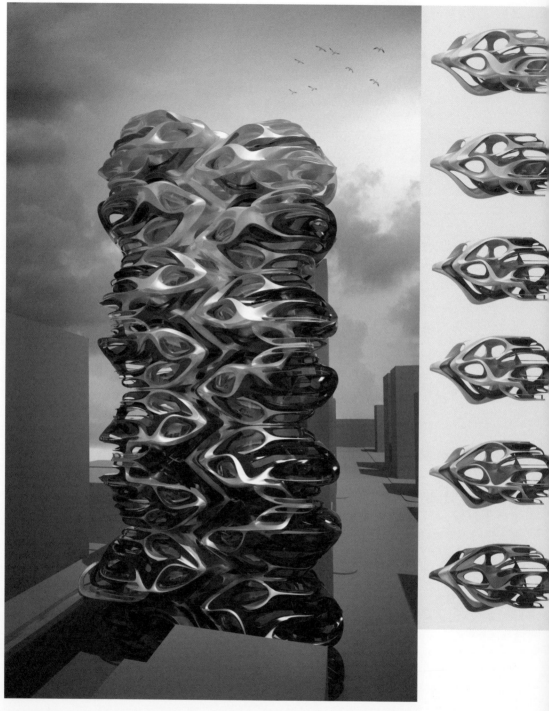

STUDENT:
Andy Shixiang Zheng

CRITIC:
Jonas Coersmeier

Located in Chelsea, this proposal speaks to hyper-densification in cities, where the need to hybridize public and private space is critical. It utilizes two interwoven colored systems, indicating the synthesis of communal and private programs from the exterior façade. Within this dichotomy of public and private, the proposal caters to both young and aging populations to positively promote understanding and learning. With the inclusion of a theater, library and other public space, this proposal is able to activate the urban fabric and blurs public-private thresholds.

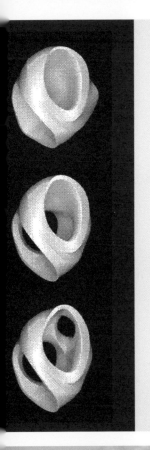

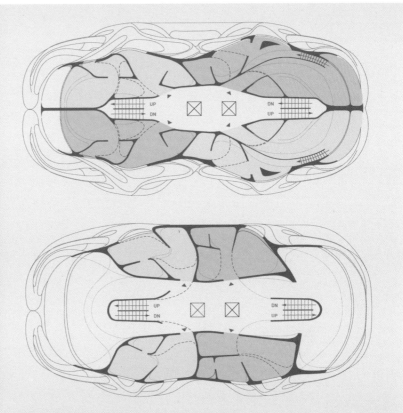

601 [MARCH]

CORE

JONAS COERSMEIER

STUDENT:
Chris Yuntao Xu

CRITIC:
Jonas Coersmeier

The design proposes a new prototype for residential towers along the High Line Park. Simultaneously exploring the possibility of integrating luxury condos and subsidized housing in both living and communal space. Using formal language, the project seeks a new form of living for residents. Lower / mid income group are emerging artistic designers, while the Luxury group are investors interested in the arts. To create interactions between users, the building offers communal spaces: a co-working space, and a gallery space, which also provides a meeting place for investors and designers.

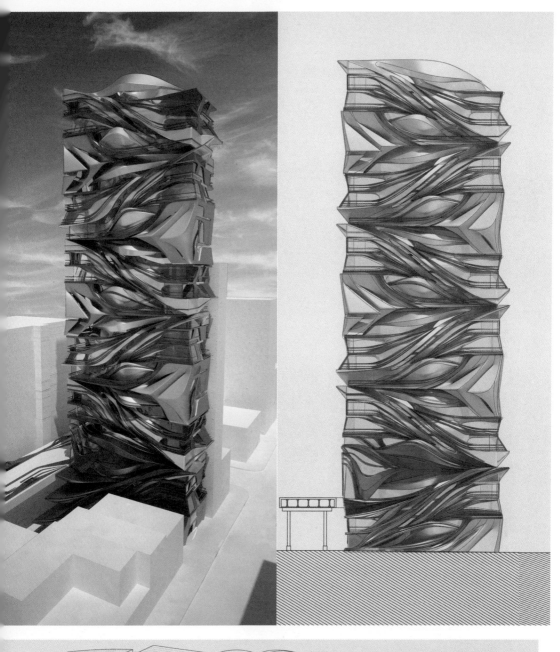

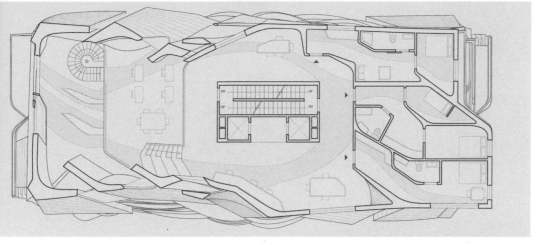

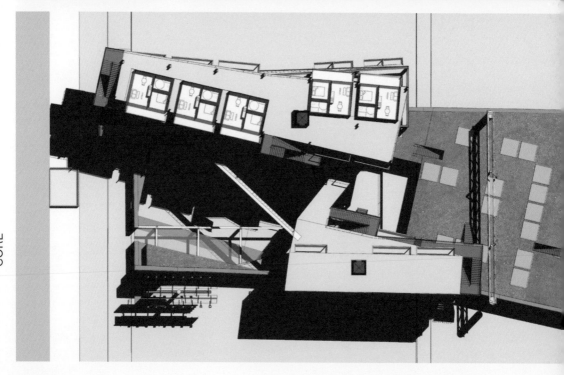

STUDENT:
Constance Chang

CRITIC:
Scott Erdy

Excavation: Sitting atop the ruinous abutment of the Reading Viaduct, the building excavates downward, uncovering multiple layers of the sites history. Using the existing abutment as fortification, the housing ascends upward as a re-constructed industrial artifact, assembled from recycled bits collected from along the viaduct.

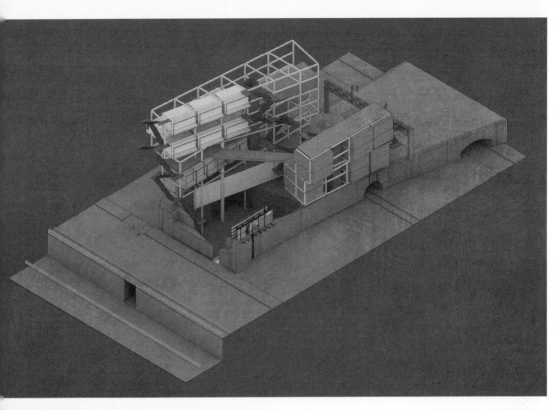

CORE

STUDENT:
Graham Perron Nelson

CRITIC:
Scott Erdy

SCOTT ERDY

The Wall: The abandoned Reading Viaduct provides the last physical connection between the Lenape's ancestral home and their forced relocation to Oklahoma. When approached from the re-emerging vegetation of the abandoned viaduct, the Wall presents itself as both threshold and barrier to Philadelphia. Although protected from "outsiders", the elitist residents are forced to live in a dystopic inversion of city fabric where their housing is literally turned upside down.

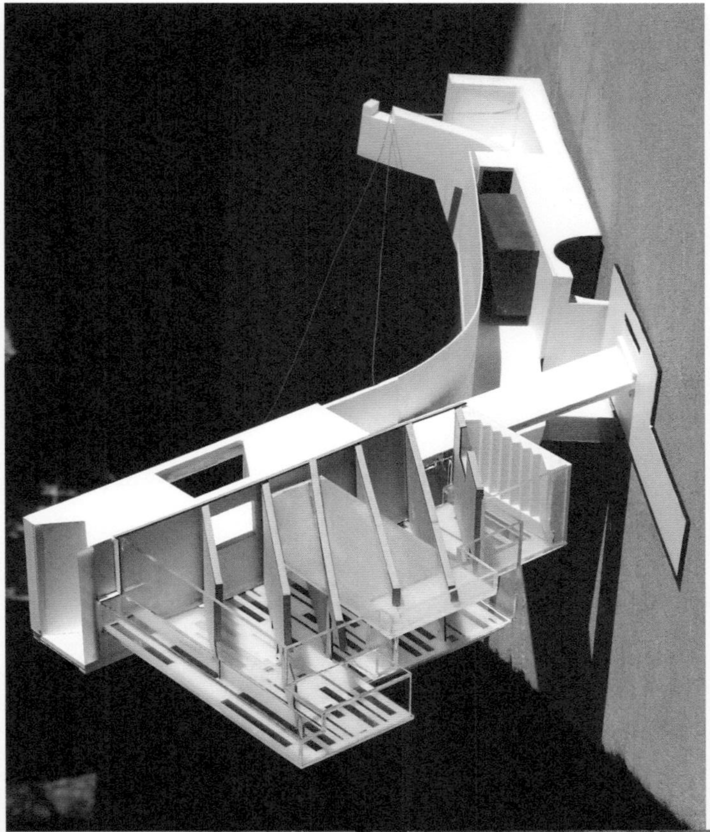

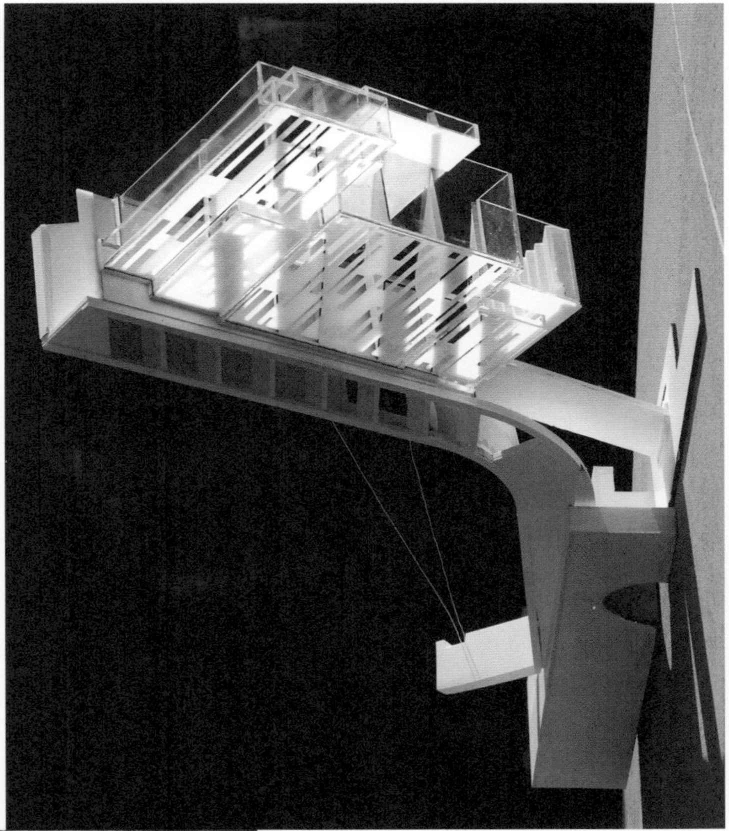

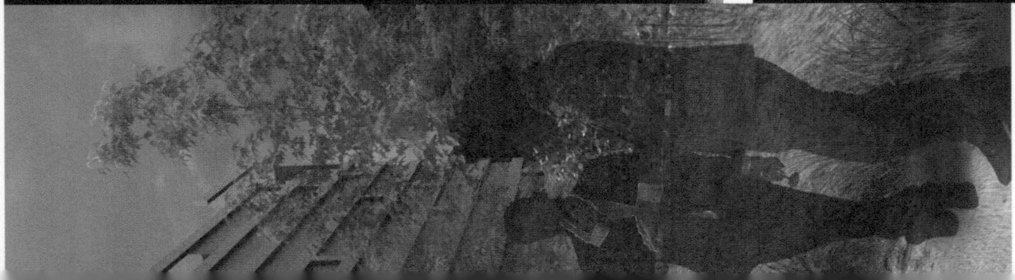

STUDENTS:
Alexander Bahr, Haeyun Kwon, Jennifer Rokoff, Ji Yoon, Madelyn Moretta, Mana Sazegara, Shuxin Wu, Tian Ouyang, Yuwei Sun.

CRITIC:
Kutan Ayata

PETER COOPER VILLAGE STUYVESANT TOWN
With 80 sprawling acres, comprising 10 city blocks north to south, 110 buildings 11232 unites, and 20000 increasingly affluent resident, PCV/ST is by far Manhattan's largest apartment complex. The complex has the exclusive advantage of being manhattans only "city within a city," combining serene pastoral living with convenient urban access. We believe the ongoing deregulatin will continue to allow new ownership to fully leverage the unparalleled competitive advantages of the complex and take advantage of the oaring rental market. Over $320 million in capital improvements and apartment renovation since 2002 have reinvigorated and refined the image of the complex. New ownership has infinite opportunities to personalize, improve, and trasform the complex into the city's most prominent market rate master community.

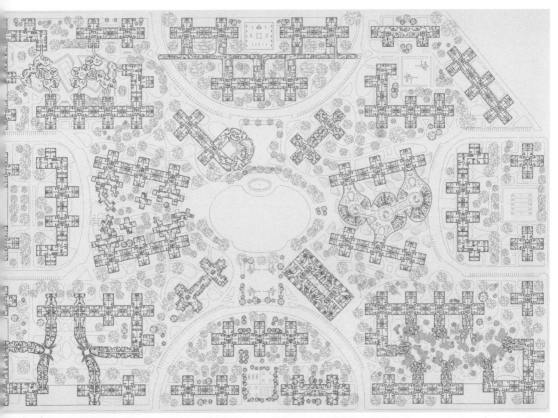

STUDENTS:
Alexander Bahr, Haeyun Kwon, Jennifer Rokoff, Ji Yoon, Madelyn Moretta,
Mana Sazegara, Shuxin Wu, Tian Ouyang, Yuwei Sun.

CRITIC:
Kutan Ayata

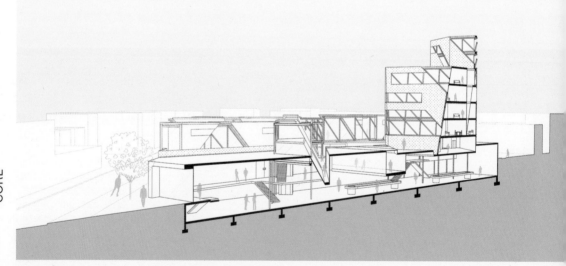

STUDENT:
Irena Wight

CRITIC:
Brian Phillips

Interwoven | A New Industrial Building Fabric. Small manufacturing is becoming increasingly important in today's political, social, and urban climates. It acts as a binding agent for a diverse group of people. Interwoven brings small manufacturing back to Philadelphia and reintroduces the relationship between making and living. A Shinola-type factory is located along the south of the site. Passersby view manufacturing through a curtain wall façade. North of the factory, an urban fabric composed of make/live units with work studio on 1st floor and living space on 2nd floor takes shape.

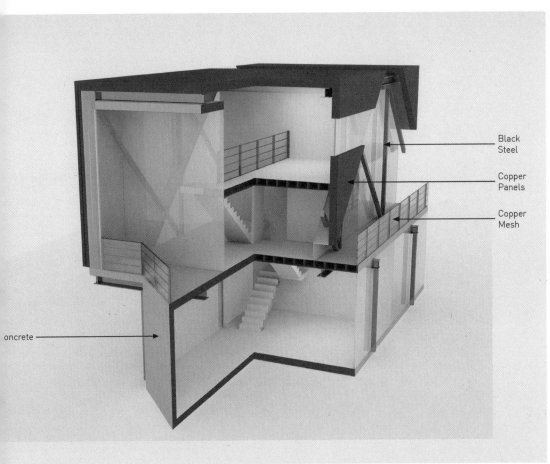

Black
Steel

Copper
Panels

Copper
Mesh

oncrete

CORE

STUDENT:
Daniel Hurley

CRITIC:
Brian Phillips

BRIAN PHILLIPS

Enhanced Perimeter reinterprets the rowhouse fabric into a new geometry that promotes community, social living, and flexible housing, while engaging the public as an urban hub. By articulating the building mass with a series of folds, Enhanced Perimeter becomes the ideal typology for a co-housing network. While traditional corridor buildings are private and anonymous, the circulation spaces of Enhanced Perimeter double as shared kitchens and lounges, becoming magnets of activity with panoptic views of the street and courtyard.

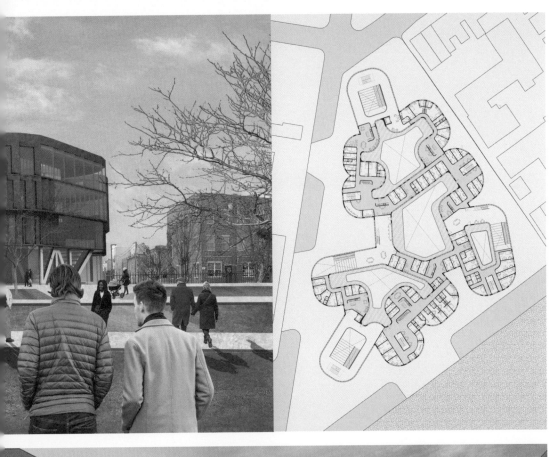

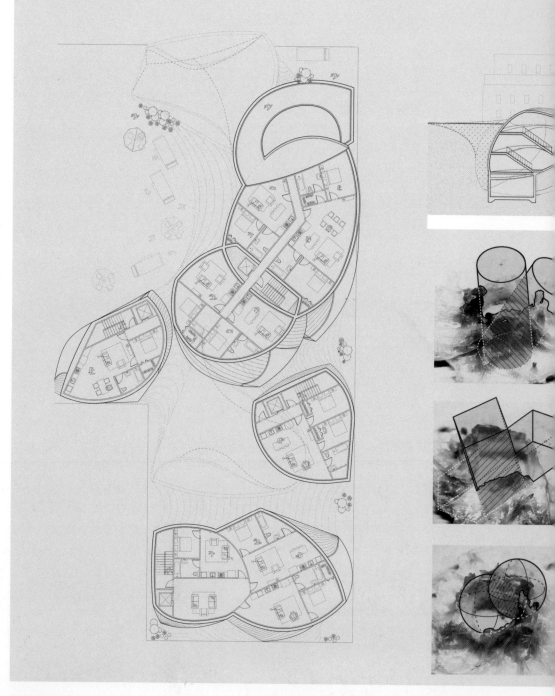

STUDENT:
Joanna Ptak

CRITIC:
Abigail Coover Hume

The Edible Collective: Through the intersection of primitive shapes, The Edible Collective integrates simultaneities and variabilities of similar geometries via overlapping, hierarchy, and scale by presenting forms as if food on a table. The project incorporates layering through the intersection of geometry, which then wraps a protective overlay holding the forms within the ground. The anomalies from the layering of these objects develop interspaces, which ultimately constitute a series of new entities and relationships that reflect an integrated program of housing and urban farming.

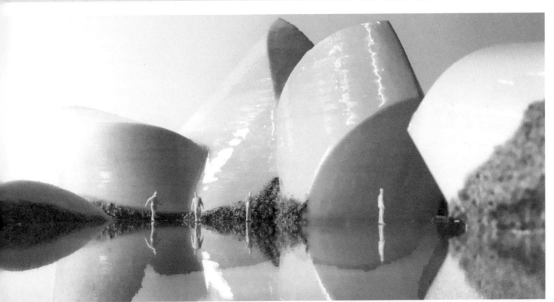

601 [MARCH]

CORE

ABIGAIL COOVER HUME

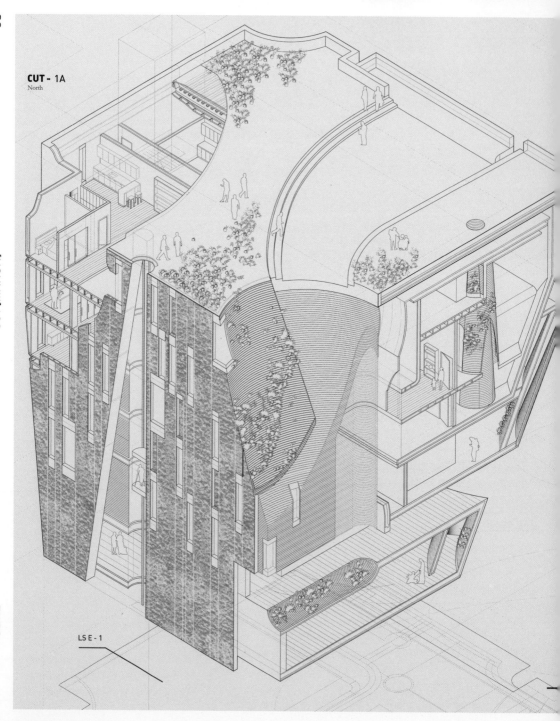

CUT - 1A
North

LS E - 1

STUDENT:
Laura Colagrande

CRITIC:
Abigail Coover Hume

This project challenges the traditional notion of horizontal layers and reinterprets the familiar operation of combining primitives (cone-cube; cube-cone; cone-cone) to create unexpected effects and experiences. The resulting system of vertical layers serves both as formal tactic to generate new volumes and as organizational strategy to curate the adjacency of the Residential-Food Coop mixed-use program. Ultimately, the vertical sequence of intersecting surfaces and textures allows for new relationships between more intimate spaces of residential units and shared ones of the Food Coop.

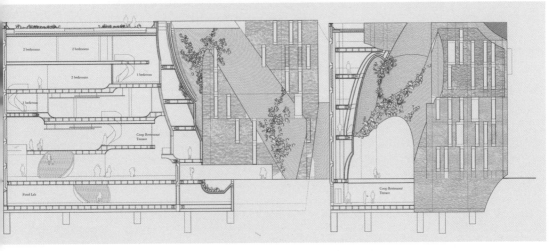

BENJAMIN KRONE

STUDENT:
Siqi Wang

CRITIC:
Benjamin Krone

For most live-work projects, the space is mixed in one unit, which may become chaotic. From an analog model, I separate the space in different tubes and study how the systems overlap and intersect. Many artists like to have private space to work without interruption. They also need public space for discussion and team work. The large tubes use perforated corten steel panels, responding to the industrial buildings in red hook. The louvers of the units are controlled by artists according to their needs. The project works as a system, and provides possibilities for artists.

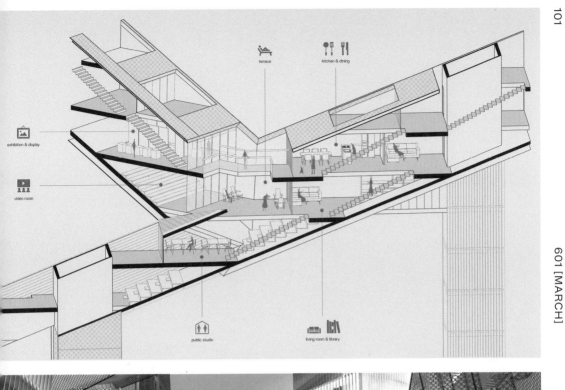

terrace

kitchen & dining

exhibition & display

video room

public studio

living room & library

STUDENT:
Sylvia Xinyu Wang

CRITIC:
Benjamin Krone

According to statistics, workers in Art & Culture Industry in Brooklyn has climbed during the years. Pioneer Works is an emerging place which works in experimental art and contemporary culture. Pioneer Homes, located across from Pioneer Works, inherits its efforts on challenging notions of art by combing gallery with dwelling. The idea came from the interlocking play of separate parts of my analog model. The collision of art and life creates interesting and innovative experience. The living units also provide cozy and affordable lives that are deeply connected to the artistic atmosphere.

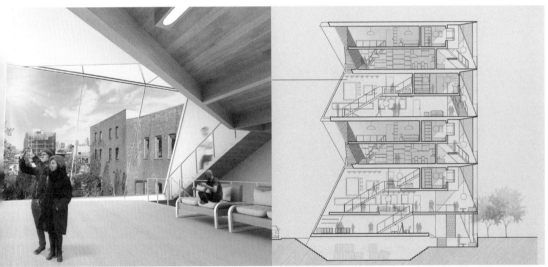

CORE

At its core, this fourth-semester design studio is the first to integrate construction knowledge developed in a constellation of core courses, within its design production. Students work in small teams with a host of internationally recognized consultants to create architecture with structural, mechanical, and environmental systems refined in organization and scale. Offices such as Buro Happold, Arup, and AKT have been involved with the studio projects. The resulting architecture, informed by the polemics of the instructors, ranges from performative air, parts to whole strategies, contemporary discourse of inside and outside, the estranged and deterritorialized, to non-human agencies.

At a disciplinary level, the histories and theories courses also come into sharper focus with new and advancing media and techniques. The milieu of architecture, as a historic tradition and a projective pursuit, continually manages the meaning and cultural production of architecture. This is not only due to the plurality of our age, but also to the higher-order ramifications of architecture in service to a global enterprise, with adjustments for a wholly synthetic and new world. When compounded with vanguard technologies, what is craft-based and what is intellectual takes on hybrid dimensions.

What is of primary importance is to ratify the often striking formal and ideological productions with a clear position, supported by equally clear planimetric and qualitative documentation.

Simon Kim, Coordinator

SYNTHETIC NATURE – THE LONGSPAN AND THE THICK ENVELOPE

CRITIC: **Simon Kim**

- Co-founded Ibañez Kim Studio, PA & MA, (1994)
- Graduated from the Design Research Laboratory at the Architectural Association (AA)
- Taught studios and seminars at Harvard, MIT, Yale, and the AA.
- Director of the Immersive Kinematics Research Group

This fourth and final in a series of the Core Design Studio Sequence is to demonstrate adaptation of the surrounding curriculum in history and building technology into an architectural design For this studio in particular, we will divest ourselves from architecture as fictive machines, towards architecture and site as sensate, nervous agents and environments.

Founded in 1986, Socrates Sculpture Park is the only site in the New York Metropolitan area specifically dedicated to providing artists with opportunities to create and exhibit large-scale sculpture and multi-media installations in a unique outdoor environment that encourages strong interaction between artists, artworks and the public. The park's existence is based on the belief that reclamation, revitalization and creative expression are essential to the survival, humanity and improvement of our urban environment.

Socrates Sculpture Park was an abandoned riverside landfill and illegal dumpsite until 1986 when a coalition of artists and community members, under the leadership of artist Mark di Suvero, transformed it into an open studio and exhibition space for artists and a neighborhood park for local residents. Today it is an internationally renowned outdoor museum and artist residency program that also serves as a vital New York City park offering a wide variety of free public services.

But next to the Socrates Park is a typology invented in the past 20 years: the single occupant big box. This Costco is fascinating in its pretensions and social inaccuracy. We will take it down and reclaim that site and its large volume of programme for the arts and the community of Queens.

BOTH/AND

CRITIC: **Nathan Hume**

Partner at Hume coover studio (2008)
- Editor & Founder of suckerPUNCH (2008)
- Earned a Bachelor of scienc in Architecture from Ohio State University (2003)

Since the time of Vitruvius, the terms "interior" and "exterior" have been integral to the manner in which architecture is discussed. A building is fundamentally responsible for distinguishing spaces, thus establishing a relative understanding of being inside of one thing and outside of another. We have, over the course of time, come to expect certain things from this relationship. In Complexity and Contradiction in Architecture, Robert Venturi posited that "[t]he inside is different from the outside;" In The Dynamic of Architectural Form, Rudolph Arnheim stated that "perceptually and practically the worlds of outside and inside are mutually exclusive. One cannot be in both at the same time." For both Venturi and Arnheim it is in this binary relationship between interior and exterior that the possibility of producing a powerful effect exists. More recent explorations in architecture of the two terms strive to produce a much wider range of spatial conditions that go on to traverse the previously established mutual exclusivity of the two terms, interior and exterior. It is in the multiplicity over the expected binary that such explorations see great potential.

We will explore the subversion of the assumed mutual exclusivity between interior and exterior as a sort of glitch, an error in a structured system that is ultimately, and perhaps unexpectedly, beneficial. The interference will not be seen as a graphic mistake but rather independent logics with moments of exchange, resisting the in-between, in favor the simultaneous. Spatially this breakage cultivates tension over the statements of Venturi and Arnheim and helps to establish the structured system that we aspire to swerve as we identify strategies for the manner in which the strict division between interior and exterior can be broken, allowing one body to occupy both simultaneously.

PERPETUAL MOTION

CRITIC: **Benjamin Krone**

Founded Gradient Design Studio, NYC (2006)
Bachelor of Architecture from the University of Florida (1999)
MArch degree from Columbia University's Graduate School of
Architecture, GSAPP (2004)
Won the McKim Prize for Excellence in Design & the Sol Kaplan
Traveling Fellowship.

For hundreds of years advancements in transport have been the marker of human progress by which most other technological achievements are measured. The future of transportation has been an obsession of countless visionaries throughout history from Jules Vern to Walt Disney. Amazingly, many of Disney's predictions from the 1940's for the future of transportation have come to fruition. These included autonomous vehicles, personal flying devices, and tubular highways. Currently, Elon Musk, founder of SpaceX and Tesla Motors, is involved with the development of compressed air hyperloop capsules and is working toward space travel for the general public. Some of his earlier innovations like the autonomous electric car are already gaining wide acceptance.

In America especially, these changes to transportation are being fueled by an aging existing infrastructure as well as a greater understanding of the environmental impacts of our current transportation systems. There has also been a shift in thinking toward the limitations of natural fossil fuels, and the acknowledgement that coastal cities must contend with rising sea levels which severely impact urban transportation infrastructures.

The electric car, magnetic trains and people movers, Compressed Air Hyperloops, drones, autonomous personal vehicles, and wind and solar powered cars and boats are just a few examples of what is likely to become a ubiquitous means of travel. We will be exploring these all as possibilities in this studio. You will be asked to design a transit hub to act as a major collector and departure point for both people and vehicles along with the necessary support programs.

ARCHITECTURAL IDENTITY UNDER TRANSFORMATION

CRITIC: **Brennan Buck**

Mr. Buck is principal of the firm FreelandBuck, based in New York City and Los Angeles. His work and writing, which focuses on technology within the discipline and its associated aesthetic culture, has been published in Log, Frame, Architectural Record, Detail, and Surface, as well as several recent books on architecture and technology.

STRUCTURAL CONSULTANT:
Andrew Blasetti, Thornton Tomasetti
ENVIRONMENTAL CONSULTANT:
Chris Sheridan, Thornton Tomasetti,

Since Alberti, architectural identity is traditionally understood primarily through the façade; read through a horizontal relationship between exterior fenestration and interior volume. The sprawling extent and intricate choreography of the interior of a contemporary courthouse suggest that the interior is too large and complex to be conveyed on the façade. Instead, the studio task proposes the design of a low 1-2 story building with a single primary façade: its roof. We will focus on the vertical relationship between the collected masses that make up the roof and volumes below.

Like a proud suburban family with more money than taste, we'll cultivate a fondness for buildings that are the product of multiple, sometime conflicting interests and concerns, the result of cramming too much under one roof. We will take inspiration from two of the more accomplished McMansion designers of the late 19th and early 20th Centuries, Frank Furness in the US and Edwin Luytens in Britain. Both invented their own unique provincial style by mixing and transforming existing elements and both had a tendency to pile on the roof peaks, dormers and gigantic chimneys beyond what their contemporaries might have advised.

VOLUMETRIC HUDDLE: A STUDY OF FORM, FOOD + MATERIAL ON THE HUDSON RIVER

CRITIC: **Abigail Coover Hume**

- Partner at Hume Coover Studio (2008)
- Editor & Founder of suckerPUNCH (2008)
- Graduated with a MArch from Yale University (2006)
- Earned a Bachelor of Science in Architecture
  from University of Virginia (2001)

The site is located in Espopus NY along the Hudson River. The site houses an existing Gothic Revival structure originally built as a farm house in 1852 and later purchased by the religious order of the Christian Brothers who built a masonry school building in 1933. These two buildings are adjacent to one another, but not physically connected. The two buildings cover a footprint of 8300 square feet on a plateau that then descends dramatically to the train tracks and ultimately the Hudson River below.

In looking at the existing site as a series of large scale volumes in relationship to the ground plane, we will study the ways in which new, large scale programmatic volumes can clump with those existing, tumble down the hillside and nestle next to the Hudson River. We will begin with a formal analysis of huddled bodies - tomatoes, penguins, football players, and corn to name a few examples. We will look at photos and paintings from popular culture to draw, study, and codify existing relationships between objects. From these studies, we will create material experiments to further examine these physical and material relationships and then use these finding to move into massing and material development.

Representation will also be heavily emphasized as a design development tool. Final deliverables for two large scale composite drawings and one large scale model will be given at the beginning on the semester and will be consistently developed through the final review.

SUPER DECORATED SPACE

CRITIC: **Jonathan A. Scelsa**
CONSULTANTS: **Yan Chu** (Heingtes Associates), **Rob Franco** (Buro Happold)

- Jonathan is an Architect, Urbanist, and an educator. Prior is a co-director of OP – Architecture Landscape.
- As an educator, Jonathan is an Assistant Professor of Architectural Design + Technology at Pratt Institute in Brooklyn and Lecturer in Architecture at The University of Pennsylvania School of Design .
- Jonathan is a Licensed Architect in the state of New York. He received his Master of Architecture in Urban Design with Distinction from Harvard University. He received his Bachelor of Architecture from Carnegie Mellon University.

Two very dirty words in a contemporary Architectural discourse are Space and Decoration, arguably due to their association with the two dominant conceptual paradigms of the 20th century which we'd like to think are dead. Space was the project of modernism, and Mies Van Der Rohe one of the chief architects. Mies made the spatial form of the grid his architectural master-work, externalities such as HVAC or private rooms would either be inside of its field, adhered within the grid or expelled. The shed's grid space is totalizing and in the soap bubble of Modernism, the Inside is the Outside.

As a studio we will adopt the interest in decoration of ordinary building typology (as well as healthy interest in figuration), but we will eschew the "envelope-only" outside-in architecture that has already been investigated, ad-nauseum. We will explore a formalism that is rooted in disfiguring the legibility of the Cartesian capital grid through various 2D optic methods of patterned illusion, deception, and trickery that hopefully will result in a new style.

We will explore methods of patterning based on mid-century graphic designers and explore how we might spatialize the graphic via Anamorphosis, or conical extrusion in order to blur the binary relationship of 2D envelope versus 3D space using shape as a medium.

OBJECTS OF NATURE

CRITIC: **Kutan Ayata**

Co-founded New York-based architecture firm, Young & Ayata (2008)
Young & Ayata are winners of The Architectural League Prize (2014)
Received a MArch from Princeton University (2004)
Bachelor of Fine Arts in Architecture from Massachusetts College of
Art in Boston (1999)

Traditionally, the discipline of architecture (as well as the arts) has always been preoccupied with questions of representing/recreating/redefining/embodying "nature" through various strains of its histories, i.e. from Baroque, Rococo to Art Nouveau, from Modernism, to Biomimicry, and even recent tendencies of green, sustainable approaches continue these ambitions by foregrounding responsible relations with our environment. Without a doubt, all these approaches generated significant aesthetic arguments. The two most common pitfalls of all such aesthetics can be summed up as follows: either the design aims for a simulacrum, resulting in literal interpretations of "what is commonly assumed to be natural," or aims for juxtaposition through absolute abstractions to posture against "the nature". Both these positions reflect the presumption of the usual nature/culture divide. What if we explore this problem yet again, but aim to operate away from these opposite poles? What if we claim that we can produce specific objects that can begin to undermine our assumptions about the culture/nature divide? What if we rather take the position that authentic "objects of nature" can be constructed and these constructions can cultivate their unique qualities, experiences, and cultures?

The studio explored an indoor/outdoor rock climbing facility in the Canal Park at the western end of Canal Street on the West Side of Manhattan. It was be understood as part of the recreational activity chain which has been developing on the waterfront with the regeneration of the Island's western edge. The central inquiry was the aesthetics of such an artificial construct and formal/material specificity of its assembly.

STUDENT:
Andy Rose

CRITIC:
Simon Kim

At the death of a building it is often demolished, or rarely collapses by itself. This creates explosions that initiate large forces, erupting in clouds of particles. At the same time the main frames of the structure itself implodes and collapses. During this brief but critical moment, the state of the building and its material component changes as the synthetic creature dies. The building once again is relegated to its initial state as materials and matter, as an object.

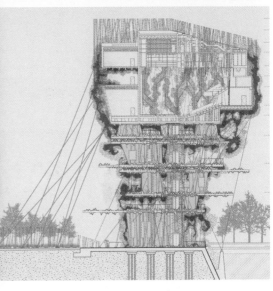

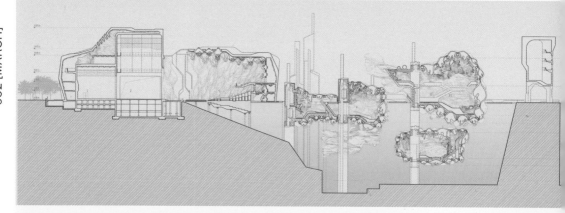

STUDENT:
Yuntao Xu & Mingxin He

CRITIC:
Simon Kim

"Thinking things as nature is thinking them as a more or less static continuity bounded by time and space". For OMA, for Zaha, for Greg Lynn, these processes are utilized in the design stages but never made manifest in the physical object. The world of non-completion and dynamic relationships were never tested in their proper environment: buoyancy in fluids. We propose an architectural urbanism of floating terrains and interiors that, like a stage or even a sentient environment, changes their configurations dependent on human interaction as well as their own self-agency.

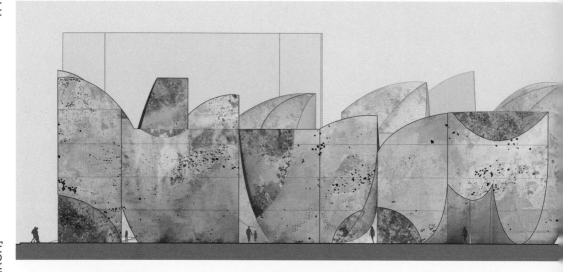

STUDENT:
Allison Koll & Mana Sazegara

CRITIC:
Nathan Hume

The geometry creates a series of choreographed experiences as one moves from the flush exterior façade to the bulbous, draping interior. The inward-facing courtyard becomes an exterior room, while also creating smaller rooms within rooms. With multiple points of entry, threshold conditions emphasize movement between layers or "slippages", and circulation through the mean-dering courtyard creates moments of surprise and interaction with the un-expected. In the façade's materiality, layers of translucent aggregates reveal other qualities, imply depth, and give hints to the other interior world.

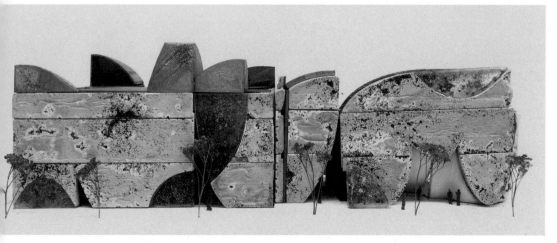

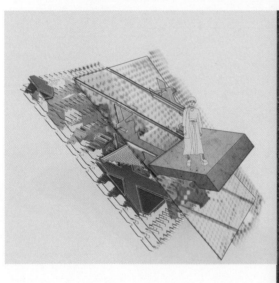

STUDENT:
Leetee Wang & Marianne Sanche

CRITIC:
Nathan Hume

A composition inspired by digital deformations occurring in images via slit-scanning and pixelation. What begins as two dimensional effects can be reimagined in architectural concepts of directionality of streaking forms, loose boundaries between objects, and vertical fragmentation where 'x' components collide.

The aggregation of such fragmented 'X' components result in changes in densities moving through the building that coincide with where physical or visual connections should manifest.

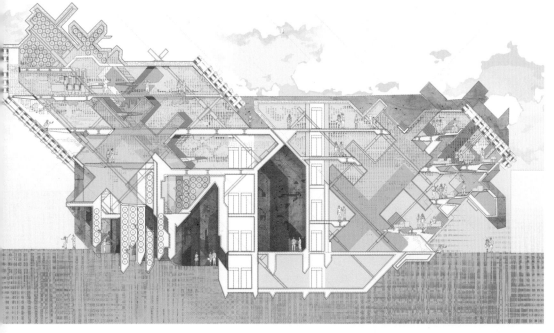

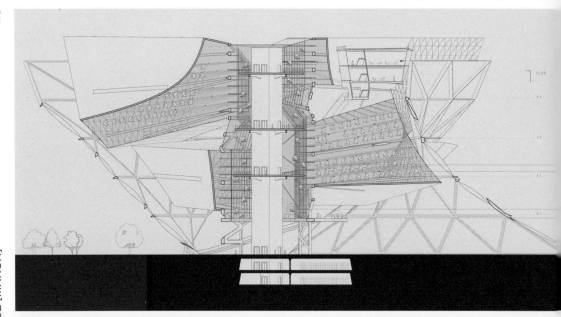

STUDENT:
Constance Chang & Tian Ouyang

CRITIC:
Benjamin Krone

It has built-in R+D offices on the research of vehicles as well as private showrooms distributed across the parking spaces. An auditorium space for new releases is also considered, all operating without interfering the collecting, sorting and redistribution. Humans will serve as the witness to this fully functioning machinery and be exposed to fascinating moments wherever they go. This self-driven yet precise mechanism casts plausible light on what else a transportation system could be, and how its uniqueness in functionality and aesthetics may help shape the its future presence.

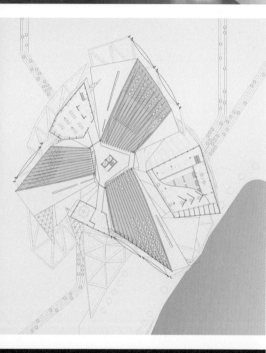

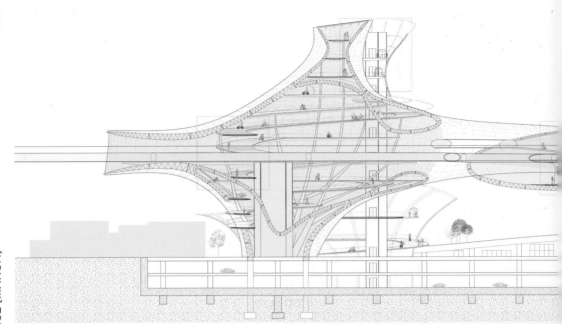

STUDENT:
Yute Chiang & Michael Hua

CRITIC:
Benjamin Krone

We are interested in the transition between systems with opposing features, sharing the common ground of environmental consciousness in terms of pollution and energy consumption. They demonstrate similar interaction between systems based on the original concept with different materials and mechanisms, which gave us new perspectives on the mediation of distinct elements. The multiple layers of skin define the program hierarchy and frequency of use, and are reshaped by the circulation of both hyperloop and biking tracks.

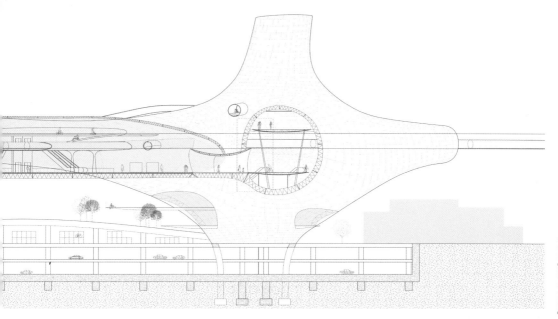

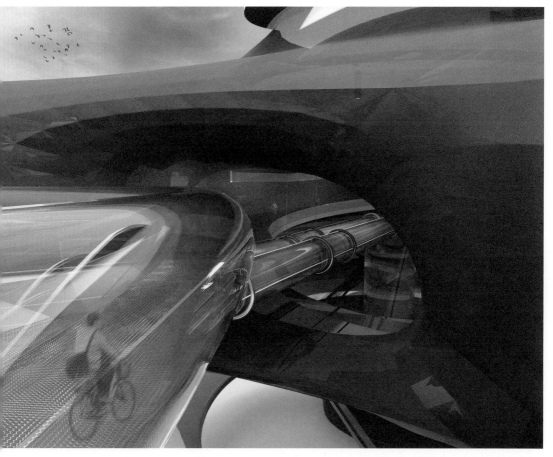

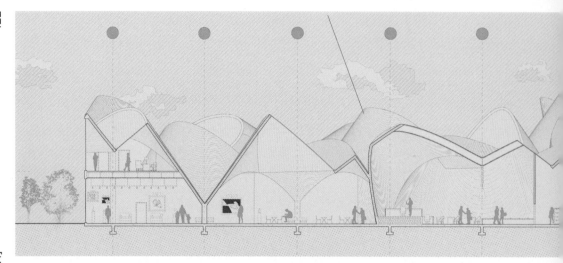

STUDENT:
Lillian Candela and Iris Kim

CRITIC:
Brennan Buck

This form is representative of the tension between individual and collective, it is both a continuous whole and an individual volume as one. Furthering the building's ambiguous nature it fluctuates between a two dimensional graphic and a three dimensional amalgamation of parts as one moves past the building on the Delaware Expressway. This ambiguity is reinforced through the changing tile roof treatment, increasing in density as more of the building is revealed and blending the individual building elements together - further confusing what is individual cone and what is aggregate massing.

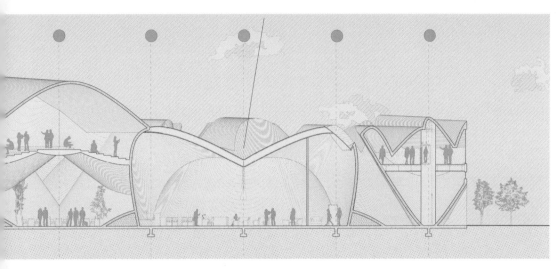

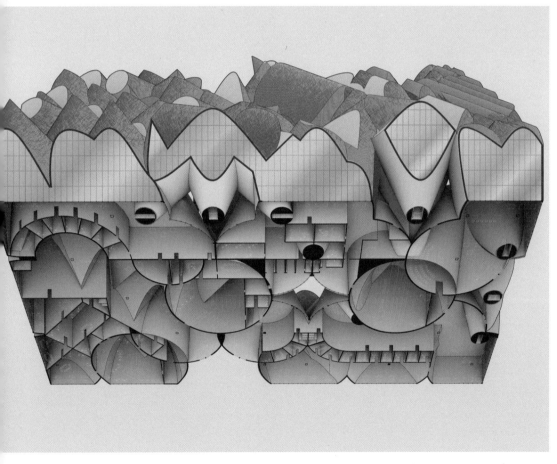

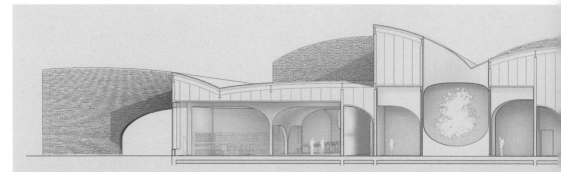

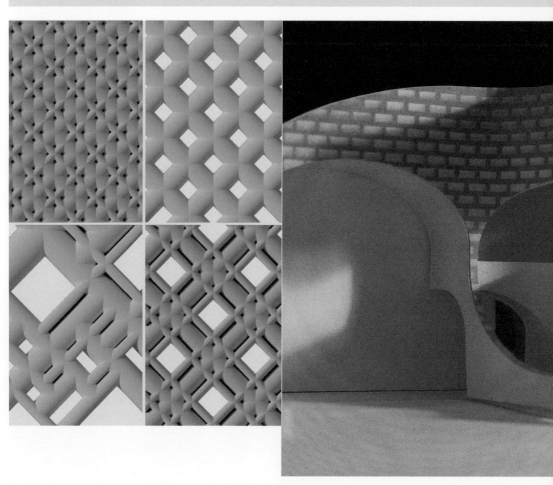

STUDENT:
Dani Lands & Ji Sook Yoon

CRITIC:
Brennan Buck

Many contemporary courthouses in the US are hyper-functional, intimidating and stressful. In these structures, the primary design driver is efficiency, and the goal is to instill a sense of authority to the occupants. Dolce Volta strives to create a space of refuge from the stress and pressure inherent in the justice system and its architecture. Filled with contemplative spaces, this novel approach gives judges, jurors, lawyers, and charged individuals a space to think clearly and come to just decisions.

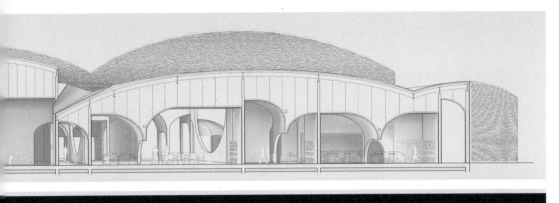

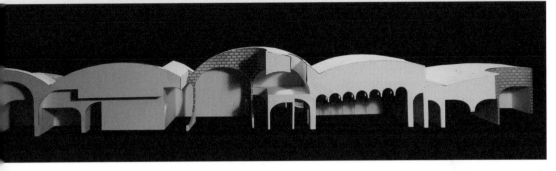

602 [MARCH]

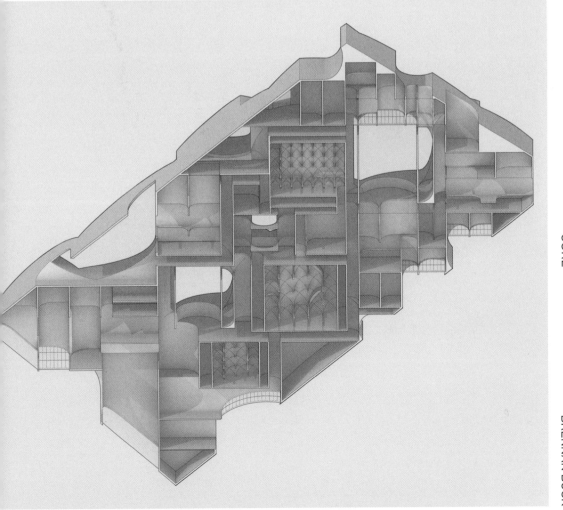

CORE

BRENNAN BUCK

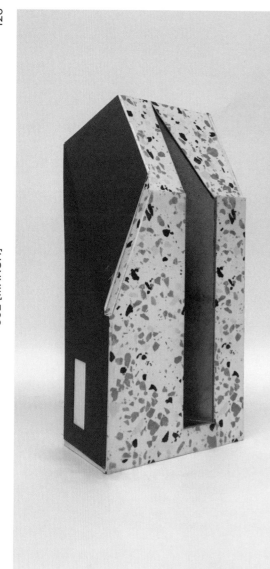

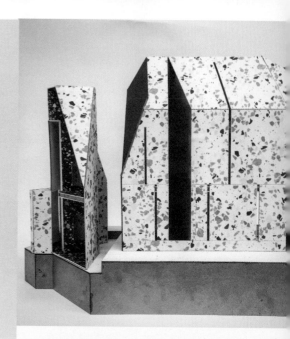

STUDENT:
Laura Colagrande and Jesus Elizondo Gonzalez

CRITIC:
Abigail Coover Hume

Kaleidoscopic Shift is hospitality experience on the Hudson Valley with a hotel, distillery, restaurants and bars overlooking the Hudson river. The project uses as a precedent the typology of the medieval village, producing an experience that is both relevant to the architectural community, while at the same time an enjoyable experience for non-architects. Following research and experimentation on the materiality of terrazzo, Kaleidoscopic Shift engages in the process of making that material: mixing, splitting, shifting, and revealing the interior material composition.

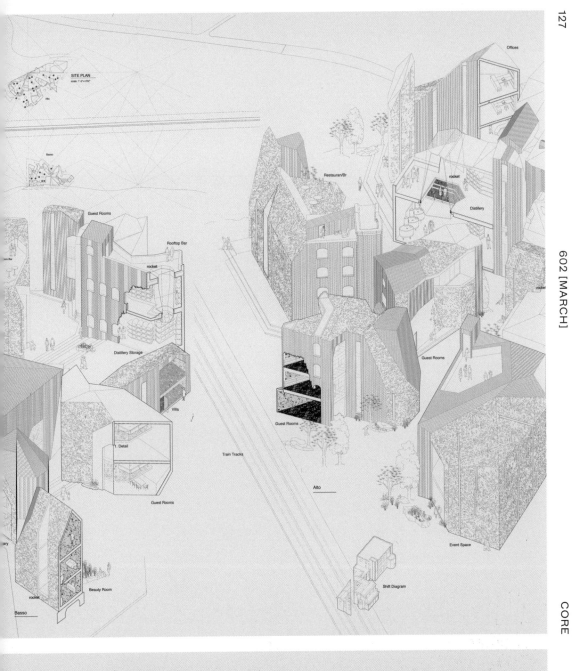

SITE PLAN
scale: 1'-0"=100'

Guest Rooms

Rooftop Bar

rocket

Distillery Storage

Villa

T. Detail

Guest Rooms

Train Tracks

Alto

rocket

Beauty Room

Basso

Restauran/Br

rocket

Distillery

Guest Rooms

Guest Rooms

Offices

rocket

Event Space

Shift Diagram

CORE

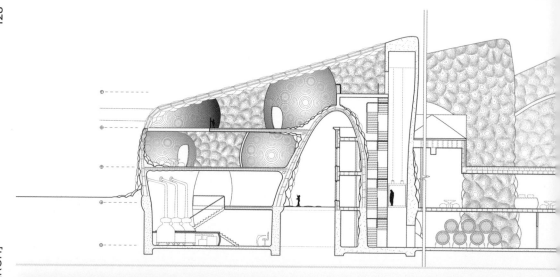

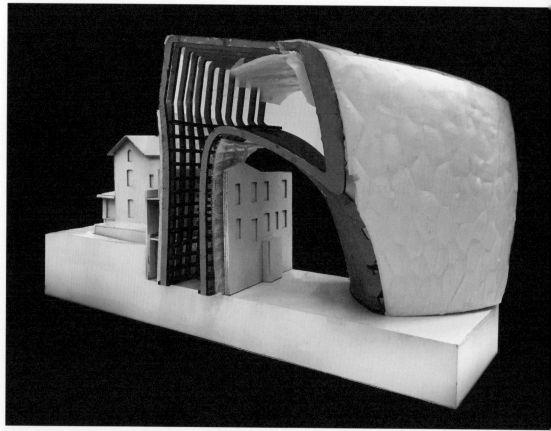

STUDENT:
Jennifer Rokoff and Kaj Marshall

CRITIC:
Abigail Coover Hume

This gradient and layering resonated clearly with a condition in which structure and program interact in strange ways, with old structure playing host to new, which layers in it and around it to form a composite form, where both existences as equally important. In this vein, our proposed structure treats the existing building as a germination point, sprouting from inside the existing, refurbished building and spilling over one side, eventually forming a new façade which shields the old, creating interstitial space between the two and enabling strange interior relationships where the two meet.

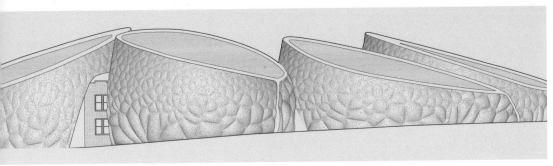

CORE

ABIGAIL COOVER HUME

STUDENT:
Alyssa Appel, Joanna Ptak, Ramune Bartuskaite

CRITIC:
Jonathan A. Scelsa

Typitecture applies the alphabetical graphic at 3 depths. The first is the structural, challenging the spatial differentiation capabilities of the letter and enabling interesting spatial experience. The secondary application of the typographic is aperture, which is generated by anamorphic views from the city. They are based on contingency and therefore contextualize the project, directly linking it to site-specific experience. The tertiary application of the letter occurs on the most superficial level, engaging the economic and corporate culture inherent in the project's parameters.

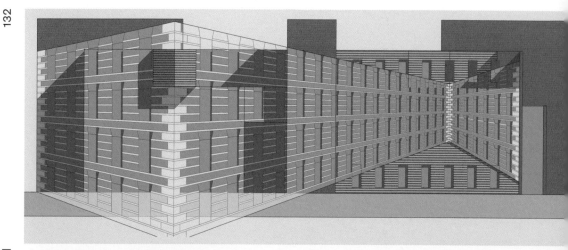

STUDENT:
Morgan Leigh Welch & Lauren Elizabeth Aguilar

CRITIC:
Jonathan A. Scelsa

The project is oriented around a series of inflection points in which the diptych view appears optically symmetrical but spatially incongruent. This effect is achieved through brick coursing manipulated to follow the view and wrap the forms. As a result the brick functions as a decoration that manipulates scale and perception and does not perform structurally. As an exterior strategy, the façade uses the language of the historic Chelsea Pier to serve as a super graphic seen from the highline.

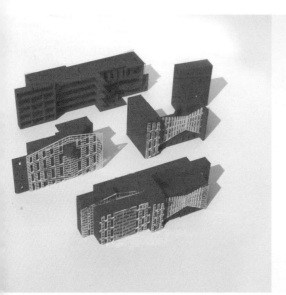
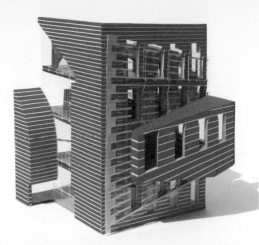
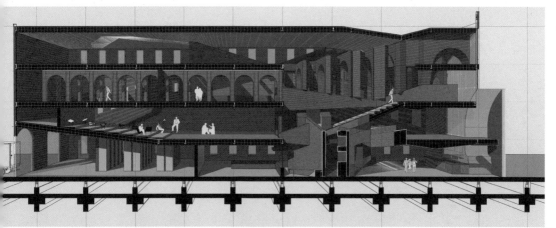

STUDENT:
John Hilla & Yisha Li

CRITIC:
Kutan Ayata

Upward movement on the interior is facilitated by tubes that are setwithin the columns. From the ground floor, these tubes exist only as structural elements, but in the basement below they are sliced open to reveal the colorful contoured surfaces that allow vertical climbers to ascend the full height of the columns and pierce through the roof of the building. Each of these tubes maintain a unique identity through the specific patterning on their surfaces that come with individualized climbing experiences, tasks, and difficulties.

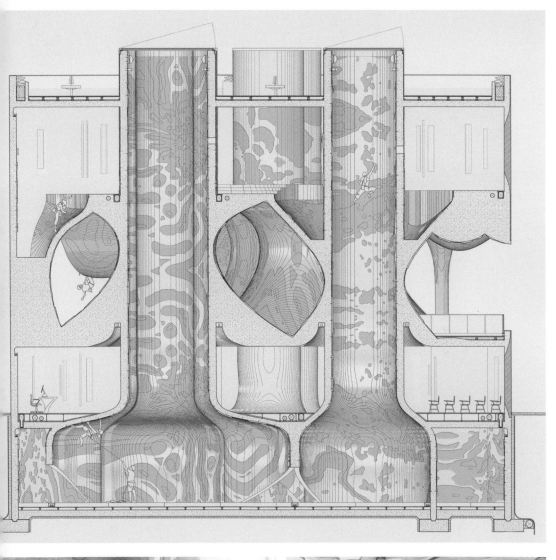

STUDENT:
Yiwei Gao & Xinyu Wang

CRITIC:
Kutan Ayata

The design basically includes two parts, form and texture. In term of the form, it starts from the boolean of four interlocking toruses which create continuous and exciting interior and exterior climbing spaces; the interior space is mainly for vertical climbing while the exterior is for bouldering, and both of them provide climbers in different levels with multiple climbing experiences. Except for climbing spaces, the building also contains a cafe on the top floor and multiple kinds of service rooms at the bottom that support the climbers.

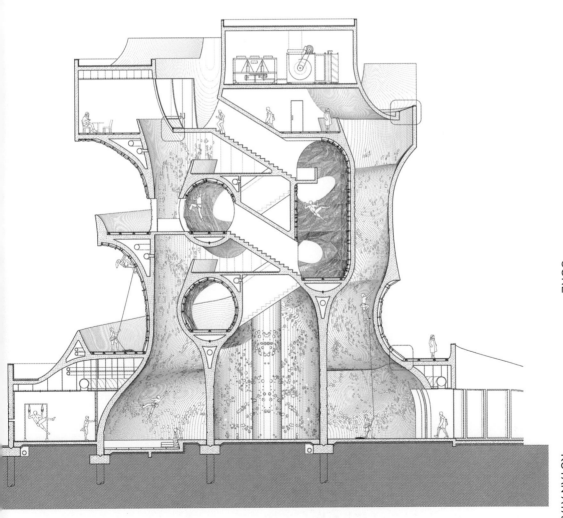

CORE

GALLERY

STUDENT:
Yi Yan

CRITIC:
Hina Jamelle

By shifting the angles of units at different levels, views are gradually changing. The shifting views not only create a montage that tells the essence of urban life but also reflect adjacent traditional building.

STUDENT:
Kirin Kennedy & Graham Perron Nelson

CRITIC:
Ben Krone

...seeks to be an extension of Lower Manhattan, with a continuous link across the river. It acknowledges the industrial nature of the site, seeks to work in concert with it, and creates an interchange concourse in the sky.

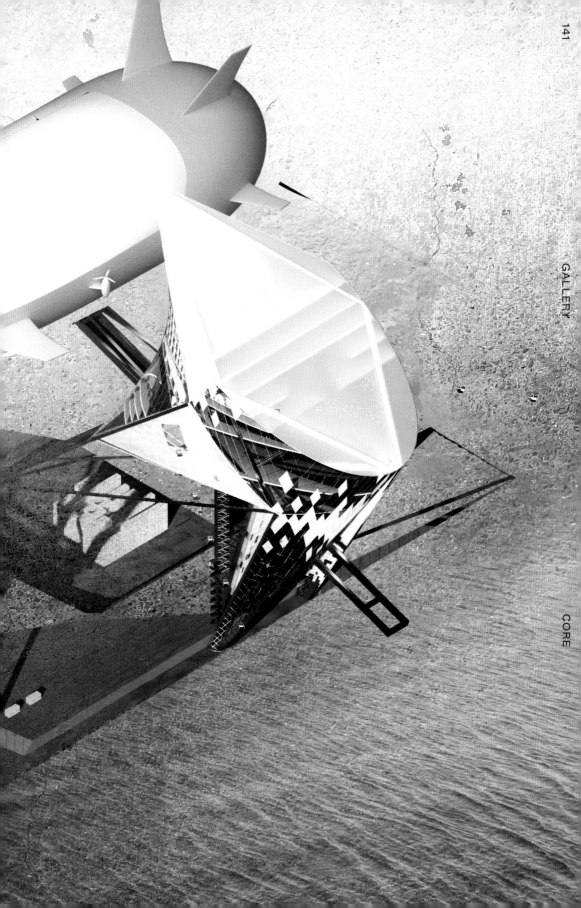

CORE

STUDENT:
Penelope Fung & Kailin Wang

CRITIC:
Nathan Hume

...layers of pipes at times disguise or accentuate the geometry of the massing, the delineation of interior and exterior is also obscured as pipes penetrate the envelope and occupying the atrium to create a fluid transition.

GALLERY

CORE

STUDENT:
Yiwei Gao & Xinyu Wang

Reference. page 136

CRITIC:
Kutan Ayata

STUDENT
Yuntao Xu & Mingxin He

Reference. page 112

CRITIC:
Simon Kim

AD
NC

VA
ED'

ADVANCED'

MASTER STUDIO

Architecture 701 is the first semester of the third year. It's an elective DESIGN-RESEARCH studio where we focus on the critical relationship between architecture and the city, and move beyond traditional planning to propose new interfaces where city and building meet. Le Corbusier declared already in his 1922 Manifesto, "Traditionalism, especially in large cities, obstructs the development of transport, cramps and debilitates activity, kills progress and discourages new ideas".

It is in this interface between the public and the private then, that a different mode of operation can be found, often shifting scales between the micro and the mega, and between public and private, thus avoiding the normative, and allowing space for new conditions.

Our diverse and renowned 701 faculty create an amazing range of interests and studios provoking the normative. Examples of themes such as; "the oversized building as object, speculative realism, and vital forms of material-ism" are found in the studio's led by Georgina Huljich: "Black Box. Mute Icon", Ferda Kolatan: "Respiratory Object", and Jason Payne: "Water and Power". Examples that operate on mega- scale and create "developments interfac-ing large urban fields" we find in studio's such as; Thom Mayne & Scott Lee's studio on Hainan Island: South Sea Pearl Eco Island, the Matthijs Bouw & Kai--Uwe Bergmann's studio on B.A.R.T. (Bay Area Resilient Trans-portation), the Tom Verebes' studio: Same-Same but Different, and of course in Simon Kim's collaboration with the University of Seoul: The Sensate and Augmented, which will be the basis for Department's exhibition at the 2017 Seoul Architecture Biennale in South Korea. Critical assessments of the norm are found in Paul Preissner's studio Cuba Libre on tourism in Cuba, while the suburban Mall as a project was revisited by Dan Wood's studio: Malltopia/Burbopolis. To summarize; the studio's goal here is not to propose a new type or typology, but to create productive responses and provocations that negate the existing urban condition, or suggest a transformative relationship between the object and the context, or from the object to itself.

GLOBAL INITIATIVES

An integral part of the 701 studio is that students travel to the location, and perform in-depth research locally. We as a Department, also have instigated a series of ongoing collaborations. Our past successes in International Partnerships have resulted in several recent requests for collaboration by international City officials, Governments and Real estate developers alike. A few examples are the collaboration with Penn alumnus Mr. Jeong from the Heerim Company, Seoul, where we partner with Seoul University under the guidance of professor Hong [Seoul] Simon Kim [PennDesign]. The resultant student team projects are to be exhibited in the 2017 Seoul Biennale. The Cairo Studio was initiated last year, starting a three-year design-research collaboration with the Government of Egypt, looking at the informal areas in Old Cairo, this Studio is taught and led by Practice Professor Ferda Kolatan. The student's work of first collaboration was exhibited in the Egyptian Pavillion at the 2016 Venice Architecture Biennale.

These are just a few examples of our 700 visiting faculty, research projects and collaborations, many of whom are steadily becoming part of our team of returning guest critics, always adding great discourse and enticing studios to our own renowned faculty.

Winka Dubbeldam, Coordinator
Professor and Chair

SUPERSTUDIO & SUPERVOIDS IN LONDON
Homa Farjadi coordinates the Annual PennDesign Masterclas at the Architectural Association [AA] in London, England.

CRITIC: **Homa Farjadi**
TA: **Eleni Pavlidou and Pierandrea Angius**

- Principal of Farjadi Architects (1987)
- Received a Graduate Diploma from the AA School of Architecture in London and an MArch with distinction from Tehran University
- The work of her office has been exhibited and published internationally.

The semester long Penn studio conducted at the AA in London takes on the landscape of large London parks considering them in their potential for high density urbanism as a more active participant in inviting high density events , structures, and infrastructures. The work of Superstudio both in their writings and their design projects is the analytic text/ source considered for the reinterpretation in the contemporary context of the London large footprint urban park exploring park urbanism.

Superstudio's work was characterized by scepticism towards the modernist ideal that enlightened architecture could change the world for the better. Instead their vision did not wish to convince you of their righteousness or propriety. They ask you 'to learn to avert your eye, to go elsewhere

to avoid and disrupt architecture as we know it' Nature was refound through enabling infrastructure of technologies and foretold a rediscovered freedom in unpredictability and limitless space.

The projects in the studio considered alter native scenarios and programs for critical logics and logistics that brought experience of nature in the city by a new set of infrastructural public spaces. They sought to allow for unpredictable experience of the reinstituted landscape whether in short term mixed use housing complex, dug out arenas for a temporary music festival, artificial climbing / camping structure of towers or a contemporary version of holiday machine with alternative transportation canal linking offered in an urban viaduct.

eview at the AA with Jurors Theo Spyropolous, Director of the DRL,
nd Chair Winka Dubbeldam.

ADVANCED'

STUDENT:
David Zhewei Feng
Haiyin Tang

CRITIC:
Homa Farjadi
Eleni Paulidou
Pierandrea Angius

HOMA FARJADI

Linear Henge, An Alternative Urbanity in Hampstead Heath
    Hampstead Heath is a precious piece of nature situated in London, the high-density metropolitan open space. We understand the value of it and propose a series of towers with small footprints in the heath to maximise our access to the valuable resources of nature, such as sunlight, air, views, etc. These towers, with maximum 150-m high and no elevators, are manmade mountains that allow extended vertical journeys of nature from the heath. The towers themselves then become an alternative nature, to provide a different way to re-experience nature, and also, at the same time, another way to urbanise the heath.

STUDENT:
Yuan Ma
Yangmei Cai

CRITIC:
Homa Farjadi
Eleni Paulidou,
Pierandrea Angius

Housing Megalith: As visionary essays Superstudio projected a total freedom of life imagining humans to have absolute free space in open natural environment metaphysically enabling freedom in a combination of freedom and unpredictability.

The megaliths dropped into Hampstead heath in our project are proto urban transitional housings confronting open nature. They consider seclusion as a new way of transition and relation with nature. The abrupt change between inside and outside, make the choice between urbanity and nature as a simultaneous possibility. The tremendous geological scale of the structure to keep it hovering between the designed and un-designed, A dense interior with two ring systems and habitable decks separate life between environments controlled and exposed to climate. The ramps, which are also the inner ring system, work with the purposefully placed amenities and the sun to create chronological population flow. This becomes the pulse of the structure. This is also creating an ambiguity between the urbanized life and circulation.

B.A.R.T.
Collaborative studio between ARCH and LARP

CRITIC: **Mattijs Bouw**

- Founding principal One Architecture
- Rockefeller Urban Resilience Fellow, PennDesign

CRITIC: **Kai-Uwe Bergmann**

- Partner at BIG
- Registered as an architect in the USA (eight states) and Canada (one province)
- Alma mater: the University of Virginia
- Is on the Board of the Van Alen Institute

In 2013, protests erupted in the Bay Area, where Google and other tech companies have organized private busses to shuttle their workers from San Francisco and Oakland to their corporate campuses in Silicon Valley. For the protesters, the busses signified many of the Bay Area's challenges, such as housing affordability and gentrification and the inadequacy of the transit networks. To many, the busses also symbolized the tendency, especially prevalent in the tech sector, toward the production of exclusionary and proprietary environments, real or virtual.

In the past decades, role of infrastructure, and in particular mobility infrastructure, in shaping cities has been extensively discussed. Infrastructure determines where and how we live and work. It allows us to interact or not. It drives our economies and resource flows.

For architects and landscape architects, exploring how to design with and for infrastructure has become of interest because the scales at which infrastructure operates and how it structures the city. It necessitates a systemic view on our urban environments. The 'Google'-bus protests are a good example of the myriad aspects that infrastructure brings together.

In this studio, we will look at the Bay Area's infrastructure through a resilience lens. The Bay Area is vulnerable to many shocks and stresses, such as earthquakes, droughts, sea level rise but also racial equity and housing affordability. Resilience can be defined as the capacity of a system to deal with these shocks and stresses, and to continue to adapt and thrive. The fact that the Bay Area's infrastructure is vulnerable became clear with the collapse of the Oakland Bay Bridge in the 1989 Lomo Prieta Earthquake. With the increasing awareness of the possible effects is sea level rise, the Bay Area is now also assessing the vulnerability of the infrastructure to coastal flooding. The challenges are enormous, not only in San Francisco and Oakland, but also in the South Bay, where much of the tech industry is located.

The challenge in the Bay Area will be to re-think the infrastructure not only from the perspective of 'coping' with stresses and shocks, but also to adapt and to transform the region, and to mitigate the climate change that causes sea level rise. The real challenge is to re-think the infrastructure in the Bay Area such that it becomes an opportunity for change, and brings what Rockefeller Foundation president Judith Rodin calls a 'resilience dividend'.

The Bay Area is also a hotbed of possible transportation innovation. Tech companies drive the 'sharing economy' and research automated vehicles. Tesla is betting big on electric vehicles and the Hyperloop project. Alphabet's subsidiary Sidewalk Labs explores the role technology can have in urban innovation. The Bay Area is planning High Speed Rail. Biking is increasingly popular. All these developments make it possible to fundamentally re-think our infrastructure, and thus the urban development of the Bay Area.

Can the resilience challenges of the Bay Area be addressed by re-thinking its infrastructure? Can we leverage new developments? Can we create a 'resilience dividend' that not only addresses possible shocks (such as earthquakes and floods) but also stresses (such as housing affordability and social inequity), while helping the economy grow and mitigate climate change?

In this studio, students will start with a group research into resilience, future transportation infrastructure and the dynamics of urban change. They will subsequently develop 'urban' or 'infrastructural' architecture and/or landscape architecture projects that can help re-think the Bay Area's transportation infrastructure. Such projects can be visionary, showing possibilities and effects on city and landscape, or take the form of proposals for pilots that can trigger large-scale change.

STUDENT:
Lei Yu
Baihe Cui

CRITIC:
Matthijs Bouw
Kai-Uwe Bergmann

SFOAK proposes to re-think the proposed BART link between San Francisco and Oakland and instead built it between the two airports, SFO and OAK. Both airports are in the floodzone. SFO is almost at maximum capacity, with little space to grow, both airside and landside. OAK has capacity to grow, and could benefit from additional programs and jobs. SFOAK would create the largest airport West, with space for growth, adaptation and redundancy. In the design, the eastern side of SFOAK is developed into a resilient landscape, with environmental features, and a concentrated commercial hub that supports the transition to a more transit oriented development. Ecological and transportation connections to the immediate surroundings are improved, and program is re-shuffled from its highway orientation to a denser organization. This will create a resilience dividend in the wider area of the airport.

[701]

ADVANCED'

MATTHIJS BOUW

ADVANCED'

MATTHIJS BOUW

STUDENT:
Nan Mu
Sean McKay

CRITIC:
Matthijs Bouw
Kai-Uwe Bergmann

The city of Alameda is a low-lying island built primarily on landfill in the San Francisco Bay. Most of the city lies on uncertain ground- unstable soils subject to liquefaction during earthquakes and inundation from sea level rise and flood events. The former Naval Air Station Alameda, comprising over 1/3 of the island offers an opportunity for Alameda to define a new relationship to the Bay. By adapting the former Naval facilities to implement a research, development and manufacturing facility for amphibious urbanism, Alameda can do so in a manner that supports local economic development and itera- tive, adaptive, community-driven innovation. The project develops an initial prototype development and strategies for wider implementation throughout Alameda. These approaches can serve as a model for strategies applicable to all the communities lining the Bay that are facing similar uncertain futures.

THE SENSATE AND THE AUGMENTED

A Studio in collaboration with SNU of Seoul, South Korea. Sponsored by Autodesk and Mr Jeong of the Heerim Company, an Alumn of the Architecture Department, PennDesign.

CRITIC: **Simon Kim**

TA: **Aidan Kim, Brett Lee**

- Co-founded Ibañez Kim Studio, PA & MA, (1994)
- Graduated from the Design Research Laboratory at the Architectural Association (AA)
- Taught studios and seminars at Harvard, MIT, Yale, and the AA.
- Director of the Immersive Kinematics Research Group

Architecture of a city - as a proposition or a form of intellectual investigation - is tethered to a built, shared environment. Its implicit and explicit meanings and affects are to be developed in material and also in behavior over time.

To do this, we will imbue architecture and urbanism with duration, with its own agency and self-governance in the location of Seoul. With new media and new materials, it is not impossible to conceptualize the built environment as a sensate and sentient field of beings. Our role as designers and as inhabitants is to coordinate and live in this new city and new nature as a shared endeavor. Korea's rapid advancement in light and heavy industries places it as an ideal post-industrial model with an apex towards advanced thinking of new environment and eco-intelligence.

This studio will break from the classical hierarchy of human-centric design and allow for nonhuman (all manner of flora, fauna, and matter) authorship and stewardship. Rather than design from a compositional position, and to dwell in a seamless zone of human comfort, this studio will engage in a design process with transformations over time, to produce environments that change and behave for other-than-human requirements (such as seasons, water, air, animal).

We will consider the postwar projects of Gordon Pask, Nicholas Negroponte, and the writings of Timothy Morton and Gilbert Simondon, while rejecting the mecha-ideologies of Archigram and Evangelion. Architecture that is sensate and nervous do not need to look like giant robots, and projects based in Korea should not be simplified to an easy reading or cliche.

PennDesign has been selected as one of the participants of the Seoul Biennale of Architecture and Urbanism (Artistic Directors – Hyungmin Pai and Alejandro Zaera Polo). The event is scheduled for September of 2017, presenting the work of this studio and other international schools as curated by John Hong, Seoul City Public Architect and Associate Professor at Seoul National University. The Namdaemun, Eulchiro, and Seoul Station areas are the loci of the Seoul Biennale International Studios. Our studio will focus on the sites of the Cheong gycheon waterways and a former US military base.

From the Seoul Biennale brief: If the term 'Anthropocene' defines the global impact of human activity, the city is at the concept's core. Although on one hand a 'human-centered' approach to urbanism can generate positive discussions on the quality of life, all too often it is used to place humans at the hierarchical apex of the ecological system. Therefore, rather than a holistic vision of the city, massive imbalances continue to degrade the global ecology; paradoxically massive social inequalities also escalate as wealth accumulation becomes a geopolitical game of subdividing the city as 'real-estate.' In fact modernist planning classifies the city along functionalist lines of housing, business, retail, production, and the like - fragments that on the surface seem to define human-centered ac vices, but in practice can easily be captured by power structures.

Within this dilemma, Seoul has the potential to become a metropolis that exemplifies an alternate form of urbanism that challenges outdated modes of city-making. Poised between the ancient and the modern, its founding principles were cosmological rather than anthropocentric: Foregoing the idea of nature vs. artifice, human settlement was considered in a horizontal relationship with the basic elements of water, earth, air, and energy flows. Meanwhile Seoul has now become one of the most technologically advanced cities in the world where almost all of its citizens are 'wired' into the internet as well as physically connected to every region of the metropolis through the smoothness of its infra-structure.

To address the imminent ecological and social crises, we have the opportunity to rethink the obsolete nouns that segregate the functions of the city and engage the city as a set of verbs. The enaction of the city as a place of making, sensing, recycling, connecting, and archiving therefore can be thought of as a new kind of commons that has spa al consequences transversely connected to social and political reforms. These technologically driven action-commons also connect the contemporary urban to the ancient cosmologies through new forms of stewardship that preserve the very elements that make urban life possible.

eoul south Korea

Workshop at Seoul National University [SNU] with prof. John Hong

STUDENT:
Chang Yuan Max Hsu
Hadeel Ayed Mohammad

CRITIC:
Simon Kim

The logic behind the assignment is to test and characterize materials and
their behaviors. It is to understand how each material react to one another
in manners of specificity and rigor. Their results will be categorized and given
traits that will later serve that motifs for Primordial giants, like the titans
of old... tasked to walk the planes until the end of time. Lumbering in their
stride, they march across the vast horizons without an aim in sight. One of
fire, and one of ice, their emergence is a reclamation of the very ground they
tread upon. In their wake, a stratification of landscapes both permanent and
temporary is formed. What was gone shall flourish once again, as land mass
is recycled and reused to generate new environments. Nothing is wasted,
as energy is simply transformed; even as the siblings fall to one another, they
are forever embedded into the terrain.

ADVANCED'

SIMON KIM

STUDENT:
Michelle Ann Chew
John Dade Darby

CRITIC:
Simon Kim

Epiphany is a schizophrenic, hallucinating architecture. She is controlled by a circadian rhythm which determines when she is hallucinating and when she is not. When she is hallucinating, she glows brightly and erratically, and wobbles frantically. When she is not hallucinating, she is dormant and not moving.

She is made of concrete and rubber. We are inverting material systems, hard and heavy on top, soft and compressive on the bottom. Epiphany is an urban farm with human producers and non-human farming harvesters. Epiphany is the mother, the center of an Internet of Things, the biomass that her farm pods are drawn to. She sends signals to and from her farm pods that are each located throughout the Cheonggyehcheon regions. She calls to the different kimchi, algae bio fuel, and aeroponic farming pods when she is ready to harvest them and have them be sent back out to the community as an economy of urban farming and exports.

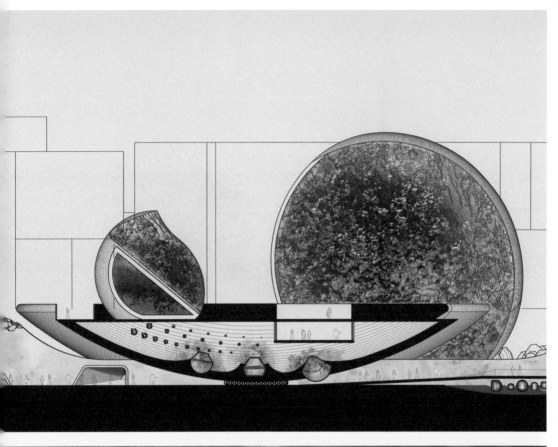

WATER AND POWER, AMBIVALENT OBJECT II

CRITIC: **Jason Payne**
TA: **Michael Zimmerman**

- Principal of Hirsuta
- Co-partenered the award-winning office Gnuform.
- Worked as Project Designer for Reiser + Umemoto RUR architects and Daniel Libeskind Studio.
- Payne holds a Master of advanced Architectural Design Degree from Colombia University.

The Los Angeles Department of Water and Power (LADWP, or simply DWP) oversees the largest municipal infrastructure in the United States. The scale of this network of streams and rivers, lakes and reservoirs, dams, aqueducts, culverts, pipes, stations, substations, and power lines is vast, spanning several western states. Physical evidence of this infrastructure is everywhere but goes unnoticed: everywhere yet nowhere at once. Usually its invisibility occurs secondarily, the inevitable side effect of ubiquity. In certain cases, however, the suppression of the system's physical presence is purposeful, a conscious decision by its architects and engineers to hide certain objects in plain sight. This is especially true of the substations, buildings that fade into the urban background through either textbook contextualism or, more interestingly, through dead iconography. This studio begins with an exploration of these substations for their potential to inform a new language for form that occurs at the intersection of infrastructure and architecture.

The development of this language occurs in the design of a larger building, the LADWP Headquarters complex in downtown Los Angeles. In terms of iconography and expression the existing headquarters building1 runs counter to the more subtle, reclusive approach taken for so much of the rest of the system. Instead the building celebrates its authority over water, its power. Indeed the word power may be understood in two ways here: the power created and distributed by DWP, as well as the power DWP has in the larger context of Los Angeles. For as we know, LA is located in a very arid semi-desert and cannot exist without water from afar. For this reason DWP may very well be the most powerful municipal entity in LA. While there are larger buildings than this one in the city and there are those more flamboyant, there is likely none more important than DWP.

This said, our relationship to water in Los Angeles has changed. A dark history and parched present render DWP's style and effects painfully naive. The curious reticence of anonymous substations seems the affect to go with now. The project proceeds through three phases, each treated as discrete design problems: exteriority, interiority, and ambivalent synthesis, described below.

A paradox: though most would agree that objects do certainly exist, they do not exist with certainty. "Certainty" refers here to a sureness of perception, asserting that our ability to know a thing in its entirety is not possible. This claim should be intuitively obvious in everyday life, as objects around us are never really completely visible or fully accessible. Even the most transparent glass cube, for example, which presents even its back sides to view cannot be seen for its exact molecular structure, let alone at scales even smaller. Philosopher Graham Harman states this principle as follows: "All human relations to objects strip them of their inner depth, revealing only some of their qualities to view."2 At issue here is the limiting condition of human perception and the implicit notion that objects have expanded lives beyond our comprehension. An old idea to be sure but one worth remembering in any serious discussion of our interaction with the things around us. From this basic observation Harman and others3 go on to build an ontology that rejects the traditional privilege given to the relationship between humans and objects (as opposed to that between objects and other objects.) Further, a world of things is described in which objects turn away, or

"withdraw"4 from one another even as they interact. Counterintuitive though it may seem, it is through interaction itself that this estrangement occurs as any specific correlation excludes all others.5 Through withdrawal comes uncertainty. At first this notion seems opaque, cryptic even, for it describes objects that move apart through the act of coming together. Prolonged consideration, however, does tend to help clarify this strange world if not to the point of absolute conviction then at least toward a curiosity to hear more.

ADVANCED'

JASON PAYNE

ADVANCED'

JASON PAYNE

STUDENT:
Michael O'neill

CRITIC:
Jason Payne
Michael Zimmerman

This proposal for the Los Angeles Department of Water and Power Headquarters seeks to subvert iconicity through the use of the doppelgänger, or the uncanny icon. The uneasiness of the two towers confuses the authenticity of the icon while disrupting its status as an urban wayfinding mechanism. The space of the plaza is charged by absence, establishing a blank urbanity. To further subvert the icon, the towers are figured as anonymous at the scale of the skyline, using warped massing tropes from familiar office typologies. This figuration blurs into spectacle at the pedestrian level, where dark mirrors create strange reflective projections of the ground level. Thus, their identity is further masked by their status as objects to be looked into, rather than looked at. Sectionally, the project seeks to leverage the kind of blankness and indeterminacy of scale found in infrastructural spaces such as electrical substations. Furthermore, the sundered nature of the program-- split between office space and infrastructure-- is manifested through a kind of ripping in section, where the interior and exterior conditions seem to be ambivalent toward one-another, creating a loose-fit or mismatching between enclosure and interior programmed space.

FIG. 5.– Golevka Section

ADVANCED'

JASON PAYNE

STUDENT:
Ryosuke Imaeda

CRITIC:
Jason Payne
Michael Zimmerman

The extensive urban setting of Los Angeles offers an interwoven network of vehicular circulation. Views from highway set a particular distance to a target, limiting visibility, and the speed of movement blurs surface characters of objects. These visual limitations give emergent qualities to this object that people perceive as a geological landform along with the surrounding textures. When people move close to the object, it reveals its detail expressions; apertures, material thickness, seams, and creases become so distinct that the object begins disclosing its geometrical qualities.

This object accommodates the existing office with a capacity of two substations inside. The overall figuration is based on these programs with a substantial spaceframe that pervades programs and that buffers the exterior qualities. This intrinsic pressure yields gigantism of the object, engaging icons on the adjacent sites; yet, given the fact that substations are mostly automated, the inside becomes extremely vulnerable despite its enormity outside.

The extrinsic tension between losing geological quality and capturing geometrical one or vice versa, and the intrinsic vulnerability against gigantism are stretchably glued by the framework. This is indeed the reality of this object in which both sensual and real qualities can bounce back and forth, and the object itself is withdrawn from a bundle of ambivalent states of the qualities.

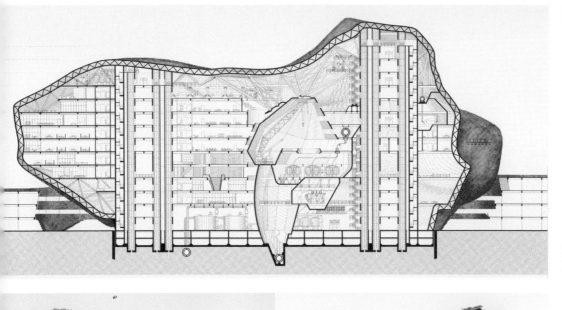

MALLTOPIA/BURBOPOLIS: PHOENIX

CRITIC: **Daniel Wood**
TA: **Maurizio Bianchi Mattioli**

- Co-fouded WORK as Architects with Amale Andraos.
- Wood holds the 2013-14 Louis I.Kahn Chair at the Yale School of Architecture, the Irwin S. Chanin School of Architecture at the Cooper Union...
- He is a licensed architect in the State of New York and is LEED certified.

Cities across America are regaining populations and cache once lost to sprawl while suburbs struggle to redefine themselves. The foreclosure crises of 2008 continues to resonate in these forgotten hamlets and clusters of McMansions as suburbs become more dangerous, less diverse and simply more boring places to inhabit. All of the suburb's formerly glorious accouterments – the meticulous lawn, the lonely cul-de-sac and – especially – the isolated shopping mall are currently called into question as viable modes of inhabitation, post crisis and post-climate.

Cities such as Phoenix, AZ – which once embraced the suburban model as a form of proto-urbanization – are at the center of this swirling maelstrom of economic collapse, policy conundrum and identity confusion. At the same time, issues such as water supply politics, illegal immigration, political tensions, and global warming all threaten the state's very existence. Ironically, however, the Arizona desert has also been home to some of the most radical rethinkings of urban and suburban life – from Wright's Taliesin West of the 1930's to Soleri's Arcosanti of the 1960's, to the Biosphere of the 1980's. There is something about the desert that has consistently inspired the avant garde and the visionary.

The studio will focus on the shopping mall as a locus to redefine suburban and urban living – channeling these prior imaginary cities in the service of creating a new paradigm of increased density, conscience-raising green living, alternative futures, newly mixed uses and a next desert phoenix to rise from the ashes of banality: the Malltopia Burbopolis

We will begin the semester with an intense period of research and thinking about Phoenix, looking at its history and possible futures and examining this often-ignored city through various lenses: history, economic, social, architectural and urban planning precedents, climate, water policy, political fiction, art, etc. This will result in a booklet summarizing our findings that we will use as the basis for the design projects.

We will travel to Phoenix and meet and work with artists and community organizers, academics including Aaron Betsky the Director of Taliesin and faculty from Arizona State University, and local architects such as Will Bruder, Wendell Burnett and and Rick Joy. In addition, we will work throughout the semester with representatives from Westfield, one of the nation's largest suburban mall developers, who are currently engaged in rethinking their sites and suburban model across the country.

The second half of the semester will be a design problem, to take what we have learned and to propose new forms of mixed-use housing and urbanism for Phoenix that transforms the shopping mall into a new model for living, work, shopping, recreation and public space – while exploring new visions of sustainable ecosystems and infrastructure for the city. Projects should both reflect and critique the current condition, using our research as inspiration. We will work first in a series of short exercises, to create hybrids of housing and malls and propose new urban conditions for Phoenix, then build up to a large, mixed-use building – a contemporary megastructure - that challenges Phoenix to rethink its future while accepting its perilous climactic condition.

The studio will attempt to weave together the varied threads swirling around these questions We will take conditions such as heat, aridity, sprawl, isolation, individualism, consumerism and boredom and try to invert them - through design thinking - in the creation of a completely new urban condition and a new vision of desert architecture and public space in Phoenix.

Biosphere 2

Cosanti - Paolo Soleri

Sinagua Cliff Dwelling - 1400AD

ASU – Left to Right: Judith Vasquez, Aly Abouzeid, Dan Wood

Rick Joy Studio

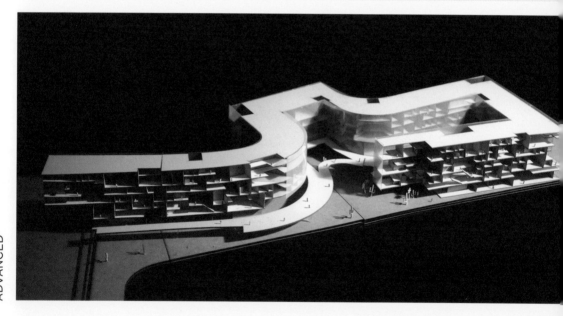

STUDENT:
Jinghao Wang

CRITIC:
Daniel Wood
Maurizio Bianchi
Mattioli

The concept is to create a living community which is consist of the hipsterville programs, material recycling ,artist live- in- studio and micro units resident. The working system here take the advantage of the canal completing the material recycling with the help of "art ship". The "art ship" collect interesting material in different area of Phoenix through the canal and carry them back to site, and then those material will be classified and assemble into different courtyards so that artists could get the material they need from courtyards. Also, the art-pieces they create could be seen in all the hipsterville programs. The idea aim to bond different programs together and create a sustainable community.

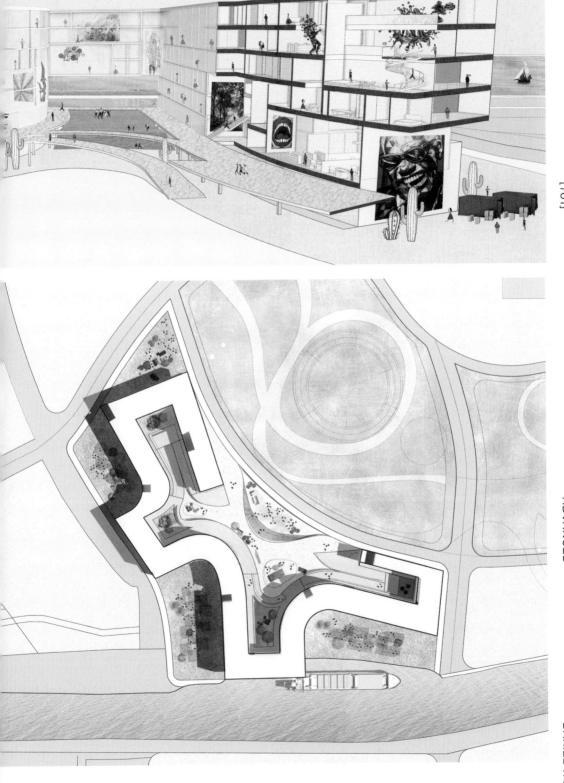

ADVANCED'

DANIEL WOOD

STUDENT:
Beidi Zhan

CRITIC:
Daniel Wood
Maurizio Bianchi
Mattioli

As an approach to redefine community and create a better living climate within the site, this building combined Water Tower/ Solar Energy as its infrastructure and Bell Making Studio as its program. In order to take advantage of the solar energy and the heat from bell furnace cooling, the building contained two water storage surfaces as its heat storage devices, higher level surface was designed to absorb solar energy, lower level surface was for furnace cooling. Absorb heat during daytime and releasing during night, residents here can live in a more comfortable living condition. The concept of community here came from Arcosanti, community space was nesting under living volume to afford more spatial variations and create a cheerful community space at the same time.

CUBA LIBRE

CRITIC: **Paul Preissner**
TA: **Jonathan Scelsa**

- Founding partner of Paul or Paul.
- AIA studied architecture at the University of Illinois (BsArch) and Columbia University (March).
- He has has taught at the University of Pennsylvania, Syracuse University, the Southern California Institute of Architecture.

Cyrus of Ancona left home in the 15th century for a trip. Unlike previous trips he had taken for family business, this trip was different. For this trip was a personal one: a tour to take a look at Mediterranean antiquities. This trip is largely accepted to be the first act of tourism. He visited Greek and Roman monuments and ruins and took notes and made drawings. This trip launched modern archeology, and a few centuries later, when the victorian era introduced the world to disposable income and leisure time, this trip also served somewhat as a template for the cultural holiday.

Centuries before Cyrus's Mediterranean Vacation, the Nisiyama Onsen Keiunkan in Yamanahi, Japan opened in 707ad as the worlds first hotel, offering the template for hospitality facilities to travelers. After the second World War, however, recreational tourism expanded with the vacationing Americans seeking beaches and cultural experiences. Hotels became people's homes away from home.

The history of modernity is the history of tourism and this history of tourism is the history of the hotel, which exists as possibly the most confused of all programs; part home, part not. In Havana, there are 265 hotels. The hotel is the one truly inauthentic program, unable to be anything else but a host to purchased experience and artificial exoticism. It is an embassy of expectation within the urban space; always populated by tourists.

If the hotel is the object of tourism, the pool is its clear symbol of leisure. Designed to project relaxation more than it ever actually provides, the swimming pool is perhaps the single most significant hotel amenity. Territorial, social, meditative, hedonistic.

The studio will also look to the city of Havana in this time just before the approaching era of mass tourism. The city of Havana, due to Cuba's relationship with the US has famously remained as a poorly preserved version of its mid-20th century self. There has never been a critical moment in Havana's architectural history when it was envisioned as anything other than a colonial project. Neoclassical, Colonial, Baroque, Art deco, eclecticism and Modernism all took their turn from the 18th century through the middle of the 20th when major development more or less halted. A city of architectural moments marking its colonial past with the beginnings of modernism prior to Cubans simultaneously retaking their destiny and finding it becoming even more complicated. The colorful, sturdy and (now) strange old buildings will inevitably serve as the constructed context for this new site of touristic activity.

Anyhow, this studio looks at the social, political and formal experiments within Havana and looks to produce a new social space that allows the para diplomacy of tourism to have a home through the party of the pool.

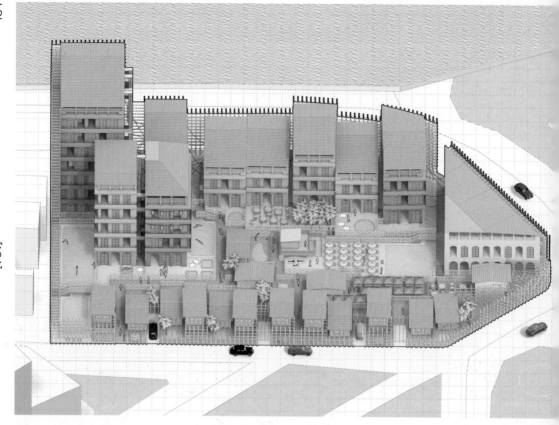

STUDENT:
Alexander Tahinos

CRITIC:
Paul Preissner
Jonathan Scelsa

Cuba Libre was a critical project looking directly at the truth and reality of "Tourism as a False Culture". The location of Havana, Cuba was the site of a new resort hotel. The end product becomes a critical stance on realism with a fake and accelerated "Cuban experience" as a typical and essential tourist experience. The tourist's position is that of an observer and experiencer of false cultures and thus the hotel reflects just that. The collection of banal and quasi-vernacular typologies help to build the argument of the distilled and simplified culture. The juxtaposition of multiple land types, amenities, and urban/suburban typologies creates the intersection of all that is stereo-typical Cuba. The exteriority is distinguished by a large wooden scaffold that doubles as public poche for local use. Hotel amenities and programs are placed sporadically inside the larger row-homes in order to hide the program to the outside. The ideal suburban community is created from a desire for authentic and "real" cultural experiences. By providing tourists with their own single room homes, the ideal situation is being provided in a more satirical way. The backyard and the pool, play a large role as the identifier of the typical suburban condition for the interior and exterior. A strange new reality is created from the banal in which tourists gain a new view on the city beyond the hotel.

STUDENT:
Yi Yang

CRITIC:
Paul Preissner
Jonathan Scelsa

Different from a lot of hotel where pools are lying on the ground, this hotel is designed base on the pools are stacking vertically into a water tower. The pools are organized from top to bottom base on how many people use it. There are water park and big slices at the lower part, and diving pool and resort pool are sitting at the top.

So that from top to bottom, is from quite to lively, from scattered to crowded. Different level is a different world. There are leisure world, diving world, falling water world, forest world and water park world. From top to bottom you could go through multiple atmosphere.

All these pools and levels are connect by water base on gravity. Water falling from top to bottom in different shape because of different type of pools. And hotel rooms are surrounded by the pools. Hotel rooms are affected by pools become different shapes and organization. Finally this hotel become a vertical stacking experiential water tower.

CONSTRUCTED PARADISE
HAINAN ISLAND : SOUTH SEA PEARL ECO ISLAND

CRITIC: **Thom Mayne**

- Founded Morphosis in 1972.
- Mayne's distinguished honors include the Pritzker Prize (2005) and the AIA Gold Medal (2013).
- He was appointed to the President's Committee on the Arts and Humanities in 2009.

CRITIC: **Ung-Joo Scott Lee**

- Principal at Morphosis Architects.
- Received his Bachelor of Science Degree from Cornell University and a Master of Architecture from the University of Michigan.
- A licensed architect in the states of New York, New Jersey and Texas.

The South Sea Pearl Studio speculates the possibility of a self-sustainable urbanism that balances and integrates the aims of culture, nature and business to re-claim the importance of intelligent ecology as the advancement of 21st century urbanism.

As we look at individual small towns and city-states that arose throughout history – from Greek city-states, such as Miletus and Samos, to the towns populating the Roman Empire, to the Renaissance fortress city of Palmanova – it should be noted that the distinctive ecological advances made within each of these urban systems were developed with a degree of autonomy and focus that has been somewhat lost to the generalizations of the current all-encompassing global era. For centuries, towns and city-states developed idiosyncratically, as micro engines of cultural, agricultural and social sustain-ability; their often remote locations and distinctly defined urban boundaries led to highly specific architectural, urban, economic, and social consid-erations as each culture addressed the questions unique to its own advancement.

In the 20th century, beginning with Ebenezar Howard's Garden City, one can easily trace the rapid integration of technology and social change through Le Corbusier and Team 10's urban master planning proposals, to the fantastic cultural re-inventions and destinations of Archigram, to the ecologically-driven agenda of Louis Kahn's car free downtown Philadelphia, to Norman Foster's Masdar City.

Now, China is poised to inherent this legacy by constructing a 290 hectare island that will become a laboratory and demonstration project of urban sustainability.

COURSE OBJECTIVES
South Sea Pearl Island aspires for a future mode of urbanism and urban organization that will catalyze tourism through cultural and ecological development strategy.

The studio begins with research and the analysis of several key precedents. Simultaneously we examine opportunities that emerge from chal-lenging traditional organizational systems within city planning and building typologies. The result-ing opportunities and challenges form the basis for each scheme's argument and determines the city's new urban context.

Within this context, the teams propose a planning strategy to support the multiple agencies of tourism and ecological development. Additional social, cultural and economic metrics is integrate through policy and infrastructural agendas. By considering the intersections of future transpor-tation, natural ecologies, tourism programming, planning policy regulations, economics and social impact, and the previously proposed development strategies, the studio works to redefine the notion of an integrated township for the next generation.

Studio Travel

ADVANCED'   THOM MAYNE & UNG-JOO SCOTT LEE

STUDENT:
Mingyue Hu
Lu Liu
Katie McBride

CRITIC:
Thom Mayne
Ung-Joo Scott Lee

THOM MAYNE & UNG-JOO SCOTT LEE   ADVANCED'

There is few natural conditions like the coastal edge that force awareness of our environment. The moment of transition from land to water offers an immediate opportunity for us to question what is, what was and what could be. Nowhere is this experience more invigorating than an island-- a place entirely defined by edge.

Prompted with the task to plan a completely man-made island, Edge Island seeks to redefine the experience of the edge condition. However, rather than define this new edge autonomously, Edge Island seeks to have a direct relationship to both Haikou and mainland China. These two regions cradle the site as the land masses that define the Hainan Strait. The coordinates of Edge Island are nearer in proximity to Haikou, but there are multiple existing modes of transit across this strait making this location highly accessible from either land mass. Though most of the existing transit is sea faring, China is planning an 18 mile long bridge to connect the edges. We propose that our island link into this system so that the bridge can connect mainland China to Edge Island and then to the Haikou.

The result of this linkage is a highly accessible island that celebrates the edge through an array of recreational, commercial and cultural edge programming. This ring of activity follows 14 miles of highly articulated and varied edge equipped with multiple landscapes and water spaces. This programmable region totals 456 acres and acts as a counter to the 186 acres of void landscape. Void of program and maintenance, the island's interior proposes a new type of national park-- one created by humanity.

Together this variable edge and void landscape generate a destination experience that cannot be found in nature and yet also cannot be found in the urban context. It is a composite experience of extremes. On Edge Island you can get lost or you can be found. It can feel like a paradise or a battlefield. It is a place for getting a way and a place for passing through. Somehow it is for everyone, but only belongs to itself.

THOM MAYNE & UNG-JOO SCOTT LEE   ADVANCED'

STUDENT:
Wenxin Chen
Jungha Lee
Matthew Mayberry

CRITIC:
Thom Mayne
Ung-Joo Scott Lee

Infrastructure city is a reaction to the pressures of expansion and development in contemporary globalized urbanism.

Cities are now no longer just amalgamations of minute changes made over an enormous timeline, but are increasingly planned, executed, and populated in less than one generation.

Infrastructure city eschews the axiomatic 2 dimensional ground plan and superimposes layer upon layer of connectivity and movement in 3 dimensions to establish a nodal network of economically fundamental anchor programs. These anchors are woven together by conduits of transportation, varying in scale from elevated tram to the pedestrian sidewalk.

Each layer of activity is not bound by its relationship to the ground, but rather influenced by the anchor programs and shifting conduits proximal to its path.

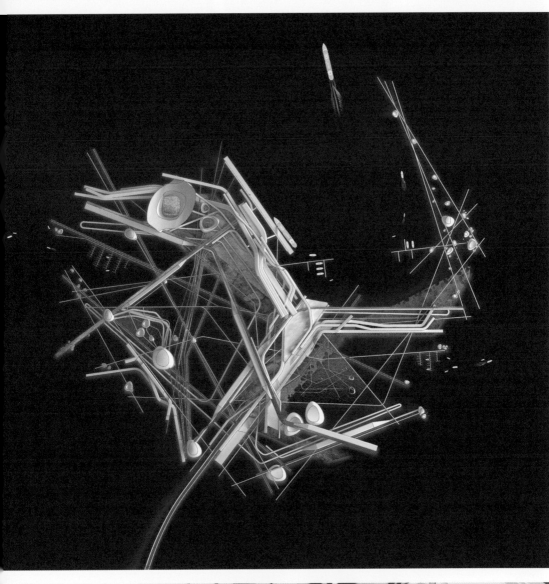

ADVANCED'   THOM MAYNE & UNG-JOO SCOTT LEE

RESPIRATORY OBJECT
A NEW DESIGN FOR THE BATTERY-TUNNEL ENTRANCE, MANHATTAN, NEW YORK CITY

CRITIC: **Ferda Kolatan**
Associate Professor of Practice, PennDesign
TA: **Michael Zimmerman**

- Founding partner of su11 architecture + design, NY (2004)
- Received an architectural diploma with distinction from the RWTH Aachen (1993)
- Received MsAAD, Architecture from Columbia GSAPP (1995)
- Selected as a Young Society Leader by The American Turkish Society (2011)

[701]

Perhaps the big project of the nonhuman turn is to find new techniques, in speech and art and mood, to disclose the participation of nonhumans in "our" world.

Jane Bennett, "*Systems and Things*"

Contemporary cultural discourse with its focus on objects, the speculative real, and vital forms of materialism, has fundamentally altered our perception of the world. Agency and aesthetics are no longer thought to be an exclusively human domain but rather qualities that reshape the world constantly even when we "don't look".

This view stands in stark contrast to the still prevailing modernist paradigm, which privileges anthropocentrism and scientific positivism as the predominant forms of access to knowledge. If we do expand the realm of knowledge to include nonhuman categories however, we are forced to fundamentally question our approach to architecture, as architecture itself has played an instrumental role in the advancement of the modernist paradigm.

Categories of nature and technology for instance, have primarily adhered to long standing traditions in architecture as separate entities with negligible relationships. Urban architecture is viewed in predetermined hierarchies, and is compartmentalized into programmatic pockets like squares, parks, and recreational zones. Below them a teeming network of mechanical systems and civil infrastructure is hidden and deemed aesthetically undesirable while above ground formulaic facades clad generic buildings often without a hint of character, originality, or authenticity.

This approach is not simply the outcome of logical organizational principles, it is also a reinforcement of ideologies of power under the guise of pragmatism and familiar practice. Therefore, as we come to terms with a world much stranger than we previously thought, our approach to architecture in the context of large cities is in desperate need of reexamination through new modes of thinking and design.

With this in mind, the studio designed a new entrance zone for the Battery Tunnel in Manhattan. The project comprised of a ventilation tower, a parking garage, recreational space, and the tunnel entrance itself. In accordance to the conceptual framework, these elements were not treated as independent categories but rather as vital components of a single hybrid object. "Respiratory Objects" ultimately aim to challenge and reorder our understanding of "value" in the accelerated urbanizations of the late capitalist city. As Jane Bennett writes, the disclosure of the participation of nonhumans in "our" world, may just be the right departure point.

STUDENT:
Insung Hwang
Wan Jung Lee

CRITIC:
Ferda Kolatan
Michael Zimmerman
Bumjin Park

Respiratory Object: The project contrasts with the city's existing public parks to provide New Yorkers with a natural environment that they can enjoy and use as an escape from their ordinary urban lives. We envision a new landscape by exposing the existing bedrock to create a new kind of urban park experience. The machines which dig into the ground are kept as a part of the park and work in 24h cycles to continuously reshape the landscape.

A concrete wall isolates the park from the city, giving it a more secretive quality, rewarding those who venture to look down into the excavated park. The new ventilation tower stands out as a beacon to garner interest with its novel aesthetic mixing infrastructural qualities with sculptural ones.

STUDENT:
Mark Chalhoub
Andrew Singer

CRITIC:
Ferda Kolatan
Michael Zimmerman
Bumjin Park

Respiratory Object: The overarching ambition of our project is a speculative reinterpretation of urban design typologies derived from existing compositional paradigms as data of realism upon which to intervene. Our design is the result of a hybridization as process of given site objects, notably infrastructure and nature, in order to synthesize and substantiate new direct relations between inherent and additive qualities of the site. Conventional ideas of designing each of these elements individually takes the back seat to the way we both design and represent our project as a singular object seamlessly combines each component, blurring the boundaries where one ends and the other begins.

In our explorations, we look to deviate from deviate further from conventional parks and tunnels through an estranged spatial experience derived from non-anthropocentric characteristics of the project components. Essentially this means that one would access the park in separate sequences rather than in a fluid manner, through a series of urban breaks that act as gaps between one level and the next, therefore inhibiting an undermining of our project as an uninterrupted promenade.

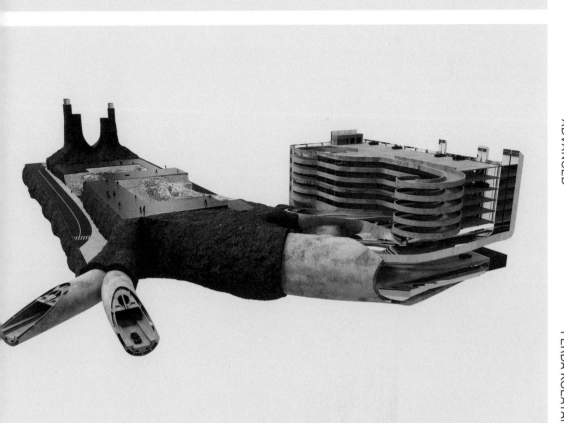

BLACK BOX. MUTE ICON

CRITIC: **Georgina Huljich**

TA: **Joseph Giampietro**

Georgina Huljich is Principal of PATTERNS ARCHITECTS, an architectural design practice based in Los Angeles which gained international recognition for its subtle approach to architecture; one that seamlessly integrates advanced technology within an extensive consideration of form, novel tectonics and innovative materials. With a decidedly global influence and working across multiple scales, programs and cultures, the office completed projects in the US, South America and Asia. Its work was exhibited and published worldwide and has received numerous prizes and awards. Huljich has previously worked at the Guggenheim Museum and Dean/Wolf Architects in New York and as project designer at Morphosis. She has lectured extensively in the U.S. and internationally, and has held visiting teaching and critic positions at several institutions including Yale University, UC Berkeley, Tokyo Institute of Technology, USC, Syracuse Architecture, PennDesign and the Di Tella University in Buenos Aires, Argentina. Together with Marcelo Spina she has been the recipient of the prestigious United States Artists 2012 Grigor Fellowship. PATTERNS Architects first comprehensive book- monograph entitled Embedded was released in 2011, followed by the forthcoming title 'Mute Icons: The Pressing Dichotomy of Contemporary Architecture' made possible by a grant from the prestigious Graham Foundation and to be published by ACTAR by end of 2017.

[701]

ADVANCED'

Architecture seems at a significant crossroads nowadays. Haunted by vast processes taking place outside itself, since 9.11, the financial collapse, the exacerbation of global warming, cultural and sociopolitical developments such as the Arab Spring and Occupy, a new epoch of economic austerity, the often ill proclaimed but certainly perceived "death of the icon" era, the impulse for social responsibility, the celebration of practices of common sense and search for common ground: all point to a challenge to the most creative and projective aspects of both discipline and field, and certainly suggest a political realignment of its establishment. While context can't be the only driver for architectural production or any form of artistic practice of cultural relevance, it is certainly an important factor to be considered and reckoned with.

The present status and contemporary role of the icon comes into a deeper scrutiny and its cultural relevance definitely under stress. While culture at large always needs icons, the question here is what constitutes a contemporary icon, and whether its image could sever its ties to former notions of iconicity. Challenging, and provoking at the same time is the notion of muteness, or the "mute icon", a kind of anti-monument. No longer concerned with either narrative excesses of meaning and communication, nor with the shock and awe of sensation making, architecture can do what it does best: express its virtues through volume and mass in its most pure state without the anesthesia of excess and ornamentation. By suppressing what have now become expected aesthetic teasers, the mute becomes intriguing by its indifference towards context and a total apathy towards the body. A mute icon in architecture is at the same time object and building. As such, it requires a strong posture and with it, an attitude that is absolute and unstable, anticipated and strange, manifest and withdrawn. By limiting its appearance, the mute icon demands closer scrutiny, its resistance conveys resilience and its introversion stimulates communication.

The relation that the term 'black box' has to questions of functional flexibility, atmospheric darkness and plain mystery, or the connotations that it entails to the most pure form of art are important aspects for the studio. Not in and of themselves, but especially if one looks at them from the perspective of a mute icon. Can a black box be a mute icon? Can a mute icon be a black box?

Given a certain semantical flexibility in the understanding of the word [from theater to popular culture and the arts], these questions become productive by suggesting a possible inversion, albeit still a dichotomic one, between interior and exterior, object and receptacle. The studio speculates on the idea of mute icons as it applies to distinct and often competing pressures. In this case, those of a university campus context with a clear neoclassical plan and an advanced multidisciplinary performing arts program destined to create new cultural audiences. In the disconnection between interior and exterior, the studio will seek new and maybe unconventional solutions to the problem of the icon. From classical notions of "poche", to ideas about "Crowded Intricacies", "Sectional Object" etc. the studio will involve advanced techniques of solid projection.

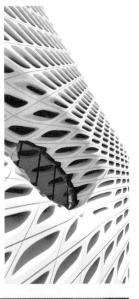

STUDENT:
Peichao Di
Jifu Pan
Lixu Wang

CRITIC:
Georgina Huljich
Joseph Giampietro

"The present status and contemporary role of the icon comes into a deeper scrutiny and its cultural relevance definitely under stress. While culture at large always needs icons, the question here is what constitutes a contemporary icon, and whether its image could sever its ties to former notions of iconicity. Challenging, and provoking at the same time is the notion of muteness, or the "mute icon", a kind of anti-monument. No longer concerned with either narrative excesses of meaning and communication, nor with the shock and awe of sensation making, architecture can do what it does best: express its virtues through volume and mass in its most pure state without the anesthesia of excess and ornamentation."

Current Dichotomies Seven Reminders to Contemporary Architects' By Marcelo Spina / P-A-T-T-E-R-N-S

The icon in our project sets up unique form and meaning within the context, which lends itself to indeterminacy and monolithicity. An icon is the one whose form resembles its meaning in some way. In our case, the theatre as a specific type of architectural design generates vast amounts of information within, yet is completely mute and withdrawn from outside. The confrontation between a noisy outside world and the silent architecture causes a finish that rusticates on the façade and interior structure: the closer in proximity to the auditorium, the smoother it becomes, which indicates that one gets eroded and the other devoured. The mute icon of the auditorium perpetually remains withdrawn from the outside world.

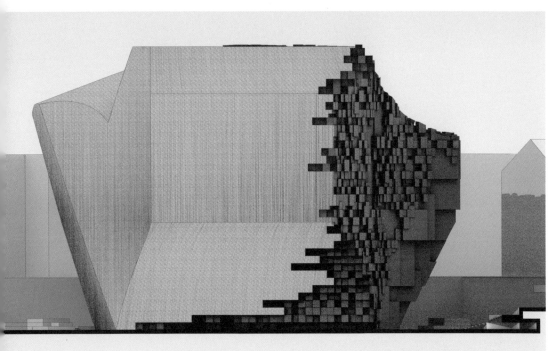

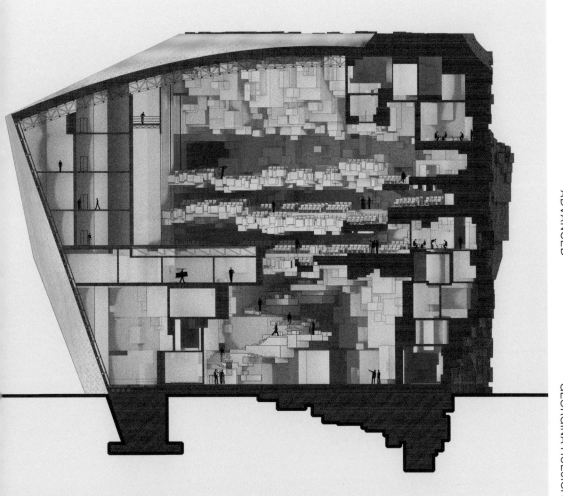

STUDENT:
Quiyun Chen
Dailong Ma

CRITIC:
Georgina Huljich
Joseph Giampietro

Fuzzy Monolith: Inspired by the unconventional motion, tension and dramatic emotion projected from the performances and choreography of dancer Ros Warby, this project experimented with the potential possibilities of mute iconicity manifested between spatial conditions of interiority and exteriority. The formal boundary and delineation between the inside and outside will no longer be communicated through conventional means as with the introduction of new configurations of building element types. These new configurations and building components destabilize your familiarity with conventional theater typologies and challenge a new understanding of performance space. Through deconstructing the conventional architectural elements, we redefine the typologies in the building, all the columns, walls, floors and stairs are adapted to their fuzzy prototypes, and extend through even to the project's context. All those contiguous programs operate with gradients of different levels of ambiguity and ambivalence transforming Royce Hall into a fuzzy monolith both in construction and in representation.

SAME - SAME BUT DIFFERENT

CRITIC: **Thomas Verebes**
TA: **Caleb White**

- Tom Verebes is the Provost of Turenscape Academy and the Director of OCEAN CN, within Turenscape in Beijing and in Hong Kong.
- Director of AA VS Shanghai (2007-2017)
- AA Visiting School Xixinan (2017). Visiting Professor roles in 2016 included: University of Pennsylvania, RMIT, SUTD and University of Tokyo.
- Former roles include: Associate Dean for Teaching & Learning (2011-2014), and Associate Professor at HKU (2009-2016);
- Co-Director of the DRL at the AA (1996-2009); Guest Professor, ABK Stuttgart (2004-2006).
- Among over 150 publications, Verebes' work has been exhibited in over 50 venues worldwide, and he has lectured extensively in Asia, Europe, North America, Australia, Africa and the Middle East.

Given the unprecedented speed and seemingly unstoppable pace of city building in the 21st century, a paramount challenge to overcome is the convergence of sameness among cities worldwide. Despite the past five decades of postmodernity, and the disciplinary promiscuity and posturing with architectural complexity and diversity, there is today a critical lack of any substantive theories of difference across the design disciplines of the built environment with which to guide cities towards the greater coherence of heterogeneous and individuated attributes. At the core of this problem lie questions as to the ways in which the qualities of cities can be amplified and differentiated to become identifiable rather than indistinguishable, during the most prolific era of urbanisation ever to occur.

The studio challenged the primacy of the GRID, as the ubiquitous organizing device for deploying infrastructure and subdividing land in China's new urbanism, and the MEGABLOCK, as an apparent modular unit of urbanism in China, ordering the road layout and hierarchy and the next scale of smaller land subdivisions. The megablock is the offspring of Modernist superblock housing schemes of the mid-twentieth century, and in part, can also be seen as a legacy of compound of the Danwei, or work unit, in post- 1949 China. The fallout of self-sufficient working and living communities has since evolved either into the prevalence of privileged gated communities, or as internalized urban environments, which relegate the street, and its vibrant culture, all but extinct. The grid, however, remains a more timeless, ubiquitous, yet insidious device, with which to dimension and to control the organisation of space and its flows.

This studio researched and proposed innovation upon Megablock Masterplannning, which is rolled out by City Mayors, Urban Planning Institutes and Transport Engineers, investors and financiers, long before architects play a role in conceiving China's urbanisation. The megablock is most often limited as tool for the standardization and routinization of the regimes of urban and infrastructural planning, and the modes of land supply and investment in architecture in Chinese cities. As such, this studio worked haptically and promiscuously to reconceive and propose alternatives to the monotony of the megablock. In a gridded array of urban blocks, the studio brief called for design proposals at multiple scales, for a series of adjacent sites on an artificial, post-industrial peninsular site on the coast of the Pearl River.

This studio confronted this disciplinary, professional, cultural and technological context – yet without nostalgia for what has been lost in China's ferocious urbanisation, nor with much naiveté of our studio's capability to change the political and economic system driving urbanisation in China. Within this dynamic and complex setting, this studio challenged the monotony of contemporary urbanism, through methods of proliferating differentiated, heterogeneous, and distinctively unique urban spaces.

ew from a boat trip to some other islands of Hong Kong.

Street view in Kowloon

Students visiting a temple in Hong Kong.
Names from left to right: Roxanna Perez, Jae Geun Ahn, Sammi Cheng, Qi Wang, Aaron Dewey, Nyasha Felder

Street view in Kowloon

Students visiting HSBC tower.

STUDENT:
Jiateng Wang
Yuheng Ouyang

CRITIC:
Thomas Verebes
Caleb White

Located at the tip of the peninsula, the project confronts ferocious subtropical nature forces such as hurricane, rainstorm, and tides, which could cause huge losses and impede everyday activities. However, those threats are also invaluable features that bring adaption to the uniform artificial site from sea reclamation.

The need of High-density communities in Shenzhen and the unwelcoming force of nature push the project to internalize the activity space and bundle individual buildings into communities. Each community is capable of sustaining all living needs with differentiated blocks. The circulation inside the community is supported by a shared podium space which connects all buildings, and cantilever corridors link buildings where frequent commute happens.

To minimize the impact of tide and waves, the ground was lifted away from the sea, only leaving arrays of legs standing in the water. The organization of legs is inspired by wave-damping instruments, with small and round legs at the frontline and huge, sharp legs staying behind. Above the lifted grounds, high-rise buildings get their outline shaped according to wind direction and daylighting requirements.

By lifting the ground, more light is introduced into the interior space from the side of podiums. Since most of the everyday-life activities are internalized inside the buildings, the whole exterior of the project gains the potential to be well-developed natural landscape. Through the opened seam which extends from buildings to podiums, interior and exterior are subtly merged.

The lifting ground also brings diversified opportunities towards the water. With a differentiated height of the podiums, the living condition varies from immersed-in-water beaches to high-rise commercial blocks which are a hundred feet away from water

[701]

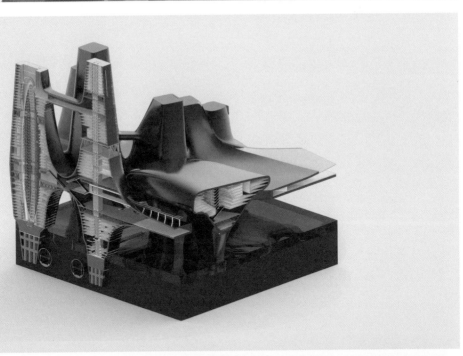

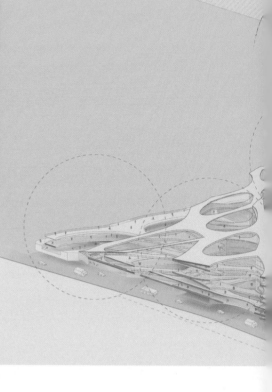

STUDENT:
Sammi Wing Sum Cheng
Roxanna Perez

CRITIC:
Thomas Verebes
Caleb White

This project challenges the isolation of Urban Megablocks from the subtropical green urbanism which pervades the infrastructural spaces of the city of Shenzhen with a proposition of a densely stratified complex of urban landscapes, topographies and building massing. A layered mat system of porous surfaces and volumes is developed as the stratification of discrete differences at various scales, densities, programs/uses, material expressions, as a result of shifting, rotating, peeling and extruding the mat system at specific instances, altogether creating extreme urban and architectural heterogeneity. A complex, artificial and highly varied topography articulates different spatial and scalar elements that create a variety of ambiences within the urban field. Referenced by two precedent studies: The mat fieldspace of the complex interior-exterior relationships of the Free University of Berlin, and the shifting and rotating of sectional massing of The Interlace by OMA.

The mat system develops a meshing of diverse landscapes, sectional routing, and variegated building types. Workspaces and habitation are intricately connected to each other and with public leisure spaces and facilities. As an alternative to conventional typologies of work environments located in isolated high-rise towers, we have shifted the role to a residential use. These challenge the notion of the existing workspaces in Shenzhen and the relationship of the building to the city.

The landscapes are programmed with different uses at different scales, while the voids (courtyards, sunken spaces, atria, etc.) create a multitude of differentiated experiences of qualities migrating across interior and exterior spaces. Residential towers peel away from the matte massing but remains highly connected on several levels. As the matte building shifts from high density areas to lower density and spread out, larger scale programs emerge to be configured as discrete masses in the stratified fields.

ADVANCED'

THOMAS VEREBES

The Architecture 704 Design Research Studio is an in-depth exploration of various architectural themes through conceptual rigor, advanced techno-logical methodologies, and overall design skill. The primary goal of this final design studio of the Master of Architecture program is to equip the outgoing students with the ability to engage in the discipline with a specific research project. The interests and skills developed in this studio extend beyond gradu-ation and provide the students with the necessary tools to become successful leaders in the field of architecture.

The challenges for architects today are unprecedented with multiple diverse trajectories defining the territories in which we operate. From global eco-nomic markets shaping our cities to the ecological realities of the anthropo-cenic age, we are entangled in forces that are seemingly elusive, yet have a profound impact on our profession. In addition, new technologies provide us with powerful tools for design and representation, while constantly altering our work-flow and adding to a growing formal/structural repertoire. Since architecture is positioned at the intersection of culture, technology, and nature, we must continuously improve our knowledge to be able to provide sensitive visions for today and the future. Each generation of designers needs to find adequate material expressions for the pressing issues of their time. These expressions cannot be simply rooted in prior models of design, but must progressively and unwaveringly engage in the now, and engage the most current paradigms of thought.

The Design Research Studio takes on this challenge and explores - through the individual expertise of leading architects in the field - various strategies and speculations that actively shape our environment, present and future. In this context, we view design-research as the indispensable element through which we critically reflect on our world, as well as the laboratory where complex design solutions are developed, tested, and applied.

Ferda Kolatan, Coordinator

Nesting
Nature

THE OAXACA ATLAS:
HOUSING AS URBAN CATALYST

CRITIC: **Alberto Kalach and Juan Rincon Gaviria**

Alberto Kalach studied architecture at the Universidad Iberoamericana, Mexico City, and completed graduate studies later at Cornell University in Ithac
In 1981 he founded the firm "Taller de Arquitectura X" with Daniel Álvarez, with whom he worked until 2002, when Álvarez left the firm. While he continue
to direct TAX, in 2002 his interests also turned to the urban planning problems of his home town, and founded the community "México: future city". He
published several articles in national and international magazines of architecture, and participates in the "Recovering the City of Lakes" project.

Juan Ricardo Rincón Gaviria, principal at Taller Paralelo Arquitectos, serves as SCI-Arc's program liaison. Rincón is the designer of Centro Creativ
Textura; the director of "Feria del Millón" art fair; and is head curator of VOLTAJE new media art show. He currently develops projects in New Yor
and for the Saatchi gallery in London.

ADVANCED'

ALBERTO KALACH
JUAN RINCON GAVIRIA

The studio concentrated on housing, public infrastructure and territorial solutions for OAXACA, one of the main historical and cultural capitals of Mexico. Since the origins of the Zapotec civilization in 2500 BCE, and continuing through the Spanish conquest of 16th century, the region holds a place of special value in Mexico's collective memory, from its own Benito Juarez and Porfírio Diaz; symbols of the Mexican history, to its very own Oaxacan cuisine and mezcal. In this sense Oaxaca has a cultural Intelligence that will be the guide of the studio itself. Although Oaxaca remains an important cultural center with a strong indigenous heritage, it is not exempt from the problems of urban sprawl, economic inequality, and environmental degradation that plague many cities in Mexico. With a rapidly expanding population of over 650,000, Oaxaca is in dire need of a new vision for the 21st century.

Students were asked not only to derive new urban solutions and possibilities for the city, but also to investigate and speculate around new typologies for a contemporary habitat of a growing city. The studio aimed to develop the potential of architecture as a catalyst of economic and cultural dynamics that to a degree could sustainably develop the city. In this regard, the value of architecture itself was determined by how the buildings are able to trigger relations in terms of social and cultural dynamics, rather than exclusively for its formal value.

Throughout the semester, the studio maintained a close working relationship with Infonavit, Mexico's affordable housing agency, and the State of Oaxaca. The final product, an 'Atlas for Oaxaca' presented the student work, and will be used in the future as a resource for State and local governments as they develop new comprehensive urban and regional planning strategies this upcoming year.

PROJECT OVERVIEW

OAXACA is a laboratory of spontaneous forms and resourceful everyday life operations of its inhabitants. We are interested in absorbing these characteristics and restating them on a larger scale; being able to generate solutions to architectural and urban problems such as actions capable of rethinking public policies and physical dynamics of the city. The studio will work hand to hand not only with Infonavit, but with government of the

State Oaxaca, where as these projects are to b the steping stone for later realized buildings.

Students will catalogue characteristics of dai life Oaxaca's inhabitants that reflect the intelligence of the spontaneous. This will be the concer tual structure that should jointly define an urban strategy proposed for the intervention perimete The architectural programs of new forms of housing and public character will be located throug social strategies that will resolve the design of buildings, public space and planning strategies the studio does not differentiate between observing, analyzing and projecting. From day one, we w define possible strategies to develop the projects that are convinced in a pragmatic and efficient wa Implying the minimal tools to produce as much as possible; minimizing a linear development of the project, but rather a parallel one where site understanding and strategy experimentation emerge simultaneously. 1

OBJECTIVES

The municipality of Oaxaca de Juárez is located i the state of Oaxaca, at the southwest end of the Isthmus of Tehuantepec, in the south Mexico. In 2015 the urban agglomeration of Oaxaca had an urban area of 168 km ^{2}. It was characterized by a expansive pattern of urbanization during the last decade, registering a rate of annual growth for homes twice the number of population (7.4% and 3.4% respectively). It has aproximatly 652,000 inhab itants, because of its stabilize demographic growth tendency, it is estimated that the population wi reach 755,000 inhabitants by 2030. In 2015 was estimated that the density of the agglomeration was 1,212 hab / km², but the municipality of Oaxaca de Juárez was above this parameter with 3, 011 Hab/km².

As a consequence of this lack of planning Oaxac has established micro urban centers that depend completely on central infrastructures. Creating urban funnels that are not well connected, nor have they their own infrastructure or housing devel opment, to operate as satellite urban centers. In this sense students will revise the current conditio of the following territories and determine possible plans of action for the urban agglomeratio of Oaxaca.

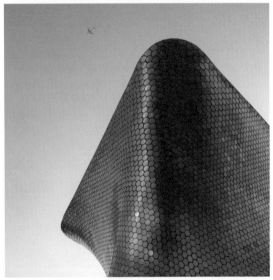

ADVANCED'

ALBERTO KALACH
JUAN RINCON GAVIRIA

ALBERTO KALACH
JUAN RINCON GAVIRIA

STUDENT:
Dongliang Li

CRITIC:
Alberto Kalach
Juan Rincon Gaviria

With the continued increase of population, the Oaxaca urban area has been expanded a lot in the past decades. The problem raised at the place that newly city area confronted the farm. In these area, most of buildings are under poor condition and city infrastructure is unorganized. Another existing problem of the city is the limited green and activity space. These two problems attracted me attention so I chose a site at the south border of the Oaxaca city which close to a well-organized farm area. I want to use my design to solve the two problems mention above and popularized to other border area of the city.

For my proposal, I first deleted some industrial buildings in the site and renovated most of the existing houses. Then, I created a park near the farm which make people have more experience and it's not only for the people at my design area but also for the people from downtown. On the north side of my site plan, I put some public buildings and activity space for the residents of the dense city. The curved green space and pavement work as an entrance to welcome citizens come to rest. The whole site design seems to like a belt to protect the farm and a smooth transition between the city and agriculture area.

[704]

ADVANCED'

ALBERTO KALACH
JUAN RINCON GAVIRIA

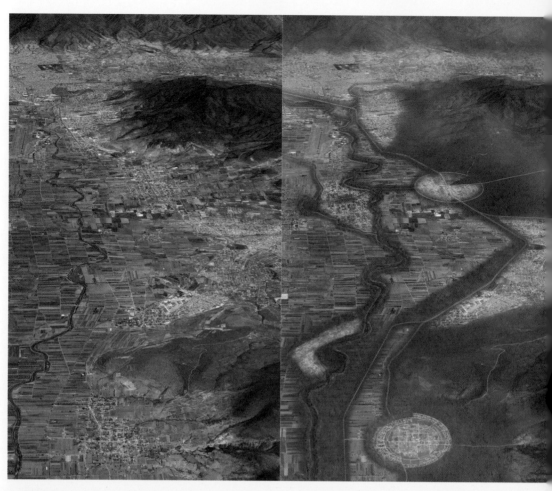

STUDENT:
Noor Al Awadhi

CRITIC:
**Alberto Kalach
Juan Rincon Gaviria**

Oaxaca began experiencing massive population growth in the 1950's, and slowly the historic boundaries of the central city have shifted as new urbanized territories are created. As the city continues to expand, new housing developments are erected in the urban peripheries, areas that lack adequate infrastructure, services and transportation. Improved connectivity and access is vital for residents of these isolated settlements, especially the thousands of commuters that travel daily to the center from the surrounding valleys. There is a need for new strategies of large-scale growth that would enrich and connect these urban nodes and control the continuing loss of agricultural land and mountain forestation due to unchecked urban sprawl.

The urban proposal consists of bands of varying widths overlaying the existing road network and encircling the small town of Santa Catarina Quiané (25 km south of central Oaxaca). The bands provide a framework for controlled urban growth. The outer bands contain new mixed use urban blocks and an opportunity to densify housing. The middle bands utilize green spaces and linear parks to integrate the existing low rise urban fabric with the new more densified urban blocks. An inner city tramline is introduced to facilitate access across the town, and a regional light rail transportation system runs adjacent to the main freeway and connects the town to the center as well as to other satellite nodes across the valleys. Adding a green belt and areas for reforestation prevent further encroachment on valuable agricultural and mountainous zones. The urban strategy is designed to be re-adapted and customized to respond to different urban scales and social, political and infrastructural needs.

[704]

TOKYO DRIFT:
SUBCULTURE PARKING GARAGE, TOKYO, JAPAN.

CRITIC: **Ali Rahim**
Professor of Architecture PennDesign
TA: **Maru Chung**

- Founded Contemporary Architecture Practice (CAP), NY (1999)
- Received an MArch from Columbia GSAPP, where he won the Honor Award for Excellence in Design & the Kinney Traveling Fellowship
- Books include Catalytic Formations: Architecture & Digital Design (2006), Elegance (2007)...

DRIFTING

Japan was one of the earliest birthplaces of drifting, a cross between drag racing and trackless driving. It originated in rural Japan with drivers racing through mountain roads, navigating hairpin curves at high speeds. The trend ultimately migrating to urban life with races occurring in parking lots throughout Tokyo. A subculture of car and motorcycle enthusiasts, known as Bosozoku/Hashiriya, emerged.

As Japan experienced a consumer revolution and the diffusion of western culture in the 1950s, Tokyo quickly became synonymous with cultural tribes and subcultures countering the Japanese norm. One can now see a mosaic of colorful outfits, with different groups emerging with their own style, influenced by Rock-and Roll, Punk, Pop stars, the French Rococo or Western Californian beach culture. Whether it was through fashion, music performance art or even a complete withdrawal from society, subcultures proliferated as escapes from reality. These trends put forth a 'new climate' of selfexpression with the ascendancy of the fantasies of the pop and fashion worlds, the pleasures of 'looking' and "being watched' and the body inscribed in the 'logic' of consumerism.

DISJUNCTIVE CONTINUITY: ARCHITECTURAL EXPRESSION OF SUBCULTURE

This shift towards new, more fragmented and hybridized cultural realities requires a redefinitio of space suitable for the new urban youth to thrive, allowing them to perform, to create and to drift literally but also figuratively, away from preconceived ideas of normalcy and success. Architecturally, Japanese 'disjunctive society' can be echoed as 'disjunctive continuity', where different qualities at times collide, overlap or merge in order to create an unexpected whole. Contrasting geometries can be woven into one another, in order to create visual sensation. The design techniques should derive from visual cues of the subcultures, generating formal, spatial, structural and material innovation. In essence, 'Disjunctive Continuity' can be defined as any blending of dissonant elements which creates an original, inexhaustible beauty.

[704]

ADVANCED'

ALI RAHIM

[704]

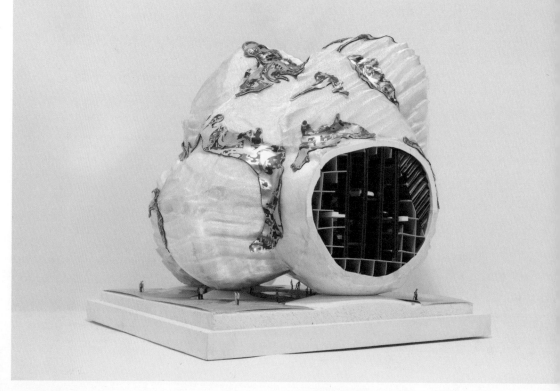

ADVANCED'

STUDENT:
Miguel Abaunza
Zachary Kile

CRITIC:
Ali Rahim

The Proposal for a new parking garage in the Chuo District of Tokyo drew inspiration from Tokyo's rich and thriving sub-culture and anti-culture scene. The parking garage is a mixed use building that accepts non-hierarchically all cultures and constituencies from urban Tokyo. The interior spaces become locations for self-reflection, performance, and group engagement, all the while allowing the density of Japan to continue growing thanks to innovative mechanical parking structures. The form of the building at an urbanistic level dismisses the conventional idea of building sidedness, this is done to ensure that no one direction of the site is given more importance than another, as the program does not privilege any single culture the form does not privilege any geographical reading. For that reason, you will find that both vehicular and pedestrian entry and exit takes place at the feet of the building. This building does not have a single reading and it should not read as such, it is for all intensive purposes this building is a cultural urban object.

ADVANCED'

ALI RAHIM

STUDENT:
David Feng
Shimou Chen

CRITIC:
Ali Rahim

This project is a huge infrastructure contains parking garage, drifting space
and Japanese sub-culture performance spaces - rockabilly performance
and Shironuri show stages. As most of the existing parking garage is not fully
enclosed, the design idea of this project is to amplify the effect and create
an extraordinary parking or drifting experience. The entire facade of the project
is covered by the hair-like structures, which filters sunlight and will not prevent water to get into the building. Also, large "weather devices" are introduced
to allow for weather and exterior conditions to penetrate through the building envelope. However, for the sub-culture programs that need to take place
in weather protected spaces, fully enclosed capsule spaces are provided
and nested into the huge parking structure. The interlocking relationship of
parking spaces and subcultural performance spaces will create a dynamic
circulation pattern with multiple significant scenes for people to explore.

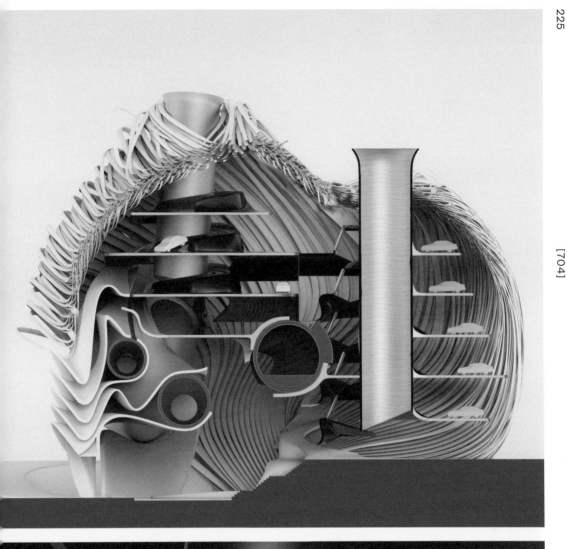

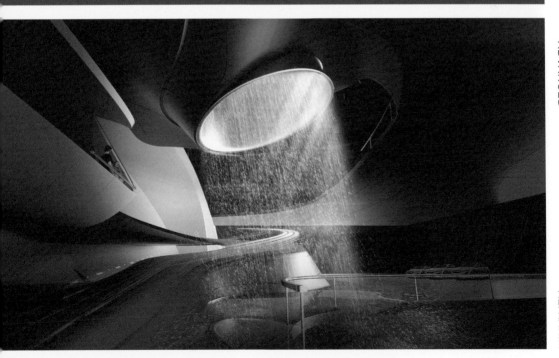

REAL FICTIONS II: OVER-UNDER

CRITIC: **Ferda Kolatan**

TA: **Michael Zimmerman**

- Founding partner of su11 architecture + design, NY (2004)
- Received an architectural diploma with distinction from the RWTH Aachen (1993)
- Received MsAAD, Architecture from Columbia GSAPP (1995)
- Selected as a Young Society Leader by The American Turkish Society (2011)

"Real Fictions" is the title of a multi-year project based in Cairo, Egypt in collaboration with the Heritage Center and the Cultural Ministry in Egypt. Last year's projects were selected and exhibited as part of the Egyptian Pavilion at the 2016 Venice Architecture Biennial. This year's studio is the second one in an ongoing investigation with a focus on Cairo's complex architectural and urban challenges.

Real Fictions, each year with a different focus, attempts to provide an architectural future for Cairo that is neither utopian nor pragmatic. We do not aim to posit a phantasmagorical idea into the bustling reality of Cairo, but we also do not believe that any meaningful shift in architecture culture can be achieved through insular problem-solving maneuvers. Instead we seek to find typical yet unique moments within the city, which already represent a fictional condition. In other words, the term "fiction" describes a "real" that has begun to withdraw from its original objectives, creating new potentialities along the way.

The studio is titled "OVER-UNDER" and focuses on an architectural object that is usually considered an undesirable interstitial leftover – the space at the landing of bridges. These zones are often dark, narrow, dominated by infrastructure, complicated to navigate, and aesthetically uncared for. Particularly, train and car bridges narrowly emphasize the main directional line and cut deep trenches into the adjacent fabric of neighborhoods, separating in the process people and traffic alike. If one were to look at these zones not as ugly divisions or inept space, but as unique moments that strangely combine infrastructure with architectural space, then unprecedented opportunities for a new kind of design arise.

The distinct quality of OVER-UNDER is that no single typological notion defines it fully. Instead a hybrid object emerges, combining parts from structure, infrastructure, and other spatial, material, and atmospheric elements found in the vicinity of the bridge landing. If viewed along these lines OVER-UNDER ceases to be the hapless resultant of a single-purpose structure and begins articulating a manifold character on its own. In other words, it transforms from a negative (passive) leftover-space to a positive (active) hybrid. Or yet in other words, it is no longer the inevitable result of other, stronger actors, but it becomes a coherent object with an agency and aesthetics of its own.

One interesting precedent for such an architectural hybrid is the medieval Ponte Vecchio in Florence, Italy, where the structure of the bridge transmutes into an "urban street" lined with homes and stores. A new aesthetic also follows as the "fictitiously" collaged appearance of the façades blend with the bridge to become a famous landmark and a prototype for newer adaptations. How could a contemporary version of this approach inform a new design for the landing area of a bridge and also manage the complex organization of the site? It is important to note that these projects do not call for the design of a bridge, or for a traffic planning solution. Rather the goal is to "invent" a new architectural type and to find an adequate conceptual-aesthetic expression for it.

Photography by: Angeliki Mavroleon

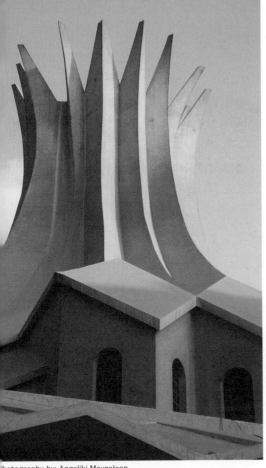

ADVANCED'

Here we see Dr Laila Iskandar (former Minister of State for Urban Renewal and Informal Settlements) giving us a talk about the history of the informal settement of the Zabaleen (Trash Collector's City) and the "Cave Church" of St. Simon.

Photography by: Angeliki Mavroleon

ADVANCED'

FERDA KOLATAN

STUDENT:
Angela Huang
Alexander Tahinos

CRITIC:
Ferda Kolatan

We looked to interrupt current norms of occupying the Nile River corniche and its implication on the architectural hybrid. Subverting the norm of the current context surrounding the Qasr al Nil Bridge western landing, the project moves towards an interesting hybridization of landscape, hardscape, and architecture. We looked to create a familiar architectural formal language which is deployed in unfamiliar ways. Creating new typologies of architectural space, the small boutique pavilions stand as signifiers of the existing within new landscapes of foliage, concrete, and infrastructure. The constructed park areas hybridize multiple conditions of traditional park spaces but never solely become classified or recognizable. Artificial rock-scapes float above glass-boxes which house contemporary office spaces. These rocks begin to hold the foliage for a proposed public park whilst creating a zone of hybridization with their own irrigation system. This water circulatory system becomes the consistent link between each typological object within the site. This ranges from large extraction tanks below the surface of the water, to fountains at the center of plaza areas, to hidden purifiers and storage systems within the roofs of pavilions. The infrastructural systems begin to express themselves in unique ways that blur the boundary between form and function of a typically "behind the scenes" system of elements.

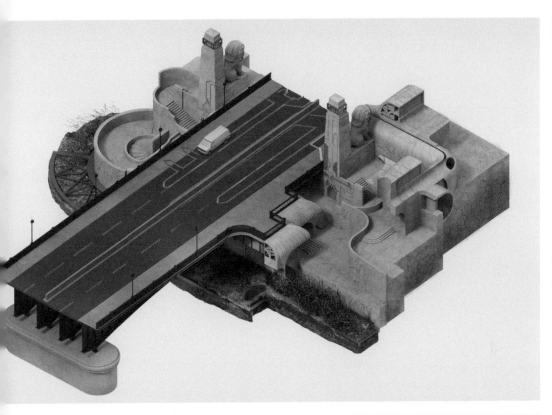

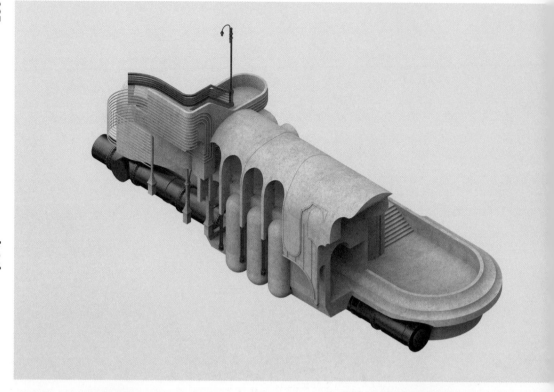

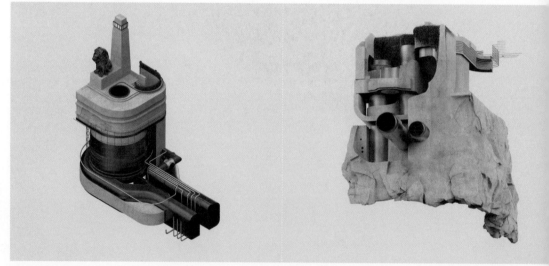

STUDENT:
Carrie Frattali
Angeliki Tzifa

CRITIC:
Ferda Kolatan

Located adjacent to Tahrir Square, a socially and politically charged area that has been reclaimed by the government as private space, our aim is to provide public open and covered space for the people of Cairo as well as complimentary programs of transportation and water purification by means of a public park. By speculating on the development of a water purification system that would be partially concealed by a public park, we were able to reconnect the streetscape with the mostly privatized Nile Waterfront. In order to provoke a curiosity among its visitors, the park slowly reveals seams and openings to the facility below and profiled of machinery. By using qualities of the site we tried to blur the line between park and machine,

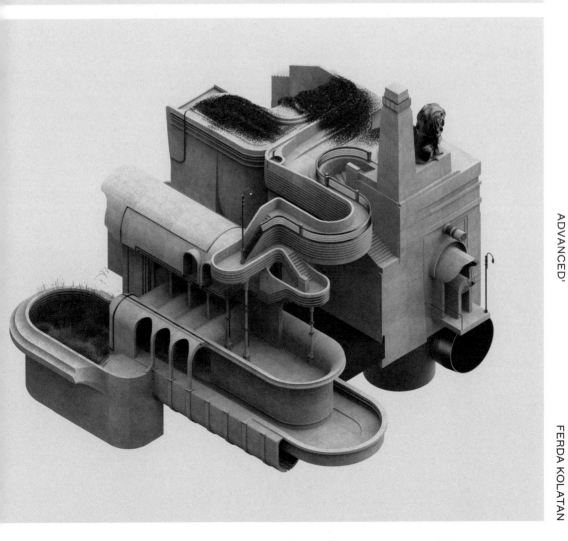

WATER-COLOR

CRITIC: **Florencia Pita**
TA: **Aidan Kim**

- Prinicpal of FPmod.
- She graduated in 1998 from the National University of Rosario, Argentina, School of Architecture.
- Her work has been widely published and received many awards.
- Her work has been exhibited in numerous museums, galleries and biennals.

This studio will investigate the fabrication of artificial landscapes and figural buildings, within the context of industrial infrastructures and a river of concrete. The LA River is undergoing mayor transformations, what once was nature, is now a hardscape of concrete that spans 51 miles. The potential of this river to shift from infrastructure to public spaces could transform the city of Los Angeles, and provide a new model of reuse, were active (as opposed to obsolete) infrastructure can perform multiple urban capacities. The LA River is not only an urban connector with un-interrupted linear path, but also it carries water, which flows toward the ocean. This extravagant expenditure of water in a desert city seems paradoxical. This studio will take on the topic of water from a painterly manner. Architecture's contribution to this topic cannot try to imitate the work done by engineers, but our potential resides in design, and design ideas. For this reason we will look at water in the manner that painters look at water, not for what it means but for what is exposes, a kind of semblance of water. Water-colour will use both water and color as the ingredients to connect landscape with building mass.

PROGRAM

In response to the water crisis that the city of Los Angeles is undergoing, this studio will design a water tank, one that will serve both as cistern and water filtration system. The water running through the LA River can be channeled to the water tower and be used for watering the park as well as other public spaces in Boyle Heights. Along with the water programs the tower will house public programs. Water towers historically populate cities across towns, they serve a functional purpose and also an iconic one, as described in the photograph catalog of Bernd and Hilla Becher (image above), these towers give profile to the city skyline.

SITE

The 'Los Angeles River Revitalization Master Plan' is an extensive proposal that takes into consideration the 51 miles of the LA river, our studio will focus on a particular area within the master plan which is located in Downtown Los Angeles Arts District. Both west and east sides of the river are currently land areas zoned for industrial use, while the further east neighborhood of Boyle Heights is a residential zone. This area is dominated by light industrial and manufacturing land uses, but the emerging residential community of the Arts District to the west call upon the advancement of public spaces and pedestrian connectivity. The lack of green spaces in these park-deficient zones, require that we reevaluate the potential of the river and its potential to rethink the idea of parks.

...ca's Final review at PennDesign

Student's site visit in Los Angeles

STUDENT:
Mark Chalhoub

CRITIC:
Florencia Pita

Boyle Heights in LA by the river is an industrial site that presents an opportunity to intervene by proposing a beautified infrastructural . The aim of this project is to give the site a new aesthetic identity while engaging the praxis of a water injection facility. The challenge itself is to tackle the notion of a park in a traditional naturalistic sense through re-appropriating our perception of "park nature". The project pushes a figural aesthetic agenda, that negotiates through form, cut and color, the merging and overlapping of the anthropocene and ecological infrastructure. The result is a colorful coordination of patterns and textures that reinterpret how inherently disparate conditions can cohabit the same site as a whole.

ADVANCED'

FLORENCIA PITA

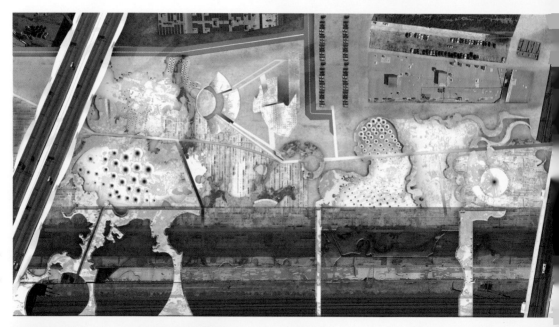

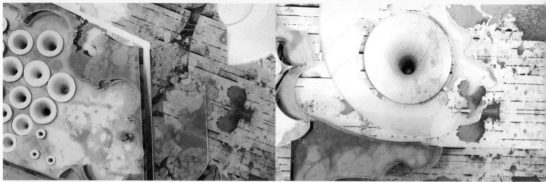

STUDENT:
Michelle Ann Chew

CRITIC:
Florencia Pita

   Los Angeles has a new spectacle. It is the LA River Spillway Park. What used to be a natural filtration system of wetlands, was covered by a closed off concrete structure of river channel and train yards. This closed off infrastructure is now becoming a new and open infrastructure drawing people to celebrate water and the LA River. What is super-flat and artificial on the surface, has a deep infrastructure below. It rains in LA only 5% of the year. The rest of the year is dry, arid, and desert- like. The site has a temporal quality in which it is only activated during a very short period out of the year. During this time, the mesmerizing spillways will implement tourism and spectacle to the site. Color will bleed and swirl, drying up into a marbleized residue. During the rain the site will be overgrown with residue of pre-existing algae and moss that creeps out of the concrete. During dry spells the artificial green algae will bloom and die transforming into arid desert areas filled with dry brush, deplete of water. Esplanades are carved out of the landscape to provide meandering paths for the aimless wanderer to explore the open infrastructure of the LA River park. The Water Tower itself serves as an icon to the city of LA, and a main observation point to the spillway reservoirs below. Tourists can ascend and view the reservoirs and beyond from various focal points of the Tower. The Tower serves as a gateway to the park, a new open area of exploration that is artificially reminiscent of a desert wetland past, but is now a new synthetic nature that is a juxtaposition of the artificial super-flat and the real super-deep.

15 MINUTES AND COUNTING.
A NEW ANDY WARHOL MUSEUM FOR TOKYO, JAPAN.

CRITIC: **Hina Jamelle**
TA: **Caleb White**

- Architect and Director, Contemporary Architecture Practice, NY (2003)
- Graduated with an MArch from University of Michigan Taubman College, where she received the Dr. Martin Luther King, Jr., Leadership Award.
- Author of the upcoming book Migrating Architectural and Structural Formations (2013) and co-author of Elegance (2007)

"The idea is not to live forever; it is to create something that will."-Andy Warhol

This studio examined eastern and western pop art and its relation to the formulation of architecture by using digital techniques in an opportunistic fashion for the generation of growth and evaluation of patterns in the development of form. Digital techniques allow us to deal with the full complexity of material systems that lead to effects that are greater than the sum of their parts.

Pop Art utilized imagery of the modern world; copied from magazines and other media, these images exposed Pop Art to the greater public. Where the early pop artists of America relied more heavily on the technique of collage and image sampling, Japanese Pop Artists are more interested in the synthesis of the borrowed symbols, images and characters into a new stylistic image narrative. As with early American Pop Art, Japanese pop art also relies on vibrant and highly contrasted color palettes. Techniques of contemporary Japanese pop art often revolve around the projection of form to the 2D resulting in graphic figuration. You can see this particularly in the work of Takashi Murakami, who created the "Superflat" Japanese pop art stylistic movement.These

graphic techniques lend themselves particularly useful to the diagram - especially when considered as a spatially generative tool.

The ability to study, research and investigate which artistic techniques are useful is key to formulating innovative systems for architecture. These innovations are accumulative and are subject to changes that shift in type and/ or in kind. In addition, the artistic technique's usefulness is determined by their eventual formation that include material, space, atmosphere, program and social interaction. The ability to identify spatial potential in buildings and developing innovative formations provide a more nuanced and architecturally sophisticated understanding of form.

The goal for each student has been to evaluate the potentials of artistic techniques in designing architecture that flows from topological surfaces and spatial arrangements, and to apply these to a range of familiar architectural issues. The final proposal of each student merged out of an interrelated working method between artistic techniques, program, space, atmosphere and materials that combine to develop an innovative new museum formation.

ADVANCED'

HINA JAMELLE

Mori Museum Tokyo

Studio Hina Jamelle with Yuko Hasegawa
Director Museum of Contemporary Art Tokyo

University, Tokyo.

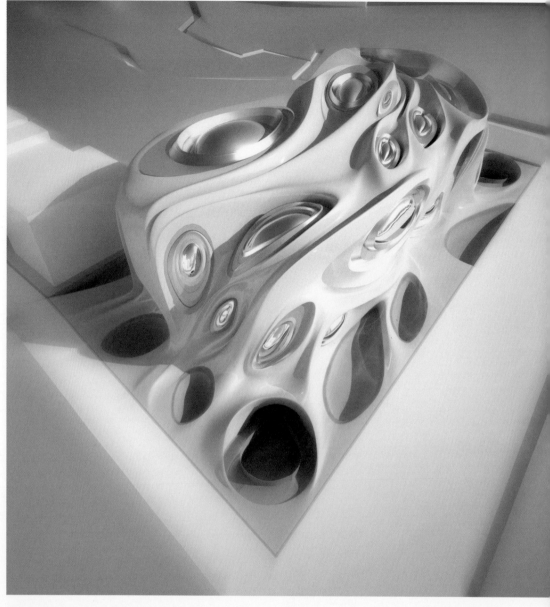

STUDENT:
Siyang Lv
Shuoqi Xiong

CRITIC:
Hina Jamelle

Our project is driven by an urban context driven strategy. Tokyo has a number of open green spaces such as Shinjuku Garden and Yoyogi Park, which are surrounded by high-dense urban buildings. These green spaces could be regarded as varying scalar voids in the city. This scalar change of voids is unique to Tokyo.

In our proposal we pick up on this condition to design a system of voids in our museum. These voids are developed as galleries in the museum, we take larger voids as public galleries, we use ramp to organize the circulation, and the paintings are hung on the wall, we take smaller void as private galleries. we also have voids on the building envelope, which spatially intersected with the interior voids, We design the intersected space as transition space between different voids. we emphasize the scale quality which are influenced by the pop culture on the building envelope and the voids are organized in hierarchy on the building skin.

[704]

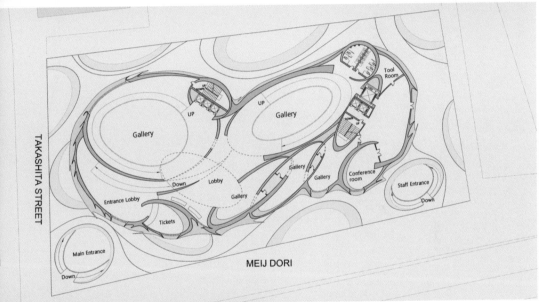

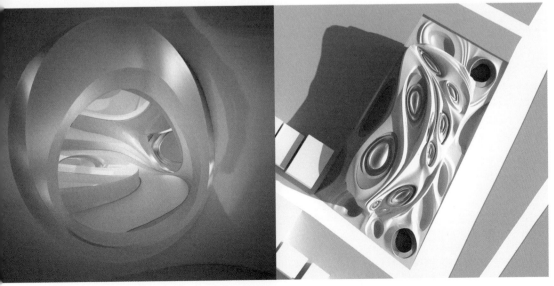

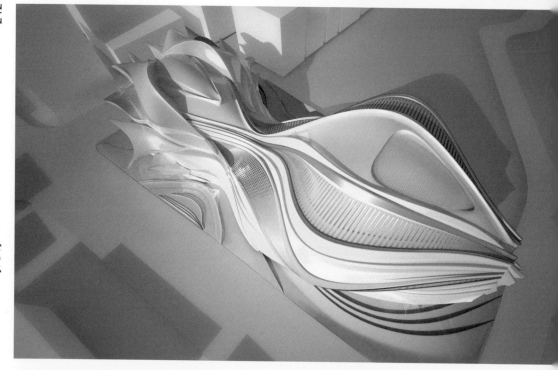

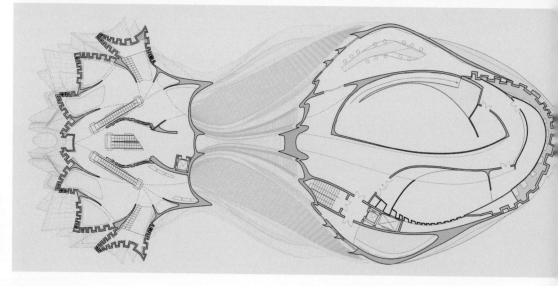

STUDENT:
Yuchen Zhao
Ge Yang

CRITIC:
Hina Jamelle

Our Museum proposal is driven by two main influences 1. the site in Tokyo and 2. pop art influences.

Our Tokyo site has unique characteristics on all four sides. Our proposals short elevation on Takashita Street picks up on the streets smaller scale idiosyncratic nature and pulls this up through the vertical bundling of small intense of digital galleries up the museum. Along the main street the larger scale contemporary galleries align with the graceful and undulating natural features of the park to the North.

The exterior skin, and main interior gallery spaces are developed through diagrammatic technique studies of brushstrokes, layering and curvature in Eastern and Western Pop Art Works.

[704]

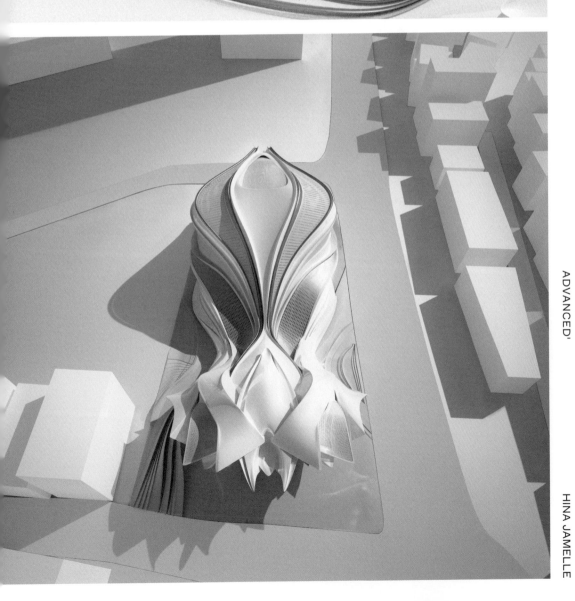

ADVANCED'

HINA JAMELLE

DRIFTING SYMMETRIES:
TOWARDS A NEW BOTANIC INFRASTRUCTURE

CRITIC: **Marion Weiss**
Professor of Architecture PennDesign
GUEST CRITIC: **Michael Manfredi**
TA: **Eric Bellin**

- Co-founder of WEISS/MANFREDI Architecture/Landscape/Urbanism, NY (1989)
- Received her MArch at Yale University and her BArch from the University of Virginia
- WEISS/MANFREDI is the winner of many architectural awards

[704]

ADVANCED'

MARION WEISS

The obligations of infrastructure inflected by the seemingly oppositional stance of botanic life raise a series of contemporary design questions. Longwood Gardens, the botanical preserve established on the Dupont estate outside of Philadelphia, has a longstanding commitment to beauty and innovation, principles which have led to their interest in both advances in conservatory construction and biological form as inspiration for building. These concerns meet in Longwood Gardens' plan for a new, biologically inflected "parking garden," pioneering a new paradigm which hybridizes car park, bridge, and conservatory.

The sites planned for the the future parking garden and new visitor conservatory are divided by a roadway, necessitating a bridge between the two structures, introducing a range of identities for the bridge – from land bridge to crystalline connector – and introducing questions about the symmetries that drift between the following:

• Car Park-car protection
/ Conservatory-botanic cultivation
• Carbon monoxide / Photosynthesis
• Mono functional infrastructure / Botanic monocultures
• Linear arrival / wandering departures

Dupont is historically noted for invention: they are responsible for innovative materials ranging from the modern formula for Gun Powder, to Styrofoam, Plexiglas, Nylon, and Teflon. Less known is DuPont's legacy in Longwood Gardens. The property was established as the DuPont family's estate and farm in 1907. Over the subsequent decades the estate was developed and expanded to include an impressive collection of conservatories and gardens, which upon the death of Pierre DuPont in 1954, was given as a gift to the public. In the years since, Longwood Gardens has grown into an internationally recognized horticultural display garden, at the center of which its conservatories host extraordinary collections of plants that, in Pennsylvania, can thrive only indoors, with temperature and humidity levels calibrated from a below level infrastructure that simulates climates ranging from humid to arid.

In 2014, Longwood Gardens announced the interest in being able to host larger groups at the property while preserving the beauty and legac of the gardens. With no public transportation options nearby, the obligation to provide onsite parking and create a new visitor center has introduced an opportunity to create one of the world' most beautiful and innovative parking facilities. This planned "parking garden," a hybridized car par bridge, and conservatory, is intended to create a new visitor experience and reveal vital connec tions between research and innovation in the field of infrastructure and horticulture, expanding the identity of Longwood Gardens as a place of sustainable innovation and invention.

The aspiration of growth in visitation to the garden is limited by the capacity of hosting cars an people, and the dual challenge of connectivity and growth will allow the Garden to meet a programmati challenge while advancing research in the terrain of botanically inspired infrastructural ecologies.

SYMMETRY AND GROWTH
Without predetermined answers, the creation of this new hybrid raises critical questions: How can the recasting of parking garage and conserva tory models inform a new form of infrastructure dedicated to advancing innovation? What are the systems that inform the surface and silhouette of the hybrid?

FIELD WORK: NEW YORK
AND PENNSYLVANIA
To understand the distinctions and common ground of innovation emerging in parking and conserva-tories, the studio will travel to Longwood Garden in Pennsylvania and New York City's Botanical Garden, Brooklyn Botanic Garden, and meets with the botanic leadership teams at each institution.

ADVANCED'

STUDENT:
Jae Geun Ahn
Jiateng Wang

CRITIC:
Marion Weiss

MARION WEISS

The sites planned for the future parking garden and new visitor conservatory are divided by a road way, necessitating a bridge between the two structures, introducing a range of identities for the bridge – from land bridge to crystalline connector – and introducing questions about the symmetries that drift between car protection and botanic cultivation; carbon monoxide and photosynthesis; mono functional infrastructure and botanic monocultures; linear arrival and wandering departures.

The project consists of three layers--surface parking which moves from exterior field to underneath the bridging structure, one level of elevated parking, and an interior visitor level. These layers are punctured and joined by a series of crystalline garden-conservatories, each of which houses a different sort of botanic environment. Expressing the journey of the interior space. Multiple functions, including amphitheater, water pond, light well, exterior garden, restaurant, café, shopping, library, education center, auditorium, musical hall and conservatories, are inlaid through the horizontal linear organization.

STUDENT:
Daniel Fachler
Elsa Listiani

CRITIC:
Marion Weiss

We are asked to design a new conservatory to expand their canvas and a garage that can park more visitors. Our brief was to design a hybrid between the two programs and to bridge over a major road that cuts their property in half. When we visited Longwood, one of the aspects that surprised us was their notion to challenge gravity. They create stunningly beautiful compositions of flowers that hang from the ceiling.

Our response to the brief is to create an immersive experience of walking through a promenade of displaced landscapes. We created a sequence of vessels that capture different climates and emotions. The first one is an intro-duction to Longwood. The surfaces of this vessel are ornamented with a diverse range of exotic flowers and colorful plants. It serves as a statement to the public about Longwood's mission. The second one displaces you to the dessert. A dry climate filled with life. The third one relocates you to the pine forest. And the last vessel captures the marbles of the tropical cloud forest. The parking garage is nested in between the vessels, in order to create a direct experience between parking and the conservatory. The experience of botany starts while you are driving your car and not when you get out of it.

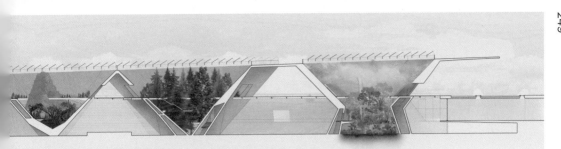

[704]

ADVANCED'

MARION WEISS

MULTIFARIOUS FUTURES:
TRANSIT IN THE AGE OF POST-HUMANIST COMMERCE

CRITIC: **Robert Stuart-Smith**

TA: **Joseph Giampietro**

Robert is a founding director of rs-sdesign, a co-founding director of the collaborative research practice - Kokkugia and a Studio Course Master i the AA School's Design Research Laboratory (AA.DRL) in London. Robert studied architecture in the UK, France and Australia and holds a Master in Architecture + Urbanism from the Architectural Association School of Architecture's Design Research Laboratory (AA.DRL). He has practiced architecture in the UK, USA and Australia for the offices of Lab Architecture Studio, Grimshaw Architects, Arup's AGU (Advanced Geometry Unit) and Balmond Studio as an algorithmic design consultant.

POST-HUMANIST COMMERCE

In 2008, communication between things exceeded communications involving people. By 2020 the "Internet of Things" will incorporate 50 Billion things. This technological shift has given rise to "Industry 4.0", where manufacturing has become a highly interconnected semi-autonomous enterprise, increasingly urban yet, decreasingly human. Architecture is historically an anthropocentric discipline with no means to address this shift. Aligned to Humanist ideology, the discipline has upheld the human as the agent and concern of architectural space. Humanism in its varied forms however, has failed to describe the complex interactions that operate in a universe which includes a multitude of non-human agencies. Post-humanism attempts to offer a more open view that upholds a respect for not only humanity, but for everything living or non-living. The Speculative Realist philosopher, Levi Bryant provides a constructive framework for architectural consideration, advocating for a "flat ontology", where the human is considered an object, positioned on the same plane as any other object. Multifarious Futures explores a non-anthropocentric future commerce and transport terminal that is concerned with a multitude of object occupants and object relations.

AMAZON 2034: ON-DEMAND MANUFACTURING, DISTRIBUTION AND TRANSIT CENTRE

The immediacy of digital content is raising expectations for immediacy in physical content delivery. In addition to their existing Kiva robot warehouse operations and autonomous delivery vans, Amazon now wishes to implement Patent No. 9305280: airship supply and delivery. The acquisition of Shapeways Inc in 2034 enables Amazon to develop a distributed network of factories each able to manufacture products on-demand. No longer requir-ing vast storage spaces, these factories can b small, located centrally in highly populated areas and directly connected to Hyperloop rapid-grou transport for material supply, with a bi-product o human transit offering additional income revenu

MONOLITHIC OR MULTIFARIOUS

It is envisioned that Amazon is able to additivel manufacture its own buildings in-situ, utilizing its own infrastructure. 3D printing allows for desigr of increased intricacy, detail, and geometrical complexity. Not requiring assembly, the compart mentalization or expression of discrete tectonic elements is not practically necessary. This enable a fuzzier, more awkward set of relationships to be explored that need not privilege a totalistic expression of assemblage, repetition, juxtaposi-tion, continuum or gradient. A formal and materia order will be developed that operates through shifting relations, providing distinct design cha acterization, and tailored relationships between spatial, urban, and aesthetic concerns. Designec to oscillate between object and field, these will be exploited to take on diverse, strange, and varie relationships at varied scales.

MALAYSIA BIENNIAL 100YC
— MEDINI FUTURE CITY

The studio is participating in the 2017 Malaysia Biennale 100YC - Medini Future City curated by Tom Kovac. Medini is a $20 Billion public-private partnership development to be constructed in the next 15-20 years. Envisioned as a "smart city," Medini will operate as the new Central Business District of Iskandar Puter. The studio will speculat on the incorporation of a new Amazon 'Manufactu-ing, Distribution and Transit Centre' within Medini masterplan. The proposal will incorporate an on-demand factory with a Hyperloop rail terminal and airship delivery center.

Robert Stuart Smith's Final Review at PennDesign

ADVANCED'

ROBERT STUART-SMITH

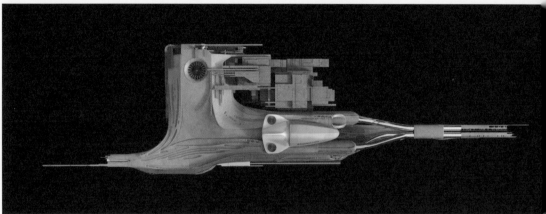

STUDENT:
Bosung Jeon
Wan Jung Lee

CRITIC:
Robert Stuart-Smith

ROBERT STUART-SMITH   ADVANCED'

The proposal addresses the studio's post-human exploration of an Amazon On-Demand Manufacturing, Delivery and Transit Centre through its design considerations for the primary occupants of the building – autonomous machines. The non-anthropocentric nature of the program has led to a design strategy that arranges space, circulation and aesthetic according to the building's robotic occupants. Activities have been arranged in a similar manner to existing Amazon Fulfilment Centers, separated into three main processes that include; receiving, organizing, and packaging. The scale and requirements of the equipment leads to a wide range of spatial scales, with some floors only high enough for small Kiva robots to pass through. Circulation for people and machines is differentiated, with robot circulation visible yet not accessible by humans. Human circulation occupies a very small portion of space at the center of the building, and is designed to not obstruct machine circulation, yet provide a view onto the activities of the building. Robot circulation involves a flexible grid system where QR Code's are utilized to track and identify deliveries. The manufacturing part of the building is a dense, and sometimes dark, yet efficient maze that is able to be re-constructed by the robots when manufacturing processes require updating. The production process therefore re-shapes the building over time. While the building is large, the on-demand manufacturing ensures the facility is considerably smaller than existing Amazon Fulfillment Centers. The appearance of the proposal is informed by the negotiation of robot-led production and a scale and articulation of space and form that relates to machine based manufacture, whilst Hyperloop and human-transit facilities inform a more continuous geometry to other parts of the building.

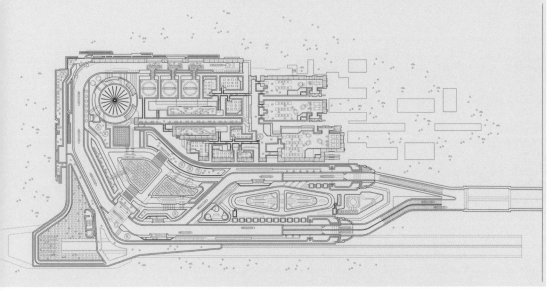

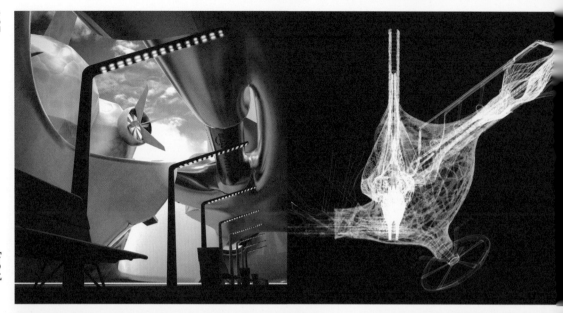

STUDENT:
Ke Liu
Yuhan Bian

CRITIC:
Robert Stuart-Smith

ADVANCED'

ROBERT STUART-SMITH

The proposal addresses the studio's speculative exploration of an Amazon On-Demand Manufacturing, Delivery and Transit Centre in the heart of a new city development – Medini in Malaysia. The city will be developed over the next 20 years and aims to become the new central business district for the region. Responding to the studios interest in post-humanism and Levi Bryant's concept of a Flat Ontology, the design proposal aims to flatten the relations between numerous transport objects and enables these to exist within the city, the building and in Hyperloop transit equally, extending their relationship to other cities. This involves equalizing the scale, operation and accessibility of the street car, building lift/monorail system, Hyperloop pods and Hyperloop capsules, so that they may co-exist and be interchangeable. Pedestrians and vehicles are to circulate through the building in similar ways to production materials and finished products. The uniqueness and immense scale of some of the project's occupants (such as the airships and Hyperloop system) are formally expressed on the exterior of the building to allow their size to visually dominate the pedestrian environment below, also further re-enforcing a non-anthropocentric reading of this new autonomous manufacturing center that is to operate in the heart of the city.

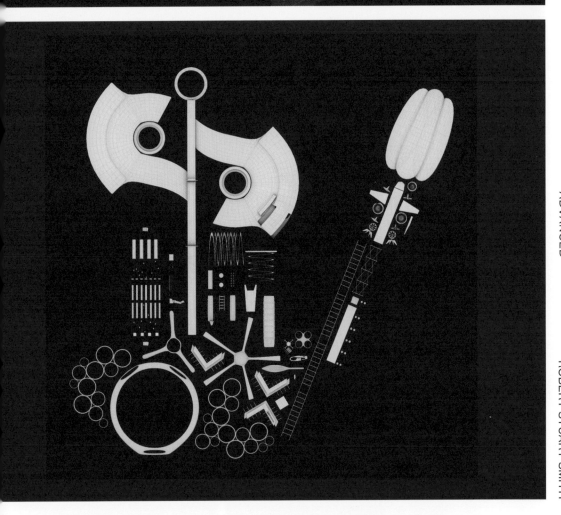

WORLD WITHOUT OBJECTS
SUPERSTUDIO @ HAMPSTEAD HEATH

CRITIC: **Homa Farjadi**
Professor of Practice at PennDesign

TA: **Hyemi Kang & Chang Yuan Max Hsu**

- Principal of Farjadi Architects (1987)
- Received a Graduate Diploma from the AA School of Architecture in London and an MArch with distinction from Tehran University
- The work of her office has been exhibited and published internationally.

As in previous years the format of this research studio is focused on the analytical conjunction of significant documents of architectural thinking, in words and in design to produce coordinate of ideas brought together to frame a dialogical discourse prompting a new conceptual premise and design parameters for a project of architecture relevant to our time.

Superstudio's work may recall seemingly impossible collages, visions of a future where speculative thought finds electrifying images contemplating urban futures that in their words ' resist design'. 'Without design' according to Super studio is where design stands still, words become mute and objects fall away. 'A world without objects' in their projects configures extensions of landscape, geology, furniture and buildings exploring limitless conditions of form and performance in their encounter with nature.

Working in mid 1960's Florence, theirs was a critical reaction to the modernist belief in design as the end all solution to urban problems. In a discipline where intentionality of the architecture solving problems in new objects spearheads its raison d'etre, theirs contemplates urbanism in geological scale to rediscover nature's operational forms and events. The aim is to bypass design, or at least its figurational/ rational logics and do away with its object fixation.

Infrastructural extrusions universalize chance forms and catch operations of surface projected into 3d. Super surface project configures worlds and objects in the same stroke projecting endless scale-less extensions of grid formations. One may be justified to think it an impossible ambition to 'forget design' in architecture, yet their forms provoke and their ideas challenge what still can be regarded as a relevant critique of architecture.

To get rid of normative design in our parametrically enlightened environment of heightened digital possibilities what are we to make of this ambitions, this impossible goal? Despite happening during 60's this is no hippy 'back to nature', nor is it a mere ethics of ecological design. There is reason for our interest. This repeal, this refrain this stoppage has a function. It is to obstruct normative design thinking as solutions, to make form avoid representational games, to resist figuration in order to explore potentials for instability and non- representational equality seen as nature's freedom and to ask how we can deny limits in making space while following each projects' line of design thinking.

London- Large Footprint Parks- Following financial boom in the last decade London has been in a hurried process of rebuilding its working priorities and its image leaving its essential urbanity to real games of real estate. Although Brexit might bring about a different end to such boom, at the moment the city is mostly driven to develop its high- density centers in the financial center in the City of London or on the southern banks of the Thames with new urban centers. Our project considers alternatives to such high-density accumulations of real estate addressing potentials of large footprint green parks in the metropolitan area.

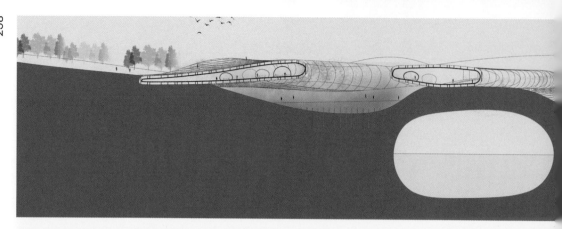

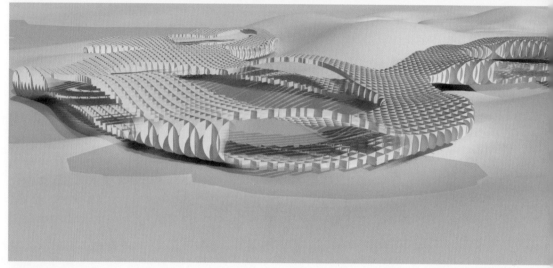

STUDENT:
Tiantian Guo
Jieping Wan

CRITIC:
Homa Farjadi

ADVANCED'

HOMA FARJADI

Hyper Nature explores the idea of an alternative experience of nature in Hampstead Heath. It envisions a technologically advanced pleasure in urbanized nature– an infrastructural system that accelerates the processes and experiences of nature. Unlike the traditional greenhouses in the UK, Hyper Nature is a layer over the landscape with two main functions. It controls flood by streaming the water into artificially created retention basins. The water collected from the flood and rain is pumped from the water tank, filtered, and sprayed as a fine mist, creating an artificial fog thereby creating a mediated environmental/ perceptual experience. The fog not only celebrates the various events that happen in the space but also irrigates the plants on the roof garden. The roof garden accelerates certain phenomenon in the natural landscape to become a hyper landscape of pleasure. In the wind room, the bamboo poles are colonized as spatial sound makers that are responsive to the distance of people. It also captures the sound of the wind in the Heath. As the wind blows, the bamboo poles produce music within the space. This artificial responsive system takes references of what people do and enhances them. Consequently, these natural phenomena happen at our pleasure.

In Hyper Nature, people are able to experience the wind, see the fog, taste the fruits produced through their interactions, and play the game of nature. Instead of simply experiencing nature, people become active participants in this pleasure.

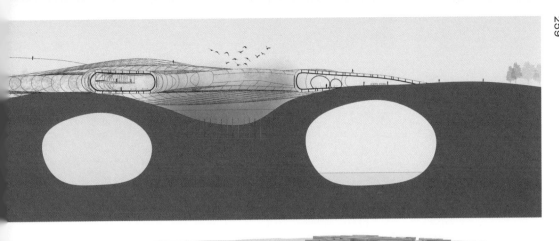

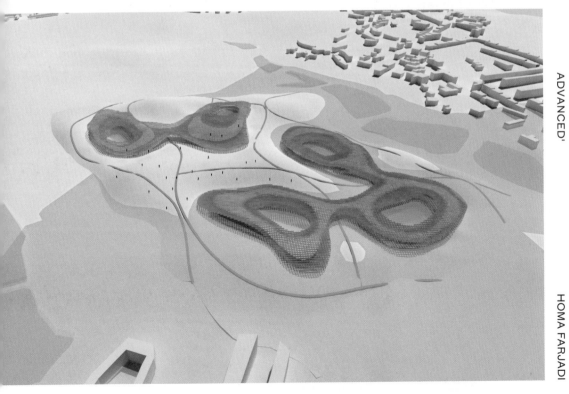

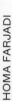

STUDENT:
Sookwan Ahn
Yunhwan Jung

CRITIC:
Homa Farjadi

Our project is based on Superstudio's idea that architecture exists in time as salt exists in water and reality exists in fiction. Based on the accumulation of time, visible entities can be seen differently. They are interpreted and remembered in various ways depending on the perspective of the individual. These diverse constructs of memory create multiple meanings in the urban environment. The project creates a structure as a landform of urbanized nature. Constructed on a geological scale it connects two high points of the existing landscape in Hampstead Heath it presents a vertical dissection of its data program and abstract urban geology.

The in-between space allows the nature of Hampstead Heath to merge with the grid structure in which the masses are organized. The two separated masses have opposite qualities. The upper mass is a mediatheque with an open floor plan to create and shared memories or information. The lower mass is an archive, a data center with a fixed floor plan to collect and accumulate memories or information. These two parts are integrated with vertical links as core, structure, and cooling towers. With the spatial and functional contrast, the whole project acts as an infrastructure that represent the urbanism of the natural environment in Hampstead Heath.

HELLINIKON PROJECT - ATHENS GREECE

CRITIC: **Cecil Balmond**
Professor of Practice at PennDesign
- Founding Principal of Balmond Studio, London & Columbo (2010)
- Received a MSc from the Imperial College of Science, London, and a BSc, from the University of Southampton
- Designed the 2006 Serpentine Gallery Pavilion with Rem Koolhaas
- He has received numerous international awards.

CRITIC: **Ezio Blasetti**
Professor of Practice at PennDesign
- Founding Partner of ahylo, Athens, GR (2009)
- Received an MSAAD from Columbia University GSAPP after having previously studied in Athens and Paris. (2006)
- Founder of algorithmicdesign.net
- Taught at Pratt Institute, the Architectural Association, and Columbia University

TA: **Shengkan Zhang**

'Each and every number has a secret number. Buried beneath the surface, hidden within the construction is another mark, a secret code that defines the original number. Like elements in chemistry, like the alphabet in language, it is a primary classification from which everything else flows. It is an imprint.' Cecil Balmond, Number Nine

Conceptual Framework: This research studio will investigate non-linear algorithmic procedures at both a methodological and tectonic level. The exploration will take the form of design research, which will be tested through a rigorous urban and architectural proposal. Design research is not defined here as a linear scientific optimization process with objective outcomes, but rather as the iterative, non-linear and speculative process with the ability to reassess and shift our disciplinary discourse.

Architecture is a singularity in the confluence of matter with time. The studio is in search of a new fundamental logos at once analytical and generative, immersed within and emerging from an environment through interference. Our speculative condition is that computation is not solely digital but omnipresent. As such, beyond the correlation of simulation, this studio positions different mediums onto a flat ontology and mines the collateral effects of the synchronicities and divergences between them. The primary territory of feedback between abstraction, matter and narration is pattern. We seek novel patterns of organization, structure and articulation as architectural

expressions within the emergent properties of feedback loops and rule based systems.

Project: During 2001, in preparation for the Olympic Games, the transfer of the airport of Athens (Greece) from the coastal area of Hellinik to Mesogeia, made available a unique site of unprecedented scale for a European Capital. At a approximate size of 6200 acres neighboring the Saronic Gulf and only 10 km from the center o Athens, the future of Hellinikon has been at the forefront of public debates for decades.

The studio will travel to Athens to research and generate a multidimensional terrain of data, which will attempt to capture and compress th various, past and future narratives of the site. This abstract construction will be our conceptua and literal site of intervention. Design will operate as a feedback tool of navigation and adaptation

The studio will re-examine the various propose masterplans for Hellinikon and propose an alternative future for the site. The participants in th studio will collaborate to provide a unique and inspired urban vision and will gradually focus or 5 pivotal projects at the building scale. Working in feedback between the various scales, from th regional to the tectonic, will allow the studio to speculate on the limits of architecture as an orga nizational, structural and aesthetic agent of innovation and change. The program will include a park, transportation, housing, a convention center, cultural and recreational buildings.

STUDENT:
Wenxin Chen
Hewen Jiang

CRITIC:
Cecil Balmond
Ezio Blasetti

In this Research Studio, we aimed to create fundamentally discrete spaces with the development of an algorithmic design strategy. Our design approach starts from a two-dimensional Turing Machine (Langton's Ant) that changes the pixel color and movement direction to generate complex patterns. In the preliminary steps of our research, we expanded Langton's Ant ruleset to three states and four moving directions. Aided by computation, we were able to run 10000 possibilities and chose the most desirable results. By combining two or more rulesets we were able to generate complex wholes that closely replicate qualities of the urban fabric.

In order to achieve spatial complexity, we further expand the rulesets to the third dimension and assign specific rules for horizontal and vertical movement (plan vs. section). With this method we were able to create different 3D configurations and assign corresponding programs to each space. With the understanding of the spatial relationships and potential inhabitation, we design several 3d configurations together and achieve higher complexity and differentiation.

In the last part of the studio, we interpreted the 2d and 3d configurations as urban infrastructure. We propose a cruise ship terminal complex as a new entrance of tourism for Athens and a new city of culture and celebration.

ADVANCED'   CECIL BALMOND & EZIO BLASETTI

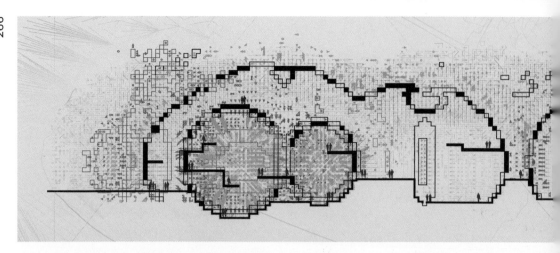

[704]

ADVANCED'

CECIL BALMOND & EZIO BLASETTI

STUDENT:
Chen Wenxin
Jiang Hewen

CRITIC:
Cecil Balmond
Ezio Blasetti

Our algorithm is mainly about the connection between points with data in grids. Basically, every point has a chance to connect another point with itself. Which point the original one connects depends on two parameters, remainder and distance.

Boundary, the core element of our concept represent the main goal we want to achieve in this proposal, creating a new lifestyle which could not only improve the quality of daily life but also the relationship between urban life and relaxing activities in nature. Besides, the form of our buildings on the boundary is defined by Mandelbrot set as well, but in three-dimensional version. It shares the attributes of two-dimensional pattern, infinite details.

What we are focusing now is to give more control to our Mandelbrot generating system, which have the potential of creating the geometry with the attribute that every single part of itself could exactly fits the specific requirement at that position in the design proposal.

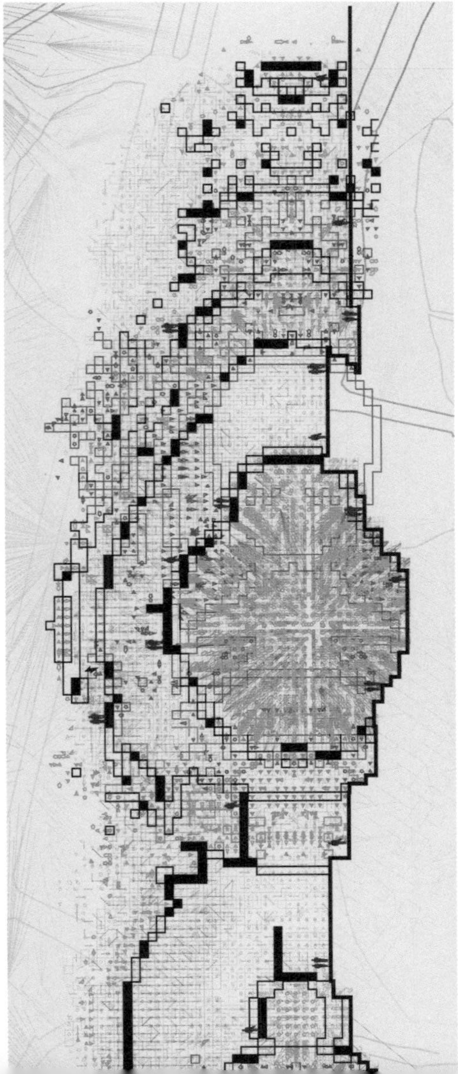

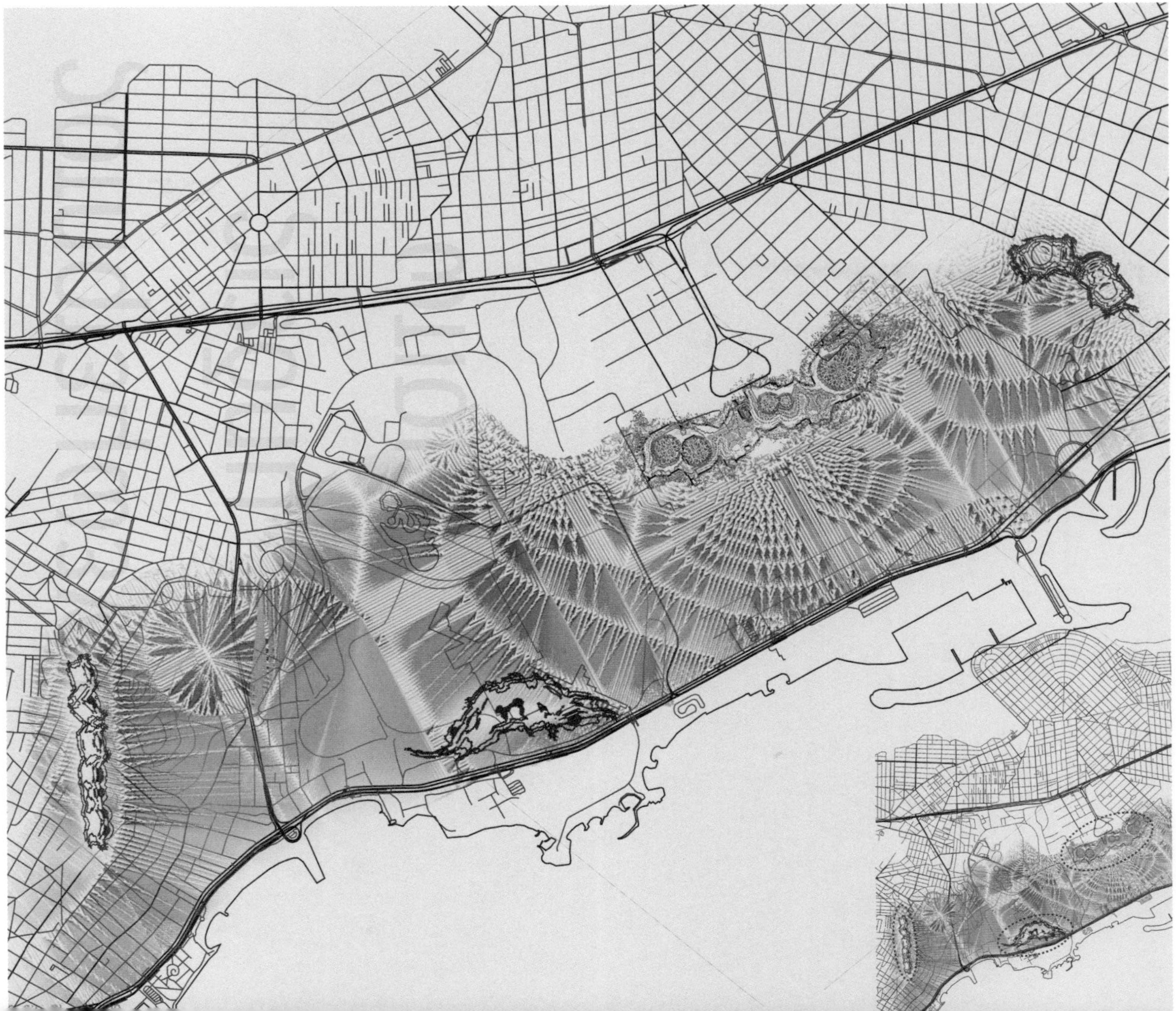

ADVANCED"
Independent Thesis

In the final semester of the Master of Architecture program, each year a small group of honors students elect to pursue the thesis as an opportunity to undertake critical and speculative exploration of their own making. Building an independent topic or set of questions, they work closely with an advisor and collegial group of students and faculty. By framing and developing a project and methodology through independent research, the thesis project initiates a set of issues and methods that students may continue to develop as they embark on their professional or academic careers. (They often do so, immediately.) But while the thesis project is oriented toward defining students' future, it also reflects on their past. By instigating their own project outside the realms of the more typical studio, students ultimately confront the scope of their education and choose to extend or alter directions in which they have been taught. The thesis at PennDesign is a self-reflective moment for both students, and the institution and its curriculum.

The thesis project at PennDesign is conceptualized as an open work, that is, its scope is limited only by the parameters of the questions posed. The question, the thesis topic, is necessarily always a disciplinary challenge, establishing a relationship to ideas formally or popularly identified as architectural, whether belonging to the realm of building or the multiple discourses embraced within the discipline. The thesis project is also essentially timely: questions are posed to address current issues and crises in which architecture is implicated, even while often drawing on historical matter. Through the year-long thesis process, these questions are concurrently researched, elaborated, edited, and finally manifested in a work of architectural dimension. A thesis project is a work of craft, building a set of ideas into a final statement and set of conclusions.

In 2016-17, the two thesis projects addressed the extremes of timely subject matter: one, the political and practical issues of the rehabilitation of the devastated Old City of Aleppo (as a dual degree thesis in Historic Preservation), and the other, a revisitation of Cedric Price's Fun Palace in an examination of the subjectivity latent in new forms of media and material.

Annette Fierro
Professor

STUDENT:
Emily Gruendel

CRITIC:
Eduardo Rega
Pamela Hawkes

ARCHITECTURE + HAVOC:
THE AGENCY OF HISTORIC SITES DURING CONFLICT

Havoc devastates the built environment. When the smoke clears, when a victor is named, when the floodwaters recede—these are the moments when havoc's vicious realities ascend to the public eye. For the fields of both architecture and preservation, such post-destruction environments can be catalysts for our work managing, manipulating, and reviving the built condition. Over the last few decades, however, technological advancements have abruptly transformed the way in which the world sees conflict. No longer must we wait for a peaceful lull to arise—havoc reveals itself immediately on our screens. Now, more than ever, it is critical for the architecture and preservation fields to extend their roles beyond pre-conflict preparations and post-conflict response. The built environment has just as much agency as warring parties do, and as such, it is essential for our fields to critically engage with the physical and humanistic realities of conflict zones.

This thesis proposes a new paradigm for the designer–that of an activist and enabler. By developing an arsenal of spatial tactics, the designer supports civilians of embattled places to sustain both life and culture within their built environment. With the Old City of Aleppo, a UNESCO World Heritage site and former battlefront of the Syrian War, as the area of study, this thesis undertakes a speculative reimaging of the historic fabric of the city as a malleable asset for survival. By means of an alternative narrative, Aleppans, through a series of enclaves and networks, transform their city into an archipelago of politically autonomous territories. While this thesis does not offer a solution for conflict nor its prevention, it does aim to mitigate the onslaught of urbicide by empowering people to preserve the tangible and intangible properties of their heritage. This alternative narrative is a means to reconsider design thinking as a tool for intervention and endurance vis-à-vis grassroots action.

706 [THESIS]

ADVANCED"

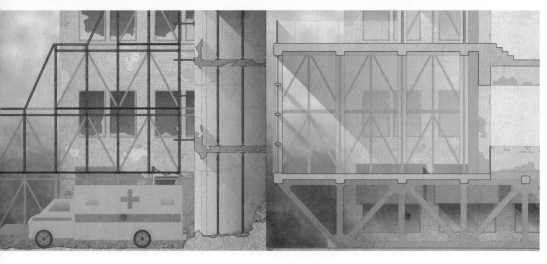

EDUARDO REGA & PAMELA HAWKES

STUDENT:
Michael Patrick O'neill

CRITIC:
Eduardo Rega
Pamela Hawkes

At the intersection of technology, identity and urbanity, this project imagines a new kind of public space for Union Square in which architecture is situated as a frame for the projection, reflection, documentation and broadcast of personal and collective identity. The project seeks to make visible the virtual layers grafted upon the built environment and to exploit the social and architectural possibilities of a multivalent urban experience in which virtual and physical infrastructures collapse into hybrid states. Both real-time and asynchronous social interactions are enabled through coordination between ubiquitous personal devices and larger infrastructural media systems embedded in the project. The project critically examines the contemporary relation between the city's occupants and the ways in which technology has augmented their relation to both their environment and to each other. Mirroring is a phenomenon orchestrated through both material and technological means, with media deployed as mechanism through with the self and the collective are "reflected", documented and broadcast. Reflection is thus presented both literally and figuratively, as both spectacle and interrogation. These infrastructures of projection become the expression of an Architecture that enables, critiques and provokes its occupants in their virtual behaviors, empowering and enticing each individual to explore the boundaries between the virtual and the real, and the threshold between themselves and their neighbors.

ADVANCED"

GALLERY

STUDENT:
Chang Yuan Max Hsu
Hadeel Ayed Mohammad

Reference. page 166

CRITIC:
Simon Kim

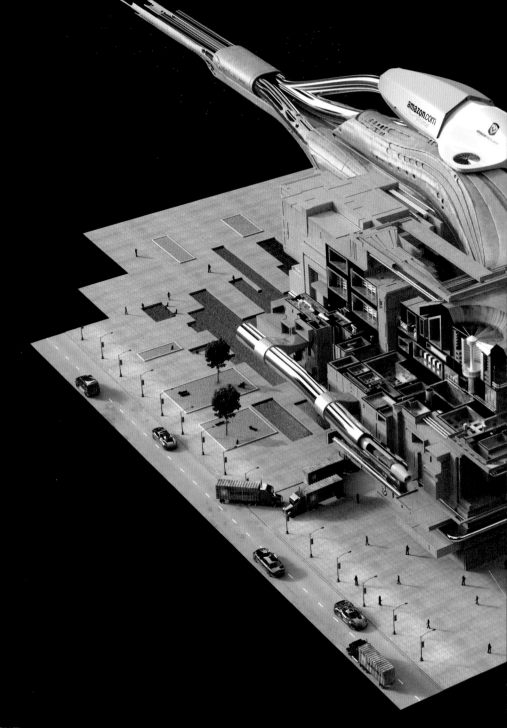

STUDENT:
Bosung Jeon
Wan Jung Lee

CRITIC:
Robert Stuart-Smith

Reference. page 252

STUDENT:
Insung Hwang, Wan Jung Lee

Reference. page 196

CRITIC:
Ferda Kolatan
Michael Zimmerman
Bumjin Park

STUDENT:
Jae Geun Ahn, Jiateng Wang

Reference. page 246

CRITIC:
Marion Weiss

ADVANCED"

STUDENT:
Mingyue Hu, Lu Liu, Katie McBride

Reference. page 190

CRITIC:
Thom Mayne
Ung-Joo Scott Lee

ADNC

VA ED"

ADVANCED"

ASSET ARCHITECTURE. MANHATTAN, NEW YORK CITY
Zombies and Ghosts: Pencil Towers in Mid-Town Manhattan

This studio will explore design techniques, the history of Manhattan Skyscrapers and combine it with an understanding of global capital markets to develop an pencil tower for Mid-Town Manhattan, New York City.

ASSET ARCHITECTURE

In times of immense growth in capital due to economies in China, India and the Middle East including the UAE and Qatar there is more capital than ever in the world today. The capital has more than doubled from 2001 to 2011 in the world from $37 trillion to $80 trillion. While monetary capital has always played a significant role in determining the built environment, recent shifts in the character of global finance have resulted in a new relationship between investment practices and buildings. Traditional assets of relatively stable locations as treasuries and municipal bonds are yielding very low returns. As the capital has grown investors have circumvented these stable assets for real estate which directly affects architecture and urbanism. Due to the amount of capital that has been channeled towards realest ate there is volatile fluctuation between growth and decay - the same as assets in the stock market. The functioning of architecture and urbanism assets has been throughout history but the degree to which space functions as an asset has increased radically. Architects and architecture have not responded to this issue in any way.

ZOMBIES

More specifically, the studio probes the notion that the increments of architecture (units, buildings, parcels of land, etc.) increasingly operate primarily as financial investment assets in contradistinction with the performance attributes typically associated with the art and science of building. New York City for example has a total of 845,000 houses and apartments and 102,000 units or 12 per cent or of its housing market vacant. This number is predicted to grow to 25% of the entire housing market if the growth of capital keeps increasing at the same rate by 2018. The people who own these condominiums are usually foreigners seeking a haven and are referred to as Skim Milk New Yorkers, only in New York 2% of their time. This number has grown rapidly and explains why so many windows dotting the imposing facade s of Fifth, Madison and Park Avenue apartment buildings are pitch dark every evening. These buildings are referred to as ZOMBIES.

GHOSTS

Speculative real estate bubbles increase in frequency and scale. Housing prices are going up and are becoming very speculative- they fluctuate up and down the same as the stock market. There is a much larger amplitude between boom and bust and frequency between these cycles. "Capital builds a physical landscape appropriate to its moment in time only to have to destroy it." The relations of cities globally are now interconnected, and prices in some cities, Beijing for example have risen 800 percent in over the past 8 years. Due to this reason the capital flows to every country in the world affecting property markets and prices throughout the world. In China there are entire cities that have been built without many people in them - GHOST cities.

Obviously Zombies and Ghosts are linked through the financial interconnectedness between them. As there is greater capital in the world, the construction industry thrives and generates more capital. As new capital is grown in the UAE for example it is invested in non-traditional instruments including real estate in New York City as interest rates in the bond markets

INSTRUCTORS:
Ali Rahim,
Ezio Blasetti,
Nathan Hume,
Robert Neumayr

TEACHING ASSISTANTS:
Maru Chung,
Kristy Kimball,
Lois Suh

STUDENT ASSISTANTS:
Ryosuke Imaeda,
Jayong Shim,
Yuchen Wen,
Yifeng Zhao

e at 1 percent. The companies or people investing in these properties live
sewhere in the world, and if these investments continue large parts of midtown
ll become a ghost town.

MANHATTAN'S RELATION TO CAPITAL

the history of the development of Manhattan with the growth of the city,
means of laying a grid over vast territory, architecture becomes the expres-
on of capital due to its increase of land value. The land value of Manhattan
as generated by modes of densification of building mass. Within the
eginning of "the liberal city" architecture becomes the outcome of vertical
pressions based on its relationship to its land. The hypothesis of the studio
sset Architecture" is to speculate on the idea that architecture incorpo-
ted elements o f the city in order to increase its value as a commodity.
as it been in the 19th century the incorporation of the land into the build-
g by the repetition of floors and in the beginning of the 20th century an
terest in aesthetic styles in order to express the building as a mode of
mmerce, then within the 30's the Skyscraper incorporated the whole city
ader one Roof. In order to search for Asset Architecture, it would mean
at we turn the building away from its means as a human inhabitation and
urely understand the architectural object by means of generating capital.
he thesis taken within the studio is that the Architecture of the New York
ity increased its value as a commodity by fusing urban elements into a new
rm of architectural interiority.

EIGHT (8) 1423-700 PENCIL TOWERS,
MID-TOWN, MANHATTAN. NEW YORK CITY. 10022

o better explain the relationship of Manhattan to capital we will have field
ips to New York City and will review the most important developments of
he skyscraper in the history of Manhattan. This in combination with the devel-
pment of techniques we will design an architecture that incorporates a
ritical position towards zombie architecture and ghost urbanism for seven
encil towers in mid-town Manhattan. The seven sites from West to East
re as follows: 225 West 57th Street, 220 Central Park South, 157 West 57th
treet, 111 W. 57th Street, 53 West 53rd Street, 36 Central Park South,
32 Park Avenue and 520 Park Avenue. The heights of the buildings will vary
om 1423 feet to 700 feet. What is common about these buildings is that
hey define the pencil tower typology with their floor plans to height ratio
eing elongated. Mid-town Manhattan is where foreigners own the most
roperty. Particularly we are (re) designing a tower typology that is now the
oster child for the creation of a zombie in Manhattan. Manhattan is uniquely
quipped to translate and speculate on Asset Architecture into critical archi-
ecture and urban proposals that do not have precedents and link global
apital to the financial capital of the world.

SITE VISITS TO NEW YORK CITY

Ve will tour New York five times during the semester to gain familiarity with
he issues that New York negotiates at an urban scale as well as tour its archi-
ectural development and ideas. These tours will be supplemented by talks by
eople involved in the development of the cit including financial experts. Currently
ve have confirmed Goldman Sachs, Arup and Zaha Hadid Architects.

STUDENT:
Ali Tatabataie Ghomi
Meari Kim
Yuchi Wang

CRITIC:
Ali Rahim
Ezio Blasetti
Nathan Hume
Robert Neumayr

BIO TOWER IN MANHATTAN — INVISIBLE TOWER

INDUSTRY:

The biotechnology industry hauled in $2.3 billion worth of venture capital investments during the second quarter of this year—a 32% increase over the prior quarter, according to the newest MoneyTree Report from PricewaterhouseCoopers (PwC) and the National Venture Capital Association (NVCA), with data from Thomson Reuters. The 126 deals struck during the period marked the biggest quarterly investment in biotech since the MoneyTree report first came out in 1995, and it brought the total for the first half to $3.8 billion. That puts the biotech industry well on track to soar past 2014's total of $6 billion of VC cash raised for the year

TOWER

Our tower is considered as the center of biological sciences ant technologies crossover. According to the accelerative development in bio-sciences and technologies and with consideration of its huge effect on our lives from every-day events such as nutrition or healthcare to military demands of having supper powerful and intelligent army, integration of this field with our life is not something far fetch. Even right now such big companies like, Johnson & Johnson, Pfizer, Bayer, Monsanto, etc. are dedicating a big portion of their investments on this topic. And some their results have been moved our living environment to another stage. Creation of Human proteins or some of the cancer drugs, or cell engineering in agriculture are some evidence of this. Even some artists have joined to this path to explore this new world. Bio Art is now an international movement with practitioners, scientists and artists in such regions as the U.S., Asia, Australia and Europe.

ASSET:

This Tower can perform the pivotal role in approaching the biotechnological dreams into the real world and magnitude the investments, sciences, technologies and techniques and be the symbol of this new era in the world. The Tower provides a range of laboratories, Huge number of gene banks, conference and gathering spaces, exhibitions and the customer services area. The investor can invest on a laboratory, or a bunch of laboratories, and can invest on a gene or a gene bank or many of them.

703 [MSD IN AAD]

ADVANCED"

ALI RAHIM

STUDENT:
Angeliki Tzifa
Ke Liu
Dongliang Li

CRITIC:
Ali Rahim
Ezio Blasetti
Nathan Hume
Robert Neumayr

VERTICAL ABYSS

The increasing desirability of calling New York home has caused a phenomenon that appears for the first time in decades: more people are moving to or staying in the city than leaving. The city's renaissance since the 1990s has drawn thousands of new residents; today's population of 8.5 million is the highest it has ever been and this number will continue to rise. However, the attractiveness of the city has led to a highly competitive housing market, with units fitting only for the uber-rich. At the same time, the available housing fails to offer a different atmosphere or "sense of place" that can lead to a different experience for its residents and differentiate the units in this increasingly saturated market.

The Vertical Abyss project, redefines the concept of housing, as an asset that can give its residents a different effect-atmosphere.

Taking into consideration the principles of micro-housing, the occupied space within the tower is maximized and optimized by stacking specific units. As for the units themselves, their height is maximized and the footprint is minimized. The extreme vertical space can command an increase to the asset value by up to 30%, in this competitive market. In addition to that the verticality that occurs can have a profound effect on one's subjective perception of their environment and their conscious feelings about those spaces. The emotional aspects of the environmental experience and the perception of space is changed, as the magnitude of the height can inspire awe and other feelings incidental to it.

Vertical voids are proposed as a transitional space between the apartments. These voids can function both as additional interior spaces that can be used by each apartment as well as a bigger vertical interior space that can be experienced as a promenade inside the building. In addition to that, the volume of these voids is calculated as an addition to the overall height of the tower. In this way, the height of the tower is maximized, but on the one hand, the tower can accommodate more units and at the same time it can be the tallest tower in Manhattan, functioning also as a landmark.

This tower consists of 136 units, each one approximately 300 square feet. The living spaces are distributed vertically in a zone that includes only the necessary equipment or furniture for each room. A moving platform can also dock to them, forming in that way a self-contained living space. For the residents to more profoundly experience these "sublime" spaces, each unit has its own private access to each floor, so in that way the residents can experience the verticality on their own. Another feature that is introduced is the balconies. These can be found on the façade as well as in the interior vertical voids. Lastly, the façade works as a massive structure that can hold the units, and encapsulate the necessary infrastructure and vertical movement for the whole tower.

At the end, these cathedral-feeling spaces can be considered as a personal skyscraper.

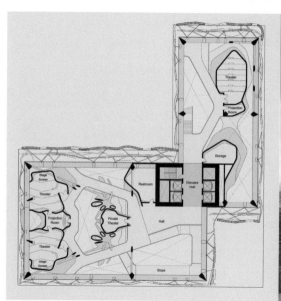

STUDENT:
Sookwan Ahn
Siyang Lv
Can Wang
Yuchen Zhao

CRITIC:
Ali Rahim
Ezio Blasetti
Nathan Hume
Robert Neumayr

ADVANCED"

The name of our project is Nested Morph, we try to maximize the value by making the best use of our tower, and our asset contains two parts.

The first one is about the facade, different pieces with specific forms can been seen as billboard for investment, and different pieces can been owned by different people, We sell the pieces on the facade .The facade is delicate and detailed with its different elegant curves, fine texture on the pieces and small detailed pieces. Besides, different layers could create different light and shadow atmosphere which is really interesting for people to experience. People are attracted by the facade, and buy the pieces on the facade as an investment, and they can go in the tower to enjoy the amazing atmosphere of light and shadow. People can also show their wealth by owning the pieces on the facade, surrounding buildings also can increase their value because of its existence . We also set five principles to price our pieces. First we analysis the surrounding's land value. It is a basic value of our building. Then, according to our facade, we made some principles. Firstly, Form. more detailed form, higher price. Secondly, Sight. The piece that people can see clearly have higher price. Thirdly, Size. Bigger size, higher prize. Fourthly, accessibility. The pieces that people can reach have higher prices. Finally, direction. Pieces that face to central park have higher price. People can own the piece that he or she likes.

The second one is about the interior spaces, the whole project does not only consider how to maximize architectures' value , but also consider how building evokes city. it is New York City Cultural Entertainment center. Theaters in NYC are of great importance in culture. Our site is near Midtown Manhattan District, almost everyone in New York would visit here and buy tickets to experience theater culture. It attracts thousands of people here. And because the immersive theatres have a sharp increase. Guests want higher participation level with actors. Smaller theater and cinema have more and more demands. Around site, there are lots of theatres which play larger performances that can not satisfy people's demand of immersive theatres. Therefore, our tower contains about 20 small immersive theaters inside to meet market requirement. Different curves and prolific space not only match theatre sound requirement but also brings people into a new world.

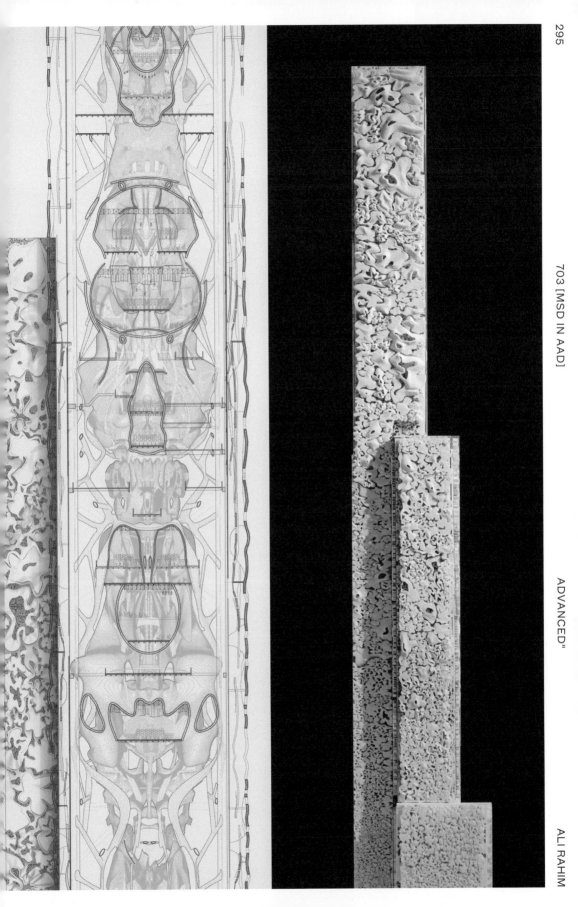

STUDENT:
Carrie Frattali
Bosung Jeon
Xiaoyu Zhao

CRITIC:
Ali Rahim
Ezio Blasetti
Nathan Hume
Robert Neumayr

VERTICAL MAUSOLEUM
AN ARCHITECTURE FOR THE DECEASED AND MOURNING

The Borough of Manhattan is "the economic engine of New York City" and is home to some of the world's most expensive real estate, yet lacks any industry aimed toward on of humanity's oldest and imminent rituals: Burial. By identifying a niche market and focusing on the optimization of the burial industry in Manhattan and Greater New York City, we are able to provide a new type of real estate. Our focus is to provide a convenient and quality space not only for the demand of burial in Manhattan, but also for non-denominational yet ceremonious private and public events.

With growing prices of burial space in Manhattan, the cost of burial on the island has skyrocketed and plots are far and few between. The vertical mausoleum lends itself to a variety of burial typologies at varying price points depending on views and relativity to ceremonial or public spaces. Trinity Cemetery & Mausoleum on Riverside Drive is the only cemetery still selling space for remains on the crowded island of Manhattan. Although, these plots are specifically priced highly and are most likely only revealed to a certain market of buyers. Compared to cemetery and mausoleum typologies around the United States, even the cemeteries within and surrounding greater New York City, are close to three or four times the price.

The Vertical mausoleum offers millions of residents and New York City fanatics an unprecedented opportunity to stay in the metropolis forever. With a height of 1400 ft, the mausoleum stands a beacon for the city's economic history and it's loyal residents. The deceased can eternally overlook Central Park and their family members will have a place of rest, contemplation, and procession in Manhattan.

Not only do the residents desire to be buried in their home city of Manhattan, but also non residents. Foreign business owners, wealthy travelers, and investors have expressed their loyalty and love of New York City as their home, even if untied to their original birth place or familial settlements. Influential people have historically invested in monumental structures as a remembrance of themselves for those to follow – and this is still happening! There is no doubt that an iconic and curious building such as a pencil tower mausoleum would generate curiosity from all levels of society. A ghostly tower would change the skyline of Manhattan in a glorious way, identifying with the city's profitable atmosphere and potentially becoming a monument to the influential people that have shaped the city itself.

The stratification of surface that doubles as the tower's superstructure and storage agent. Vertically and densely stacked niches are contained within the structural elements of the building and are designed to maximize availability and profit. The organization of the interior consists of a procession of programs in which are enclosed by the stacks of urns and caskets. The construction of the elevational elements is a series of louvers that change direction and depth, highlighting program changes on the interior as well as providing a variety of light quality throughout the tower. The interior is arranged as a series of processional spaces - from the crypt at the base, an underground burial chamber, to the cemetery at the top. As one goes through a process of mourning after a loved one's death, going in and out of moments of doubt and vision, the tower's undulating transformations of light lead the visitors through spaces of darkness and spaces of extreme brightness and vision. Although the tower has rotated this traditional ceremonial progression vertically, the process of healing and ritual have been elevated.

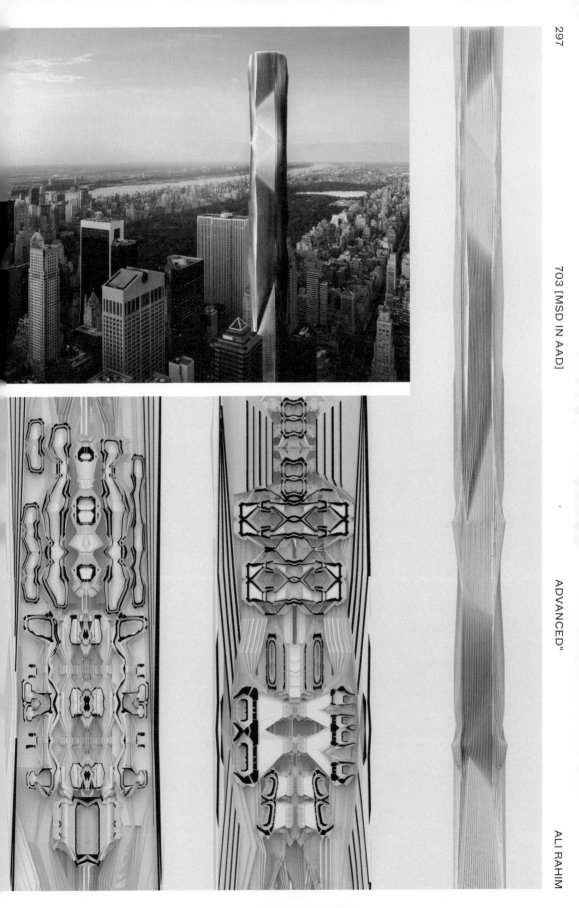

ADVANCED"

ALI RAHIM

ADVANCED"

ASSOC. PROFESSOR: **William W. Braham**
Received an MArch and a PhD from the University of Pennsylvania and a BSE from Princeton University
Organized the Architecture and Energy symposium and published the books Rethinking Technology: A Reader in
Architectural Theory (2006) and Modern Color/Modern Architecture: Amédée Ozenfant (2002)

LECTURER: **Mostapha Sadeghipour**
- Researcher at Environmental and Energy Design Departement at Building and Housing Research Center.
- Environmental Consultant at CARBON Ideas Studio
- Integration Applications Developer, Thornton Tomasetti, CORE Studio
- Master in Environmental Building Design University of Pennsylvania

BIOCLIMATIC AGENTS: 4 TEAMS, 4 CLIMATES

Contemporary buildings are inherently hybrid, combining the traditional, bioclimatic elements of buildings—walls, windows, doors—with increasingly intelligent technologies for delivering modern services. These systems of power and control have mostly been used to compensate for the inadequacies of building envelopes, but when they are successfully hybridized, innovative and powerful new forms of building emerge.

Within the broad category of Design with Climate, the work of the studio focused on the design of responsive or intelligent envelopes that selectively enhance the performance of the building-as-a-shelter. This was largely achieved through the careful selection of material properties and the thoughtful configuration of building form, as well as through the design of openings that can sense their environments and change their properties accordingly. Taken together, we can called them the building's bioclimatic agency: "the capacity, condition, or state of acting or of exerting power," whether that is the power of human or nonhuman action.

Climates (and weather) are inherently variable and difficult to predict, even more so with the uncertainties of global climate change, and bioclimatic agents mitigate those uncertainties by their design and by different modes of response and adaptation. From the opening and closing of venetian blinds to the tactics of machine learning routines coordinating multiple modes of environmental exchange, environmental buildings must adjust their capacities to enhance their performance as shelters.

Enhancing the bioclimatic agency of building enclosures remains the foundation of any approach to environmental modification, and also provides the elements of architectural expression. Responsive building elements bind human and nonhuman actors together in new configurations that have to be fit into social and cultural contexts, raising critical questions about the appropriate degrees of autonomy and human engagement for each process and device.

The project for the studio was The New Chautauqua Institute, an international research and development corporation, leading the transition to a prosperous, renewable economy. The Institute was inspired by the travelling Chautauquas of the late 19th and early 20th century, which Teddy Roosevelt called, "The most American thing about America". Institute buildings were designed for sites in four different climates: Cold, Temperate, Hot & Dry, and Hot & Humid.

The studio employed multiple forms of advanced performance simulation —comfort, energy, daylight, and air flow—primarily through the parametric interface of Ladybug and Honeybee, and explored the design methods with which they become effective.

William W. Braham

mi Trip - Brillhart House

ngapore Trip - 60 Cecil St

ngapore Trip - Waterloo St

Singapore Trip - Waterloo St

ADVANCED"

W. W. BRAHAM & M. SADEGHIPOUR

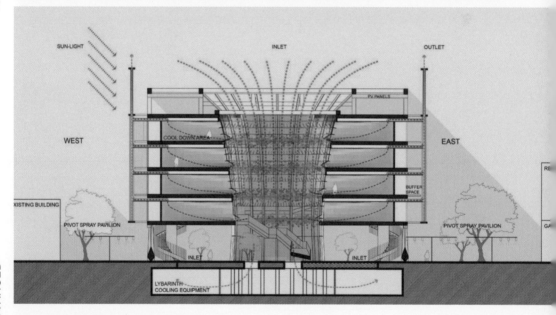

STUDENT:
Shengji Tan, Mitra Sajjadi

CRITIC:
William W. Braham
Mostapha Sadeghipou

Tempe is a desert climate, so the project was conceived around two internal atria that serve as chambers of evaporative cooling for the air is drawn through the buildings by solar chimneys around the perimeter. One atria is configured and scheduled for the residential portion of the building, while the other is focused on institutional activities.

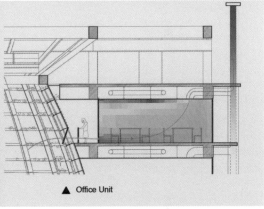

▲ Office Unit

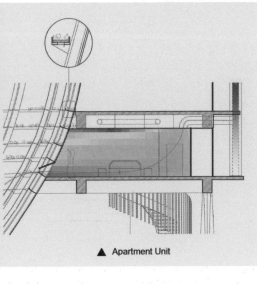

▲ Apartment Unit

STUDENT:

José Barría, Bhakti Kothari, Neeharika Siram

Singapore is a hot, humid climate, with almost no variation through the year, so the institute building was configured to enhance air movement through the building with a sequence of thermal chimneys, using internal waste heat to draw air though carefully configured openings. The envelope was designed to both shade the internal spaces and support plant materials, which keep the exterior surfaces cool.

CRITIC:

William W. Braham
Mostapha Sadeghipou

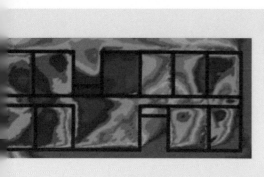
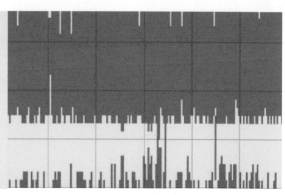

708 [MEBD]

ADVANCED"

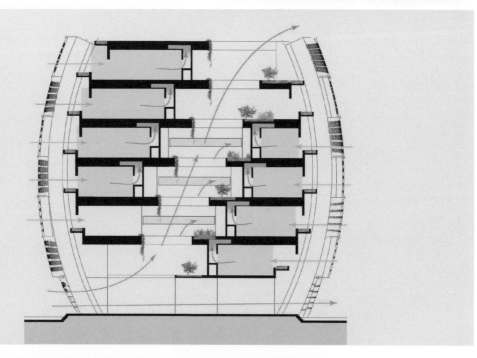

W. W. BRAHAM & M. SADEGHIPOUR

ADVANCED"

PROFESSOR: **Sarah Rottenberg**
- Directing Associate at Jump Associates, a growth strategy firm
- Received a Master of Science in Social Sciences from the University of Chicago (1997) and a Bachelor's in Foreign Service from Georgetown University (1995)
- Prior to her career in consulting, Sarah worked as an assistant to the Cultural Attaché at the Israeli Embassy in Washington, DC.

IPD 528/ARCH728, DESIGN OF CONTEMPORARY PRODUCTS: SMART OBJECTS

Smart objects are information-based products that are in ongoing dialogs with people, the cloud and each other. By crafting rich interactions, designers can create expressive behaviors for these objects based on sophisticated programmed responses. At the same time, sensor technologies have enabled us to introduce natural gestures as a means of interacting with a product. (Not only can we push, pull and twist data value, but we can wave at, caress, tilt and shake it as well.) With an explosion of new possibilities for object interaction and human control, it is the designer's role to envision new solutions that are both meaningful and responsible. Students will learn through a series of lectures and hands-on studio exercises, interaction systems, ergonomics, data networks and contexts of use. The course will culminate in a final project that considers all aspects of smart object design within the context of a larger theme.
Carla Diana

IPD 551, DESIGN PROCESSES

This studio is structured for IPD students as an intensive, interdisciplinary exploration of Design. The goal of the studio is to give students a firsthand experience of various processes involved in creating successful integrated product designs. Students will go through various stages of the design process including problem definition, concept development, ideation, prototyping, and idea refinement. The purpose of the IPD design studio is to offer options of ways to approach and resolve larger design objectives.. This year, students were asked to conceptualize, iterate, and build a toy for a child. They were first introduced to the child through a watching videos of their client telling stories about themselves, including explaining what he or she likes to snack on, or what superpower she or he would want. In the middle of the semester, students visited their client at home to get feedback on their prototypes. Finally, they refined the implementation of their ideas.
Sarah Rottenberg, Carla Diana

IPD 799, FINAL PROJECT

The last two semesters of the IPD studio sequence consist of the IPD Final Project. Students are given the opportunity to work on design problems that follow their passion or to work on a real world problem provided by our partners in academia, industry, or the non-profit world. The Final Project enables students to put the skills that they have developed in engineering, design arts and business into practice, following the process from initial opportunity identification into the development of a working product with a complementary business plan. Interdisciplinary group work is encouraged on final projects. Working in teams offers students the opportunity to collaborate across skill sets and learn from teammates from different disciplines. Final Projects provide students with ample opportunity to learn leadership and collaboration skills that are invaluable in today's workplace.
Sarah Rottenberg, Peter Bressler, JD Albert.

STUDENT:
Zac Bensing and Lila Cohn

CRITIC:
Carla Diana

COUNTABLE TRAY

Countable is a product that allows you to reinforce your commitment to causes you feel strongly about. Through an ecosystem that includes an online donation service, a key chain and a charging tray it provides both a virtual and physical presence of your selected causes. Glowing lights remind you when an event linked to your cause is taking place nearby, and then prompts a decision to grab your keys and go or stay home and donate instead.

Workout control module

Music control module

Stretchable tube

Bone conduction pad

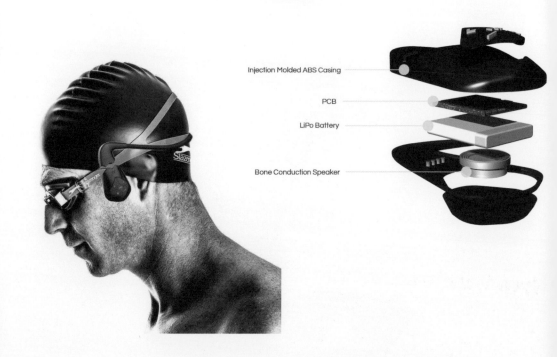

Injection Molded ABS Casing

PCB

LiPo Battery

Bone Conduction Speaker

STUDENT:
Xixi Jiang , James Lovey, Forrest Milburn and Han Xiao

CRITIC:
Sarah Rottenberg
Peter Bressler
JD Albert

Wavtrac is a wearable swimming coach and entertainment system designed to help amateurs get into swimming and stick with it. Worn on the head, Wavtrac can reliably detect swimmers progress and using bone conduction technology, will coach swimmers through their sets. It can also store music and playlists to keep swimmers entertained while in the water.

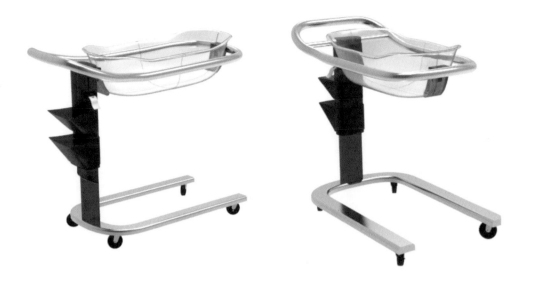

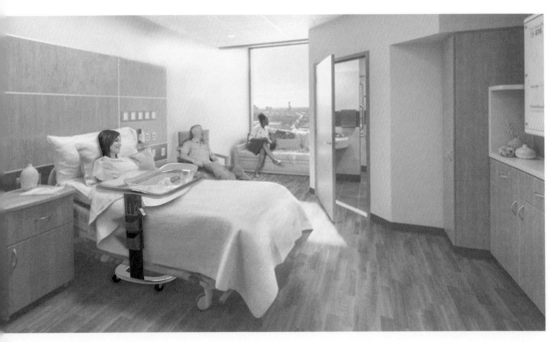

STUDENT:
Carissa Lim and Jessica Soe

As hospitals become more baby friendly and encourage new mothers to keep their babies in the room with them, an unfortunate side effect has occurred: babies falling out of their mother beds. When this team looked into why babies were falling they found that it is difficult form new moms to take their babies out of traditional cribs, and, more importantly, put them back in the cribs after breastfeeding. 2me is a newborn hospital bassinet that allows mothers to easily, safely, and painlessly transfer her baby to and from the crib because of its unique cantaliever design, adjustable height and tilting mechanism.

CRITIC:
Sarah Rottenberg
Peter Bressler
JD Albert

DOCTORAL DEGREE

For many years, scholarship in Penn's Ph.D. Program has operated under a double constraint: the development of knowledge that is both descriptive and productive. Although dedication to productive knowledge may not be common in other fields, it is entirely relevant to architecture. Marx's dream for philosophy—to change, not merely interpret the world—is nothing special in architecture; rather, it is a fairly obvious commonplace. Architecture is a form of engagement par excellence, aimless if not oriented toward given conditions, intent on their transformation. The particularity of architecture's productive sort of knowledge, that it gets its hands dirty in the actual transformation of the environment in which we live, has been and remains a central concern of Penn's architectural scholarship.

Dedication to both descriptive and productive knowledge may be apparent in the titles of some of the books published by Ph.D. graduates. Among the recent books are: Jin Baek, Nothingness: Tadao Ando's Christian Sacred Space; Raffaella Fabiani Giannetto, Medici Gardens: From Making to Design; Thomas Beck, La Villa; Nathaniel Coleman, Utopias and Architecture; George Dodds, Building Desire: On the Barcelona Pavilion; David Haney, When Modern Was Green: Life and Work of Leberecht Migge; Zhongjie Lin: Kenzo Tange and the Metabolist Movement in Japan; Alex Anderson, Modern Architecture and the Commonplace; Claudio Sgarbi, Vitruvio ferrarese De Architectura, la prima versione illustrate; William Braham, Modern Color/Modern Architecture; Judith Major, To Live in the New World: A.J. Downing and American Landscape Gardening; Harry Mallgrave, Gottfried Semper: Architect of the Nineteenth Century; Gevork Hartoonian, Ontology of Construction; and Cornelis van de Ven, Space in Architecture.

These books clarify developments in a number of periods and investigate a range of subjects related to architecture, landscape architecture, building technology, and urbanism. Concepts are examined— space, style, or surface color, for example— but also particular figures: Le Corbusier, A.J. Downing, Gottfried Semper, and Mies van der Rohe. This range indicates the real possibility of striking a balance between architecture's disciplinary identity, ultimately based in practice, and its engagements with several subjects and dimensions of scholarship in the university at large.

Yet more than balance is at issue here, for we have learned that neither scholarship nor practice in architecture can be realized fully without reference to the other, that neither drawing nor writing can realize its potential when pursued in isolation. In reciprocity, though, they can help us know the world by productively engaging in its transformation.

iel Genadt

Iwang Yi

STUDENT:
Daphna Half

SUPERVISOR:
David Leatherbarrow

FROM FRUGALITY TO EXUBERANCE,
ARCHITECTURE AND THE CITY IN ISRAEL 1923-1977

This dissertation argues for the emergence of a new materiality in Israeli architecture in the 1950s, 60s and 70s. It examines these decades in an extended historical time frame beginning with the British Mandate for Palestine. Materiality refers to local Israeli socioeconomic and geopolitical conditions. It also reflects the literal use, handling and finishing of materials in architecture. During this period first and second stages are described. The first was shaped by objective circumstances in which architecture operated in response to scarcity and demonstrated a realist attitude, one also embedded in the concept of asceticism. It was manifest in restrained formal gestures, abstention from material extravagance, the use of local materials, and an appeal to rational building procedures. The second stage emerging in the 60s had a different syntax. The analytical, skeletal frame constructions of the 50s turned synthetic, monolithic, and earth-bound. Compositions turned sculptural and exuberant. An appeal to the architect's expressive ingenuity became a recognized design objective. The issue of banality versus extraordinariness in design surfaced at this point.

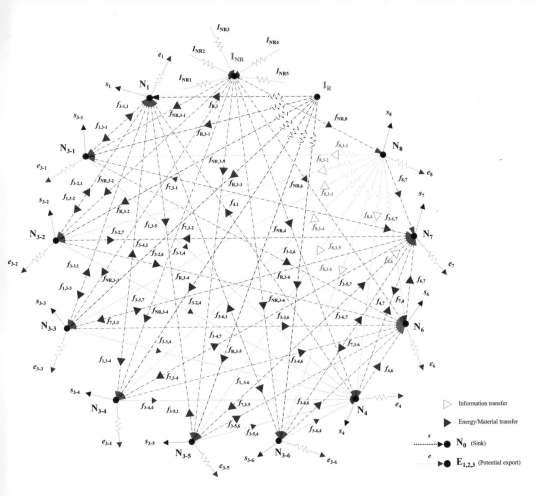

STUDENT:
wang Yi

SUPERVISOR:
William Braham

FORMATION IN ENVIRONMENTAL ARCHITECTURE:
COLOGICAL NETWORK ANALYSIS
ND NEW INDICES OF BUILDING PERFORMANCE

his dissertation suggests a new framework and indices of building performance
valuation based on an eco-systemic approach. The energy-efficient build-
g construction and operation are important to achieve sustainability.
evertheless, efficiency does not fully account for the building's complex
nvironmental phenomena in which nature, art, and human living are insepa-
bly involved. In particular, increasing efficiency cannot clearly associate
e robustness and stability of building's internal energetic organization
nd trade-offs between energy efficiency and material use) with building
rm and occupant behavior. Based on ecosystems theory, this study defines
uilding as a thermodynamic system that utilizes, transfers and self-orga-
izes the useful environmental resources energy, material and information
rough an emergy (spelled with an "m")-networking process. The defini-
ons and formulas of information measures and ecological indicators from
hannon's information theory, Ulanowicz's ascendency principle, and Odum's
aximum empower principle are discussed and adopted to develop a new
ethodology of integrating building information and emergy and a systemic
odel of building emergy flow. Findings demonstrate that buildings self-orga-
ize internally, like ecosystems, with inputs and outputs of the resources. This
ventually suggests that increasing complexity, total information, and power
e the final goal of building sustainability and environmental building design.

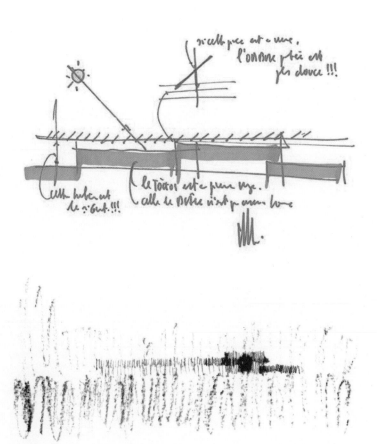

STUDENT:
Ariel Genadt

SUPERVISOR:
David Leatherbarrow

THE ARTICULATE ENVELOPES OF RENZO PIANO AND KENGO KUMA

The study defines building envelopes as articulate when they selectively conceal
and reveal their constitution, allowing the expression of something beyond
their construction. It demonstrates how such envelopes can help situate
buildings in place. The first part of the study defines a semantic framework
for articulation and then identifies five operations of articulation, demonstrating them in the work and words of architects Renzo Piano and Kengo
Kuma. The second part begins by surveying different meanings of place and
related terms, especially those that set the ground for transcending a
dichotomy between objective, subjective and collective understandings. It
then examines six case studies of buildings by Piano and Kuma, showing how
the combination of operations of articulation in the envelopes' design was
symbolic or evocative of people's relationship to place. By relying on both
sensory stimulation and comprehension over time, articulate envelopes can
provide a focus for social life and make their agency manifest.

TUDENT:
artin Hershenzon

SUPERVISOR:
David Leatherbarrow

OWSHEDS AND ADMINISTRATIVE HEADQUARTERS:
UNCTION AND FRUGALITY IN THE INSTITUTIONS OF
RAELI AGRICULTURAL COOPERATION, 1940-1976

he dissertation examines notions of functional economy in the designs for
gricultural cooperatives in Israel between 1940 and 1976. Connecting the
istory of modernist architecture with the sociology of knowledge and insti-
utions, I analyse the roles played by key cooperative institutions and their
rchitects in disseminating inter-war methodologies of utilitarian design
nd translating them for use in Israeli public welfare regime. In particular, I
ocus on the works of architects Arieh Sharon and Emmanuel Yalan, for urban
nd rural workplaces, which I argue disclose the representational charge,
nd civic servitude of Israeli functional design, as an approach to the man-
gement and aesthetics of resource scarcity. Studying built works, com-
mission history and architects' writings on design economy across locales
nd tasks, contributes to a new understanding of the processes through
vhich Israeli modernism was vernacularized. It also joins ongoing discussions
mong historians of architecture and development planning on the nature
f endogenous institutions of territorial development in mid-20th century
rchitecture culture.

EVENTS

SPRING

JANUARY 2017

Overcast and ArchDaily.com! Winning Pavillion Chosen!

A juried pavilion competition of studen
group concepts was a program highlight
with the 2015 winning design Over Cast
named one of the world's top student
design-build projects by ArchDaily.com:

"OverCast is the winning proposal in the
collaboration between PennDesign at the
University of Pennsylvania and the Russel
Wright Design Center. To celebrate the
legacy of the late industrial designer,
first year M.Arch students were instructe
to analyze Wright's mid-century modern
pieces. The winning design takes inspira
tion from the curvature of Wright's 1937
American modern collection. Copying the
fabrication process of the mid-century
pieces, similarly curved thermoformed
polystyrene pieces were used as "bricks" t
constitute a larger sculptural pavilion."

FEBRUARY 2017

Climatic Effects: Architecture, Media, and the Great Acceleration

Daniel Barber receives URF grant!

Climatic Effects: Architecture, Media,
and the Great Acceleration
From the 1930s to the 1960s - just as
HVAC was also developing - numerous architects explored design methods to manage seasonal climatic changes or

provide comfortable living and working
nditions in extreme locales. Climatic
fects explores the images produced by
ese design strategies. Meteorologists,
onomists, biologists, physiologists,
surance agents, and many others devel-
ed climate knowledge in relation to
chitectural images. What emerges is a
dia-architecture history of the Great
celeration.

ngratulations on your University Re-
arch Foundation grant, Daniel!

Archinect's Top Ten "Student Work" featuring: Mingyue Hu, Lu Liu, Katie McBride

Congratulations to our 700 students Mingyue Hu, Lu Liu, and Katie McBride for
being featured on Archinect's "Top Ten
Images' post!
This project was part of their Fall semester studio with Thom Mayne and Scott
Lee.

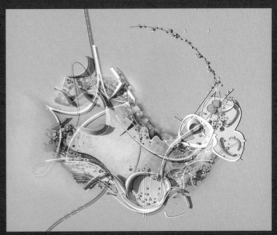

MARCH 2017

700 Travel Studio Update

Some of our third year masters students
were in Los Angeles a few weeks ago with
Florencia Pita! Here are a few photos
from their travel!

700 Travel Studio Update

Some of our third year masters students
are in Mexico this week with Alberto Ka-
ach and Juan Rincon! Here are a few photos from their travel.

INCS Zero Factory, Nagano, Japan

Museum of Modern Art, New York, NY, USA

JANUARY 18TH, 2017
FROM PENN TO PENN

Eugene Kohn, Chairman & Founder, Kohn Pedersen Fox

The World Bank Headquarters, Washington D.C., USA

APRIL 14TH, 2017
[RE]FORM: THE FRAMEWORK, FALLOUT & FUTURE OF WOMEN IN DESIGN

While recent studies have found that women comprise nearly half of architecture graduate programs in the United States, only 22% of licensed architects in the field are women and only 17% partners/principals in architecture firms. This is worrisome.

MISSION

PennDesign Women in Architecture hopes to examine this historically male dominated profession while providing networking and mentorship opportunities to all its member We want to not only understand what drives women out of the profession, but to offer guidance and support to our peers practicing in the field. PennDesign Women is excit to host our first ever symposium on Women in Architecture in Spring of 2017, in addi tion to several other networking and social events slated throughout the school yea Our goal is to mobilize a community of designers and thinkers alike, with the purpos of increasing the incidence and visibility of women in architecture. Our hope is to bring awareness to the gender disparity that exists in the profession and empower eacl other by fostering growth, promoting the success of women architects, and above all, cultivating the next generation of leaders in the industry.

STUDENT ORGANIZERS:

Ramona Adlakha
(MArch'18),
Communications Chair,

Kirin Kennedy
(MArch'18),
Programming Chair,

Ramune Bartuskaite
(MArch'18), Outreach Chair,

Mary Swysgood
(MArch'18), Media Chair,

Rose Deng
(MArch'18),
Fundraising Chair,

SPRING EVENTS

Panel 1 - THE FRAMEWORK
Joan Ockman (Moderator)
Lori Brown
Ila Berman

Vanessa Keith
Mary McLeod

Panel 2 - THE FALLOUT
Daniela Fabricius (Moderator)
Danielle DiLeo Kim
Annelise Pitts

Despina Stratigakos
Marilyn Jordan Taylor

Panel 3 - THE FUTURE
Franca Trubiano (Moderator)
Shirley Blumberg
Margaret Cavenagh

Nicole Dosso
Winka Dubbeldam

[R E]

F
O
R
M

THE FRAMEWORK, FALLOUT & FUTURE OF WOMEN IN DESIGN

SYMPOSIUM
FRIDAY, APRIL 14 2017
LOWER GALLERY, MEYERSON HALL
9AM-6PM

ILA BERMAN University of Virginia

SHIRLEY BLUMBERG KPMB Architects

LORI BROWN Syracuse University, ArchiteXX

MARGARET CAVENAGH Studio Gang

NICOLE DOSSO SOM

WINKA DUBBELDAM Archi-Tectonics, University of Pennsylvania

DANIELA FABRICIUS University of Pennsylvania

VANESSA KEITH StudioTEKA

DANIELLE DI LEO KIM Leong Partners, Platt Byard Dovell White

MARY MCLEOD Columbia University

JOAN OCKMAN University of Pennsylvania

ANNELISE PITTS AIA Equity by Design

DESPINA STRATIGAKOS University of Buffalo

MARILYN JORDAN TAYLOR SOM, University of Pennsylvania

FRANCA TRUBIANO University of Pennsylvania

KEYNOTE ADDRESS BY

MARION WEISS University of Pennsylvania, Weiss/Manfredi

Presented By WOMEN IN ARCHITECTURE
A Student Initiative

PennDesign

THE FIRST-YEAR 501 STUDENTS PRESENT THEIR LIBRARY DESIGNS AT THE COMMUNITY EVENT IN PARKSIDE, PHILADELPHIA // MAY 1, 2017

ARCHITECTURE STUDIO IN PARKSIDE ASKS WHAT A LIBRARY COULD BE

As Philadelphia has begun the long process of reinvesting in parks, recreation centers and libraries in neighborhoods across the city, students in a spring graduate architecture studio are being asked to imagine a major new public amenity for Parkside, the West Philadelphia community that was built up around the Centennial Exhibition in 1876.

Fair Grounds, as the studio is called, includes 63 students split into five sections, and is led by Annette Fierro, Associate Professor of Architecture, Associate Chair of the Department of Architecture. The object of the studio is to design a community library that goes beyond traditional thinking about public archives. Included in the syllabus is a program outlining the physical needs and limitations of the space, including a lobby and cafeteria, reading rooms, administrative offices, storage, and circulation, along with flexible internal space and a large public landscape that are meant to be designed with feedback from community members.

But, according to Fierro, the real challenge of the project is to develop ways of thinking about architecture as a holistic venture undertaken in full partnership with a community. To that end, students are working with members of Centennial Parkside Community Development Corporation, a year-and-a-half-old neighborhood group, to talk through what community members would want and need from such a site.

The studio was designed to fit into the larger agenda of the 2016 Venice Biennale of Architecture, Reporting From The Front. In his introduction to the Biennale, curator Alejandro Aravena said, "On the one hand, we would like to widen the range of issues to which architecture is expected to respond, adding explicitly to the cultural and artistic dimensions that already belong to our scope, those that are on the social, political, economical and environmental end of the spectrum. On the other hand, we would like to highlight the fact that architecture is called to respond to more than one dimension at a time, integrating a variety of fields instead of choosing one or another."

The syllabus for the Fair Grounds studio was also crafted in response to the controversy surrounding the U.S. Biennale pavilion in Detroit. Some of the designers of that exercise were criticized for overemphasizing the architect's imagination as a tool to address social problems, at the expense of true involvement with "actually existing communities."

One of the exciting things about the studio, Fierro said, is that it coincides with Philadelphia's Rebuild initiative, a $500-million effort to refurbish parks, recreation centers, and libraries throughout the city. A collaboration with the Centennial Parkside Community Development Corporation and PennPraxis, the engagement and consulting arm of PennDesign, the studio includes not only a traditional review, but also an open exhibit and roundtable discussion with students, community members, and city officials. The event, open to the public, will be held at the Christ Community Baptist Church, 1224-30 North 41st Street, Philadelphia

ARCHITECTURE STUDENTS PRESENT BIG IDEAS FOR LIBRARY DESIGN IN PARKSIDE

At a packed community meeting in early May, a group of graduate architecture students met to share a semester's worth of research around libraries and design with residents of East Parkside, the West Philadelphia neighborhood that backs up against Fairmount Park.

The context for the studio, called Fair Grounds, includes the 2016 Biennale of Architecture and a $500-million effort by Philadelphia to rebuild parks, recreation centers, and libraries around the city. Hosted by Centennial Parkside Community Development Corporation, the meeting convened more than community residents. City Councilwoman Jannie Blackwell was there, as were State Representative Vanessa Brownand Anne Fadullon (MCP'88), the City's director of planning and development.

The students' goal was to think through the various roles that a library could play in East Parkside—a neighborhood that currently has no library. And they thought big.

"The library of Philadelphia should not be static, but an urban network of mobile architectures, portable facilities and distributed learning laboratories that re-envision underutilized city resources, infrastructures and buildings," said Prince Langely (MArch'17), a student in one of five sections of the studio.

JANUARY 30TH, 2017
ENVIRONMENTAL HISTORIES OF ARCHITECTURE

A Panel Discussion on the new book by Daniel A. Barber, 'A House in the Sun:
Modern Architecture and Solar Energy in the Cold War' (Oxford University Press, 2016)

Daniel A. Barber's book, A House in the Sun: Modern Architecture and Solar Energy in
the Cold War, was published in November of 2016. In January, he gathered together a
number of environmental and architectural historians to discuss the ways the methods
and narratives of these histories interconnect. The panel discussion, held as part of
the public lecture series, touched on historical narratives of urban farming, of zygotes
as models for architectural form, and on why cattle won't cross graded pathways.
Particpants included Mark Wasiuta, Daniela Fabricius, Sophie Hochhausl, and Etienne
Benson; Penn/Mellon fellow Anna Vallye moderated.

Panelists include:
Daniel A. Barber, PennDesign
Etienne Benson, University of Pennsylvania
Daniela Fabricius, PennDesign/Pratt
Sophie Hochhausl, Boston University
Mark Wasiuta, Columbia GSAPP
Moderated by:
Anna Vallye, Penn/Mellon Fellow

Degrees of Design

Student Work From Local Architecture + Design Schools

The University of Pennsylvania is excited to showcase our student's talents in partnership with the AIA Philadelphia. The opening reception will take place on Thursday April 6th. The exhibition runs from March 23rd to April 27th.

For more information visit the Philadelphia CFA website: http://www.philadelphiacfa.org/events/degrees-design

APRIL 2017

PennDesign Students Shortlisted in LIXIL Competition

A team of graduate students in the Department of Architecture led by faculty members Jonathan A. Scelsa and Ariel Genadt was shortlisted for LIXIL's 7th International Student Architectural Competition for the design and construction of a sustainable "Spa in Nature" in Hokkaido, Japan. The team's entry, The Veiled Garden, was selected as one of three finalists from 13 Invited universities around the world. The team will present their design to a jury led by Kengo Kuma in Tokyo on April 19 alongside teams from Vienna Technical University and Kyushu University.

According to the competition brief: "The public baths of ancient Rome, the Great Bath in Pakistan's Mohenjo-daro, Germany's Baden Baden, England's city of Bath, Finnish saunas or Japanese onsen (hot spring) or steam baths going back to a time long before the Middle Ages - there are a variety of bathing customs found throughout the world. Even in earlier times, baths were not merely intended to remove soil and stains. They were also places of social interaction, public areas as relaxing as a living room. In the rich natural setting of Taiki-cho Hokkaido, what would a relaxing bath spot be like? One should do more than simply soak. Imagine places to stretch or enjoy massage, stroll through the lush natural setting, dally away a day, or other kinds of activities. Under a roof or not? Do men and women share spaces? Aren't there new and untried ways of thinking about a bathing spot and its pleasures?"

The team's advisors are Richard Farley (structure) and Evan Oskierko-Jeznacki (thermodynamics).

What's Going On...

In College Hall

The Philomathean Society has curated an exhibit about the Philadelphia School architectural movement of 1960-2000. What Was the Philadelphia School? An Architectural Exhibit:

How Philadelphia Architects Formed a Movement Unified by Ideas, Reinvented Modernism, and Influenced the Entire World.

If you look carefully, you will notice that the buildings of the last 60 years that you see in Philly look quite unlike those elsewhere. They are tense: they don't smooth over the multiple and often conflicting aesthetic desires and functional needs that accompany the build-g process. They draw on history, rather than a glass-and-steel-and-concrete aesthetic of the future — which is to say that we lack the purist sculptures of Europe and Boston and Chicago. Our post-war buildings don't usually shout for attention: they reflect a sense of architecture as more or less modest — befitting function rather than showing it off, fitting a place rather than reinventing it. It is these buildings, and the group of formally unaffiliated architects who produced them, that we call the Philadelphia School.

The exhibit will be one of the first attempts to interpret the school as a bona fide movement reflecting a distinctive culture and set of ideas, rather than just a collection of architects united by affiliation with the university and physical proximity.

among those great architectural leaders previously honored with the George M. White Award."

MAY 2017

Students Honored by Dorot, eVolo, Gensler, and ALSA-NY

Joshua Harrington Davidson (GCP'17) won the Dorot Fellowship for Jewish Leadership in the 21st Century. Each year, 12 Fellows are chosen by the Dorot Foundation to live in Israel, where they gain skills to observe where change is needed, assess and interpret the actions needed to bring about change, and then become active players in the social change process.

Hao Fu (GAR'17), Yunlong Zhang (GAR'17) and Ge Yang (GAR'17) received an Honorable Mention in the 2017 eVolo Skyscraper Competition for their submission "Flexible Materials Skyscraper" that "hopes to explore a new architectural model to meet people's pursuit of architectural form while reducing the tedious construction process." The competition recognizes ideas that redefine skyscraper design through novel technologies, materials, programs, and spatial organizations.

Farre Nixon, a student in the Department of Architecture, is the Second Prize Winner of the Gensler Selects 2017 Diversity Scholarship. Nixon's submission proposed a live-work mixed-use building in Red Hook, Brooklyn that marries exceptional aesthetic considerations with creative functionality. The Gensler Diversity Scholarship is a juried program that recognizes emerging talent among African-

WHAT WAS THE PHILADELPHIA SCHOOL? AN ARCHITECTURE EXHIBIT

AF honors Marilyn Jordan Taylor

On Thursday, April 13, 2017, at the American Architectural Foundation's 28th Annual Accent on Architecture Gala, Marilyn Jordan Taylor, FAIA, Professor of Architecture and Urban Design, Former Dean, University of Pennsylvania School of Design, was honored with the George M. White Award for Lifetime Achievement.

AAF President and CEO Ron Bogle said of this announcement, "Marilyn Taylor is among the world's most respected architects and is recognized globally as a thought leader in urban design. Her humor, warmth, and passion also contributes to her down-to-earth demeanor. Marilyn exudes deep enthusiasm and compassion in her dedication to enhancing the vitality of urban communities through design. AAF is very proud to include Marilyn Taylor

American students enrolled in architecture programs.

Rivka Weinstock, a student in the Department of Landscape Architecture, has been awarded the ASLA-NY Designing in the Public Realm Scholarship. The Scholarship is intended to support future leaders who will strive to make living in urban environments healthier and more enjoyable. Weinstock's work is community-centered, prioritizing flexible and equitable spaces within contemporary urban landscapes.

MASS Design Group Wins Cooper Hewitt Design Award

Cooper Hewitt announced its annual National Design Awards with recognition ranging from lifetime achievement to fashion design. The Architecture Design Award was given to MASS Design Group for their work on the UK Holocaust Memorial, a hospital in Rwanda, and a primary school in the Congo. The Boston-based firm is a collaborative of 75 employees working in more than a dozen countries. MASS's practice focuses on architecture's relationship to health and behavior, and on designing systems necessary for well-being. Among the alumni employed at MASS Design Group are Kordae Henry and Sierra Bainbridge.

Seminar Will Challeng Students to Rethink Connections Between Wellness, Healthcare and Design

To design its new patient Pavilion on th former site of the now-deconstructed Pen Tower, Penn Medicine has enlisted the design expertise of world-renowned archi tecture firm Foster + Partners. But the final product, a 13-story structure with 700 new beds and 50 operating and procedure rooms, will be the work of multiple inputs, including some conceptual design proposals from PennDesign graduate archi tecture students.

The project, expected to be completed in 2020, is being developed through a process known as Integrated Product Delivery, or IPD, in which all parties, from architect to developer to construction contractor, act as stakeholders, collabo rating and sharing risks.

Mikael Avery, Lecturer in the Department of Architecture and founder of the desig studio and fabrication lab Draft Works, and Joyce Lee, president of IndigoJLD Green Health, will co-teach a seminar in the Fall 2017 semester, challenging students to rethink the impact design can have on healthcare. In particular, said Avery, students will focus on designing some of the internal and adjacent public spaces, like visitor lobbies, waiting rooms, and, potentially, spaces where healthcare professionals themselves can decompress. The students will keep the "triple aim" of healthcare in mind in their approach to the design: improved health outcomes, lower costs, and an overall better healthcare experience.

"People want to be more connected," he said "How does a hospital respond to that?"

The seminar came to be when Lee and Avery each separately pitched classes dealing with the intersection of healthcare, wellness, and architecture to Professor and Chair of Architecture Winka Dubbeldam, who paired up the instructors following a tip from Sarah Rottenberg, director of Penn's Integrated Product Design program.

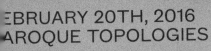

EBRUARY 20TH, 2016
AROQUE TOPOLOGIES

drew Saunders Architect, principal
ofessor, PennDesign Dept. of Architecture

Summer Program

SUMMER PROGRAM

COLOMBIA

The Summer Study Abroad Program in Colombia is a four year project. It researches and tests archi-tectural design in its role to provoke change within the Forms of Informal urban development in three cities in Colombia: Bogota, Medellin and Cartagena. An important part of the program involves visits to neighborhoods, buildings, events, architecture offices, interviews to politicians, urban and community activists and architects. Last year, the first installment of the program, was invested in understanding and unpacking the overall forms of informal dynamics in the three cities in a broad level. A week-long workshop allow for meeting and collaborating with local students.

REECE

The Summer Study Abroad Program in Greece organizes a series of visits to both archeological sites as well as modern and contemporary architectural sites. PennDesign students exchange and collaborate with a selected group of Greek architecture students during a week-long design workshop. There is a series of lectures from professionals and academics, which frame the proceedings of the workshop. The final presentation takes the form of a symposium and an installation in Athens.

PARIS

This five-week long program is a long-established academic program based in Paris, where students live near the Latin Quarter, go to lectures and visit sites all around the French capital. The program combines evening talks about Parisian architecture and urbanism from the city's most prominent architects, engineers and scholars, with accompanied morning tours to buildings, parks and professional offices. Recent programs have addressed issues of technology found within architecture, urbanism and landscape in a particularly Parisian frame of reference.

COSE

Course Descriptions

DESCRIPTIONS

COURSES

A = Spring Summer
B = Summer Semester
C = Fall Semester

Arch 511
History and Theory I
Joan Ockman – 2016C

The century between the Crystal Palace and Lever House witnessed the emergence of a dramatically new building culture with far-reaching consequences. In this overview of international architecture from the second half of the nineteenth century through the first half of the twentieth, we will situate the icons and isms, the pioneers and hero figures within a broad technological, economic, sociopolitical, and cultural context. The thirteen lectures will move both chronologically and thematically, tracing architecture's changing modes of production and reception; its pivotal debates, institutions, and tendencies; and its expanding geography, highlighting the ways the culture of architecture responded to and mediated the unprecedented experiences of modernity. We will also reflect on modernism's legacy today. The objective of the course is not just to acquaint students with seminal buildings and their architects but also to foster a strong understanding of history and of architecture's place in a modernizing world. Readings drawn from primary and secondary literature as well as a recently published text that is among the first to place modern architecture into a global perspective will supplement the lectures and provide a rich introduction to the historiography of the hundred-year period.

ARCH 512
History and Theory II
Daniel Barber – 2017A

This course examines the history of modern architecture since World War II, with an emphasis on relationships between architectural practices and increasing knowledge of the environment. Buildings, projects, and texts are situated within the historical constellations of ideas, values, and technologies that inform them through a series of close readings. Rather than presenting a parade of movements or individuals, the class introduces topics as overlaying strata, with each new issue adding greater complexity even as previous layers retain their significance.

Arch 521 – Visual Studies I
Nathan Hume – 2016C

Visual Studies-I is the engagement of graphic and visual information found in the world and in media, and its ability to contain – and more importantly, to convey – meaningful information. Intelligence in visual information is deployed to transfer cultural values, to educate and influence, and to create new relationships not easily expressed through mathematics, linguistics, and applied science.

One of the challenges in the course is the re-invention of a means of assessment, the development of notations and techniques that will document the forces and the production of difference in the spatial manifestations of the generative systems. Tactility, material, scale, profile, shape, color, Architecture works primarily in the assertion of these modes, and the meaningful production and control of these modes of communication are imperative for all designers.

Arch 522 – Visual Studies II
Nate Hume – 2017A

Visual Studies-II extends the use of the computer as a tool for architectural representation and fabrication by engaging in digital three-dimensional modeling. Modeling is approached first of all as a set of techniques for exploring and determining design intent and direction. Attention is given to precision and detailed modeling, paralleled by the development of the critical understanding for the constructive translation between physical and digital working environments.

This course analyzes the intensive and extensive properties at the scale of the city through a series of mapping exercises. Computational strategies of transformation are deployed to create explicit formations, by utilizing the analytic methods as generative procedures. The resultant systems become the basis for experimentation with computer aided manufacturing tools of the school. In parallel to the development of modeling skills, exercises in visualization emphasize both the analytic and affective possibilities of computer generated imagery.

ARCH 531 – Construction
Franca Trubiano – 2016C

Lecture and digital modeling course exploring the basic principles of architectural technology and building construction. The course is focused on building materials, methods of on-site and off-site construction, architectural assemblies and the performance of materials. Topics discussed include load bearing masonry structures for small to medium size buildings, heavy and light wood frame construction, glazing, roofing, sustainable construction practices, emerging engineered materials, and integrated building practices. The course also introduces students to Building Information Modeling (BIM) in a series of 5 workshops that result in construction documents for a residential masonry load bearing/wood frame building.

ARCH 532 – Construction
Phillip Ryan – 2017A

A continuation of Construction I, focusing on light and heavy steel frame construction, concrete construction, light and heavyweight cladding systems and systems building.

ARCH 535 - Structures I
Richard Farley – 2016C

Theory applied toward structural form. The study of static and hyperstatic systems and design of their elements. Flexural theory, elastic and plastic. Design for combined stresses; prestressing. The study of graphic statics and the design of trusses. The course comprises both lectures and a weekly laboratory in which various structural elements, systems, materials and technical principles are explored.

ARCH 536 – Structures II
Richard Farley – 2017A

A continuation of the equilibrium analysis of structures covered in Structures I. A review of one-dimensional structural elements; a study of arches, slabs and plates, curved surface structures, lateral and dynamic loads; survey of current and future structural technology. The course comprises both lectures and a weekly laboratory in which various structural elements, systems, materials and technical principles are explored.

ARCH 611 – History and Theory III
Daniela Fabricius – 2016C

This is the third and final required course in the history and theory of architecture. It is a lecture course that examines selected topics, figures, projects, and theories from the history of architecture and related design fields during the 20th century. The course also draws on related and parallel historical material from other disciplines and arts, placing architecture into a broader socio-cultural-political-technological context.

ARCH 621
Visual Studies III
Nate Hume – 2016C

The final of the Visual Studies half-credit courses. Drawings are explored as visual repositories of data from which information can be gleaned,

netries tested, designs refined and trans-
ed. Salient strengths of various digital media
rams are identified and developed through
gnments that address the specific intentions
challenges of the design studio project.

ARCH 631
Tech Case Studies I
Lindsay Falck – 2016C

udy of the active integration of various
ding systems in exemplary architectural
ects. To deepen students' understanding of
process of building, the course compares the
ess of design and construction in buildings
imilar type. The course brings forward the
ure of the relationship between architectural
gn and engineering systems, and highlights
crucial communication skills required by
h the architect and the engineer.

ARCH 632 – Tech Designated
Elective: Daylighting
Jessica Zofchak – 2016C, 2017A

s course aims to introduce fundamental
lighting concepts and tools to analyze day-
ting design. A wide range of topics includes
planning, building envelope and shading
imization, passive solar design, daylight
ivery methods, daylight analysis structure
l results interpretation, and a brief daylight-
and lighting design integration. Each session
composed of a lecture and a workshop. The
ture part will cover the fundamental knowl-
ge and case studies that focus on effective
ylighting design. The workshop will cover key
ylight analysis tools currently used in the
ustry, and students will have opportunities
explore them to work on assignments and
e final project. In addition, in order to orient
students to understand actual light levels,
udents will keep a daylighting journal with
ght meter to discuss interesting daylight
counters via photos and measurements.

ARCH 632
Deployable Structures
Mohamad Al Khayer – 2017A

he objective of this course is the introduction
the history, theories and application of the
pidly growing field of deployable structures
d folded plates (complex geometric structural
nfigurations that are used as temporary
d rapid assembly configurations) through
nds-on experiments conducted in a workshop
vironment. The course's objective is to
troduce various concepts and techniques to
e design, modeling, simulation and the physical
uilding and execution of deployable structures.
xperiments will be conducted using the hand
uring the construction and observation of
hysical models), and computer Modeling of de-
oyable structures using computer simulation
oftware (Solid Works). The course is divided
to two parts: in the first part, students work
dividually on weekly assignments building de-
oyable structures related to the topic taught
at week; in the second half of the semester,
tudents work as one team in the fabrication
hop, designing and constructing a full-scale
eployable structure (working prototype). Stud-
s include geometric studies of Platonic and
rchimedean solids, space filling geometries,
pology and morphological transformations,
tudies of different mechanical joints, and com-
uter simulation.

ARCH 632 – Geometric
Structural Design
Masoud Akbarzadeh – 2017A

eometric structural design I provides a
omprehensive introduction to novel geometric
methods of structural design based on 2D and

3D graphical statics (Rankine, 1864; Maxwell,
1870; Wolfe, 1921; Akbarzadeh, 2016). The main
emphasis of the course will be on developing
a general understanding of the relationship
between structural forms in equilibrium and
the geometric representation of their internal
and external forces. This relationship will be
used as the main apparatus in designing pro-
vocative structural forms using only geometric
techniques rather than complicated algebraic/
numerical methods. Moreover, special consideration will be given to materialization of the
structural geometry and the proper fabrication
techniques to construct the complex geometry
of the structure.

ARCH 632 – Principles
of Digital Fabrication
Mike Avery – 2017A

Through the nearly seamless ability to output
digital designs to physical objects, digital fabrication has transformed the way designers work.
Over the past several years the techniques of
sectioning, tessellating, folding, contouring, and
forming have received a great deal of attention
and have become standard methods of practice
in the field. Drawing from the tradition of the
architectural installation as a test bed for new
technologies, this course will review the established modes of digital making while focusing
primarily on the exploration of 3D printing and
its place within this continuum. It is our belief
that the 3D printed component has the ability to
offer a unique perspective on digital fabrication,
one that sidesteps the subtractive and material
intensive 'traditional' digital techniques, and can
bring with it novel ways of looking at assemblies
and structure at the level of the detail.

ARCH 632 – Material
and Structural Intelligence
Mark Nicol – 2016C

The semester long project will involve a gradual
development of architectural ideas that are inti-
mately informed by and centered on knowledge
of Structure and Materiality. Employing both
physical and digital simulations, the students
will synthesize knowledge acquired in previous
courses in structures, materials, and construction methods to develop architectural solutions
within a carefully selected set of determinants.
Work will begin with individual research and experimentation into formal systems using a given
set of material and structural constraints. It will
grow into a collaborative small group effort with
a focus on the rationalization, resolution and
execution of the design for a small scale architectural intervention. The students will learn to
develop solutions by starting with a wide variety
of ideas which are then funneled through critical
assessment, elimination, and enriched through
the constant inquiries into efficiency and elegance. The process would thus take them from
concept design to design development, culminat-
ing in the development of detailed drawings and
building systems for a well resolved design.

ARCH 638
Building Acoustics
Joe Solway – 2017A

This six-week course covers the fundamentals
of architectural acoustics. The lectures cover
the following topics: overview of acoustics in the
built environment, the role of the acoustic consultant and the interaction with the architect,
fundamentals of sound - sound measurement
and representation, sound generation and
propagation, sound absorption and reflection and sound isolation and transmission,
acoustic materials, case studies of acoustics
in building projects, the history and future of
performance space design. The course includes
measurements and testing in Irvine Hall and two
assignments, one practical (Boom Box) and one

theoretical (Sound Space).

ARCH 638
Architectural Workflows
Richard Garber – 2017A

This seminar in design and technology would focus on the concept of the architectural workflow
as it pertains to both contemporary operations
in design practice as well as novel project delivery methods. It follows a recent interest of mine
explored in a writing project titled Workflows:
Expanding the Territory of Architecture in the
Design and Delivery of Buildings (Wiley 2017). In
current business practice, a workflow is defined
as a 'progression of steps (tasks, events, interactions) that comprise a work process, involve
two or more persons, and create or add value to
the organization's activities'. However, workflows
date back to the industrial processes developed
in the 18th century.

ARCH 638
Mechanisms for Design
Aaron Pavkov – 2017A

Mechanisms enable everything from scissor lifts
and corkscrews to elevators and accelerator
pedals. To design a properly working mechanism
requires knowledge of how to achieve the
desired motion and a source of power to make it
happen. We will examine a variety of mechanisms
to understand how they work and how to apply
those concepts to solve mechanical problems at
a human scale and beyond.

ARCH 638
Building Envelopes
Charles Berman – 2017A

This class will provide an overview of enclosure
design with a focus on materials, methods,
and detailing strategies that contribute to
a high-performance building envelope. An
overview of design criteria, structural design of
framing members and cladding materials with
consideration of governing codes and standards
will be given. Performance standards and rating
systems such as LEED, Passive House, and Net
Zero will be compared in the context of envelope
design. How the design of the envelope inter-
sects with the design and development of other
building systems (including mechanical system,
lighting, finishes, and structural systems) for
a total building performance will be discussed.
Case studies of new construction as well as
retrofits of various building types will provide a
basis for analyzing the development of the cur-
tain wall through all phases, including schematic
design, design development and construction
detailing, the bid process, mock-up testing, field
installation, and on-site field testing. Research
developments such as adaptive facades and
energy-generating facades will be examined.

ARCH 638 – Water
Shaping Architecture
Jonathan Weiss, Stuart Mardeusz – 2017A

While efforts in sustainable design have focused
on energy use, carbon footprint, light and
materials impacts on human occupants, it could
be argued that water is the ultimate test of
sustainability. Without water, there is no life.
Water impacts, influences and shapes architecture in many different aspects. As our planet is
ever more challenged to provide for increasing
populations with finite resources, our approach
to water will need to evolve to meet our new and
future realities. This course is an investigation
of the ways that architecture is informed by the
water resources and availability of each specific
project region. We will cover a range of subjects
including; the physics of water, the systems to
gather, distribute, supply and treat potable
water, grey water, waste water, including the

correlation to energy and recycling that are integrated into the architecture of buildings. How do our choices as architects impact access to water, and how are those issues predetermined on a building, local, regional and continental scale? How can our projects react resiliently to changing climate and changing reality? If Sustainability is about providing for our needs while allowing for future generations to do the same, how does our outlook on water shape our decision making process?

ARCH 671
Professional Practice I
Philip Ryan – 2016C

Arch 671 is the first of a three course sequence that discusses the issues and processes involved in running a professional architectural practice and designing buildings in the contemporary construction environment. Arch 671 will begin by briefly outlining the overall course sequence in order to locate the first section in the context of the next two courses, Arch 672 and Arch 772. From there the course will describe the methods involved in getting, designing, and constructing a building project. The lectures will draw connections between the student's studio design knowledge to date and the instructor's experience in practice including local building examples and guest lectures by relevant professionals. The second half of the semester will build on the understanding of the project execution process to then shape how an office is formed and managed. This foundation will set up the segue to Arch 672 which will delve into more detailed analysis of legal, financial, and risk/quality management practices.

ARCH 672
Professional Practice II
Charles Capaldi – 2017A

A continuation of ARCH 671. Further study of the organizational structures of architectural practices today, especially those beyond the architect's office. The course is designed as a series of lectures, workshops and discussions that allows students and future practitioners the opportunity to consider and develop the analytical skills required to create buildings in the world of practice.

ARCH 711 – Topics in
Arch Theory I: Doodle Cities
Paul Preissner – 2016C

This looks at themes for urban areas from existential (albeit derided) city circumstances, as well as accidents, mistakes, art, sociology, etc. etc. including the subjects: plain cities, messy grids, sister cities, corporate fantasies, suburbanized urban experiments like cul-de-sacs and dead ends, and small, weird buildings. Additionally, the course will explore themes and actions like doodles and scribbles, glitch art, un-organization and carelessness, etc. Each of these will be looked into as both visual and organizational
phenomena that allow for cities to introduce new freedoms, and provide opportunities for subversion of dominant ideologies.

ARCH 711 – Topics in Arch
Theory I: Urban
Imaginaries, From
Thomas More
to Rem Koolhaas
Joseph Watson – 2016C

The city in its various forms has provided a consistent source of inspiration for visionary thinkers throughout history and across cultures: in works of fiction it is the centerpiece of a transformed society; in works of modern architecture it is the starting point from which transformation will spread. This course explores how architects, novelists, filmmakers, theorists, and other intellectuals have used the city as a medium through which to imagine alternative spatial, social, and political worlds.

One goal of the course is to develop an understanding of works of architectural and literary speculation as historically produced objects of collective hopes, desires, memories, and anxieties, as much as the unique visions of individual authors. Another goal is to consider through discussions and drawings how the history of these ideas continue to bear on the globalized context of contemporary design discourse. Themes to be explored include the relationship between ideal visions and material realities; the intertwining of memory and anticipation; the roles of technology, forms of production, and habitation; gender and race relations; the relationship between architectural form and social change; and the globalization of the economy and society.

ARCH 711 – Topics in Arch
Theory I: The Agency
of Autonomy, Tools For An
Architecture of Translation
Eduardo Rega – 2016C

Architecture cannot be reduced to an introverted disciplinary discourse, nor can it be understood solely through its actions and relations with other entities outside of itself. The debate developed in the last 40 years between architecture's project for autonomy vs architecture as an instrument for social and political change, serves as a premise for this seminar, which analyzes and seeks to instrumentalize both theoretical positions. Adopting Graham Harman's terms, the seminar positions itself in a theoretical territory that neither undermines architecture through an essentialist discourse (Autonomy) nor overmines it through a purely relational one (Agency), but rather does both at once. The readings, presentations, debates and projects will capitalize on the differences and transferences in order to develop research and design tools that enable the translation between architecture as an autonomous discipline and its potential to provoke change in the social and political milieus of which it is a part.

ARCH 711 – Topics in
Arch Theory: Architecture
of Patterns
David Salomon – 2016C

From the structure of the universe to the print on your grandmother's couch, patterns describe a vast array of conceptual and physical phenomena. For architecture, something that so easily traffics between scientific rigor and personal taste demands attention, which partly explains their revival. While traditionally marginalized as frivolous decoration or overly deterministic principles, recent advances in digital and materials technology have helped produce a new generation of patterns with protean vitality and multifarious intelligence. These current versions are imbued with properties of elasticity, aperiodicity, opulence, variegation, and idiosyncrasy – qualities that enable them to simultaneously engage numerous operative and material domains. Their newly developed capacity to link seemingly disparate intellectual and cultural categories – such as organization and sensation, graphics and behavior, and process and content – provides an opportunity for a more precise and expansive role for patterns in architecture.

ARCH 711 – Topics in Arch
Theory I: Culture, Climate
and Techniques of Modern
Arch in Japan
Ariel Genadt – 2016C

This seminar surveys modern architecture in Japan since its so called "opening" to the West and its rapid process of industrialization in the second half of the nineteenth century. It looks built case studies in particular through cultural, aesthetic, climatic, technical and material perspectives. Each session discusses a group of architects whose work exemplifies salient topics and turning points in the history of the practice in Japan. The seminar seeks to develop a critical understanding of the diversity of interpretations of modern architecture in Japan in relation to its particular climatic, historic and cultural setting. By studying graphic, textual and audio-visual accounts of key buildings and architects techniques and ideas, it will establish a vocabulary to discuss contemporary works in relation to their context and antecedents.

ARCH 711 – Topics in Arch
Theory: Architecture's
Cultural Performance:
The Façade
David Leatherbarrow – 2016C

This course will ask about the interrelationships between topics of design that seem to be categorically distinct: the project's functionality and its style, its provision of settings that allow the enactment of practical purposes and its contribution to the image and appearance of our landscapes and cities. Our concentration will be at once historical and thematic. We will study and reconsider buildings from the twentieth century and we will ask questions that resonate through the past several decades into the present, questions about the building (its materials, construction, and figuration) as well as the process of design (description, projection, and discovery). Throughout the course we will return to the building's most visible and articulate surface, the façade. Added to the typical concerns with production and representation will be a topic of design and experience that is often overlooked: performance. A simple analogy should show the environmental import of this topic: what adaptation is to the organism performance is to the work of architecture. The attributes of the façade: its materials, fixed and moving parts, dimensions, and spaces give it capacities to act in response to its encompassing milieu. Seen as a whole, the course will argue a simple thesis: the way the building's looks is largely determined by what the building does – how its acts, adapts and performs, in the city, the country, and the environments that bind these places together.

ARCH 712 – Building
Envelopes: Articulation
and Performance
Ariel Genadt – 2017A

In the 20th century, building envelopes have become the prime architectural subject of experimentations and investments, as well as physical failures and theoretical conflicts. This seminar examines the meaning of performance of 20th-century envelopes by unfolding their functions and behaviors in salient case studies, in practice and in theory. While the term performance is often used to denote quantifiable parameters, such as exchanges of energy, airs and waters, this seminar seeks to recouple these with other, simultaneous actions performed by the envelope and by the building it encloses. Albeit numbers cannot describe those performances, their consideration is key to the interpretation of quantifiable ones. Ultimately, the articulation of the polyvalence of envelopes becomes measure of their architectural pertinence. h class meeting includes a lecture, students' e studies presentation and documentary film enings. Lecture topics address construction niques, environmental conditioning, percep- nd representation, while each lecture tes one kind of performance to specific build- where it was articulated most poignantly.

ARCH 712 – The Idea of an Avant Garde in Architecture
Joan Ockman

e seminar will undertake a close reading ne of Tafuri's richest and most complexly ceived books, The Sphere and the Labyrinth: nt-Gardes and Architecture from Piranesi to 1970s. Initially published in Italian in 1980 and nslated into English in 1987, the book came a pivotal moment in Tafuri's career and rep- ents the first sustained effort to define and toricize the idea of an avant-garde specifically he domain of architecture. Tafuri's narrative ters on the architecture of the first three ades of the twentieth century and traverses erimental theater designs, the American scraper and its impact on the European hitectural imagination, and urban planning Germany and the Soviet Union. Surpris- ly, however, Tafuri begins his account in the hteenth-century with the "wicked" architec- al inventions of Piranesi, and he concludes h a critique of neo-avant-garde practices in e 1960s and '70s.

ARCH 712 – Detroiters Spatial Imagination. Architectural Translations of Grassroots Networks
Eduardo Rega Calvo

lected as the subject matter of two recent ar- itecture and design events (the US Pavilion at e Venice Biennale and the Ideas City Festival, th in 2016), Detroit has been a key protagonist American architecture discourse attracting ternational attention both within and beyond e discipline. The Detroiters' Spatial Imagina- n seminar aims to reflect and develop col- ctive architecture research on contemporary etroiters' visionary architectural and urban ttivist practices vis a vis the city's economic ansformation, from top-down disinvestment bottom-up self-provisioning and organizing. hrough reading discussions and mobilizing vari- us tools of inquiry on the city, the seminar will vestigate those involved in the long-term and mall scale processes that have been revitalizing ommunities in Detroit using architecture, art nd design to facilitate people's participation the production of their built environment. he work produced in the seminar will be part f upcoming international exhibition and will be eatured in UrbanNext, an online platform by ctar Publishers.

ARCH 712 – Topics in Architecture II: Baroque Parameters
Andrew Saunders – 2017A

Deep plasticity and dynamism of form, space nd light are explicit signatures of the Baroque Architecture; less obvious are the disciplined mathematical principles that generate these ffects. Through art historians, Rudolf Witt- ower, Heinrich Wölfflin, and John Rupert Mar- in in addition to philosopher Gottfried Leibniz via Gilles Deleuze), Robin Evans and the history f mathematics by Morris Kline the course will examine how geometry and mathematics were ntegral to 17th-century science, philoso- hy, art, architecture and religion. The new evelation of a heliocentric universe, nautical

navigation in the Age of Expansion, and the use of gunpowder spawned new operative geometry of elliptical paths, conic sections and differ- ential equations. The geometric and political consequences of these advances are what link Baroque architects Francesco Borromini and Guarino Guarini to other great thinkers of the period including Descartes, Galileo, Kepler, De- sargues and Newton. Through the exploitation of trigonometric parameters of the arc and the chord, Baroque architects produced astonishing effects, performance and continuity. Generative analysis by parametric reconstruction and new speculative modeling will reexamine the base principles behind 17th century topology and reveal renewed relevance of the Baroque to the contemporary paradigm.

ARCH 714 – Museum as Site: Critique, Intervention and Production
Andrea Hornick – 2017A

In this course, we will take the museum as a site for critique, invention, and production. As architecture, cultural institution, and site of performance, the museum offers many relevant opportunities. Students will visit, analyze, and discuss a number of local exhibitions and produce their own intervention in individual or group projects. Exhibition design, design of museum, the process of curating, producing artworks ranging from paintings to installation and performance, as well as attention to con- servation, installation, museum education, and the logistics and economics of exhibitions will be discussed on site and in seminar. These topics and others will be open for students to engage as part of their own creative work produced for the class and an online exhibition.

ARCH 717 – Philosophy of Urban History
Manuel DeLanda – 2016C, 2017A

Cities are among the most complex entities that arise out of human activity. For some of these cities (Versailles, Washington DC) the process through which they emerge is not hard to grasp because it is planned up to the last detail by a human bureaucracy. Other cities, such as Venice and its labyrinthian system of streets, emerged spontaneously without any central agency mak- ing the relevant decisions. But even those cities in which urban structure was the result of a de- liberate act of planning, house many processes which, like Venice, represent the spontaneous emergence of order out of chaos. This seminar will examine a variety of these processes, from markets to symbiotic nets of small produc- ers, from epidemics of urban diseases to the creation of new languages and urban dialects. It will also explore the interaction between these self-organized phenomena and centrally controlled processes which are the result of human planning.

ARCH 721 – Designing Smart Objects
Carla Diana – 2016C

Today's children enjoy a wide array of play experiences, with stories, learning, characters and games that exist as physical stand-alone objects or toys enhanced with electronics or software. In this course, students will explore the domain of play and learning in order to develop original proposals for new product ex- periences that are at once tangible, immersive and dynamic. They will conduct research into education and psychology while also gaining hands-on exposure to new product manifesta- tions in a variety of forms, both physical and digital. Students will be challenged to work in teams to explore concepts, share research and build prototypes of their experiences in the form of static objects that may have accom- panying electronic devices or software. Final design proposals will consider future distribu- tion models for product experiences such as 3D printing, virtual reality and software-hardware integration. Instruction will be part seminar and part workshop, providing research guid- ance and encouraging connections will subject matter experts throughout the Penn campus.

ARCH 724 – Technology in Design: Immersive Kinematics/Physical Computing: Body As Site
Simon Kim – 2016C

The aim of this course is to understand the new medium of architecture within the format of a research seminar. The subject matter of new media is to be examined and placed in a disciplinary trajectory of building designed and construction technology that adapts to material and digital discoveries. We will also build proto- type with the new media, and establish a disci- plinary knowledge for ourselves. The seminar is interested in testing the architecture-machine relationship, moving away from architecture that looks like machines into architecture that behaves like machines: An intelligence (based on the conceptual premise of a project and in the design of a system), as part of a process (related to the generative real of architecture) and as the object itself and its embedded intelligence.

ARCH 724 – Technology in Design: A Periodic: The Mathematics of Tiling in Architectural Design
Josh Freese – 2017A

Repetition and difference in geometric tiling patterns produce visual complexity, intricacy, economy and articulation. From textiles and ceramics to architectural design, the tradition of tiling has culled from mathematical systems that inscribe two- and three-dimensional geo- metric conditions, ultimately yielding cultural effects that are unique to their time. By exam- ining this tradition across time and disciplines, this course will explore a range of mathematical systems, tools and media as well as how they advance contemporary architectural topics such as parametrics, optimization, fabrication, and implementation.

Through lectures, readings and work- shops, the course will lead students to develop contemporary and future-oriented methods that establish new parameters for tiling sys- tems. Students will identify particular tiling fam- ilies from guest lectures, historical precedents and readings, and will establish conditions for scripting new assemblies for generating three- dimensional patterns and assemblies.

Fabrication methods will consider an economy-of-means, using minimal variation in base models and molds to achieve maximum differentiation in the aggregation of tiles into 3-dimensional volumetric models. It is through this negotiation between fixed rules and variable freedoms that tiling systems have historically asserted their cultural value – and this will be the ultimate goal of the course.

ARCH 724 - Technology in Design: Data and Adaptation
Mark Nicol – 2017A

Data + Adaptation seeks to study emerging tools and workflows that allow designers to tap into abundant sources of data and leverage them towards crafting adaptable, dynamic constructions. Low cost sensors and simple scripting techniques will be used to collect and visualize complex data fields. Design tools within the Rhino/Grasshopper or Maya ecosystem with the capability of designing and simulating dynamic responses to shifting data fields will be explored. In the end, students will take a position with regards to how data might affect design and furthermore how architectural constructions might be designed with the capacity to dynamically adapt to those fluctuating data.

ARCH 726 – Contemporary Furniture Design
Katrin Mueller-Russo – 2017A

This course provides a platform, in the form of furniture, to execute and deploy architectural and engineering principles at full scale. It will be conducted as a seminar and workshop and will introduce students to a variety of design methodologies that are unique to product design. The course will engage in many of the considerations that are affiliated with mass production; quality control, efficient use of material, durability, and human factors. Students will conduct research into industrial design processes, both traditional and contemporary, and will adapt these processes into techniques to design a prototype for limited production. Instruction will include; model making, the full scale production of a prototype, its detailing; design for mass production and the possibility of mass customization; design for assembly, furniture case studies; design techniques, software integration, optimization studies; Computer Aided Manufacturing (CAM) and a site visit to a furniture manufacturer.

ARCH 728 – Design of Contemporary Products
Carla Diana – 2017A

Smart objects are information-based products that are in ongoing dialogs with people, the cloud and each other. By crafting rich interactions, designers can create expressive behaviors for these objects based on sophisticated programmed responses. At the same time, sensor technologies have enabled us to introduce natural gestures as a means of interacting with

a product. (Not only can we push, pull and twist a data value, but we can wave at, caress, tilt and shake it as well.) With an explosion of new possibilities for object interaction and human control, it is the designer's role to envision new solutions that are both meaningful and responsible. This course will explore product design solutions through a combination of physical and digital design methods. Beginning with an examination of case studies, students will gain a sense of the breadth of product and interaction design practice as it applies to smart objects. Through a series of lectures and hands-on studio exercises, students will explore all aspects of smart object design including expressive behaviors (light, sound and movement), interaction systems, ergonomics, data networks and contexts of use. The course will culminate in a final project that considers all aspects of smart object design within the context of a larger theme.

ARCH 730 – Techniques, Morphology, and Detailing of Philadelphia City Pavilion
Mohamad Al Khayer – 2017A

The course will focus on the design morphology, detailing, and the construction of "Moment Lab Pavilion" which is to be constructed in Spring 2015 at the southeast corner of Philadelphia City Hall. The course will develop through hands-on workshops and will focus on acquiring knowledge through making (Techne), understanding the morphological transformation of a given geometric packing, and building using readily available materials. The process consists of building and testing physical models that simulates the actual pavilion. In addition to digital simulation sessions to realize the desired design, which answers to the program developed by the Moment Lab curators*

The second half of the semester will focus on using lightweight materials to fabricate the pavilion's actual components, including structural members, panels, and joints, which are required for pavilion's superstructure and envelop.

ARCH 731 – Experiments in Structure
Mohamad Al Khayer – 2016C

This course studies the relationships between geometric space and those structural systems that amplify tension. Experiments using the hand (touch and force) in coordination with the eye (sight and geometry) will be done during the construction and observation of physical models. Verbal, mathematical and computer models are secondary to the reality of the physical model. However these models will be used to give dimension and document the experiments. Team reports will serve as interim and final examinations.

In typology, masonry structures in compression (e.g., vault and dome) correlate with "Classical" space, and steel or reinforced concrete structures in flexure (e.g., frame, slab and column) with "Modernist" space. We seek the spatial correlates to tensile systems of both textiles (woven or braided fabrics where both warp and weft are tensile), and baskets (where the warp is tensile and the weft is compressive). In addition to the experiments, we will examine Le Ricolais' structural models held by the Architectural Archives.

ARCH 732 - Advanced Enclosures
Charles Berman – 2017A

This seminar seeks to expand a framework of understanding enclosures as integral to the student's architectural intentions. We will seek to move beneath the numerical facts of

what is accepted as facade design (criteria, codes, loads, forces and consumptions) to seek a deeper understanding of the generat process underlying these physical criteria in order to evade the mere acceptance of thes external facts to the intentions of the Architect. The nature of enclosures will be explor through methods of analysis and interrogati of materials, their attributes, their forms of assembly and the natures of their manufactu The vehicle for this interrogation will be the act of drawing and assembling. Case studies of new materials, new processes and new applications will provide the basis gaining thi dissecting /cutting ability (Frascari). In addit the students will engage in generative detaili exercises, at simultaneous scales, to analyze and apply these decontextualized results to reveal their nature manifest in facade.

ARCH 734 – Ecological Architecture Contemporary Practices
Todd Woodward – 2017A

Building is an inherently exploitive act – we ta resources from the earth and produce waste and pollution when we construct and operate buildings. As global citizens, we have an ethical responsibility to minimize these negative impacts. As creative professionals, we have a unique ability to go farther than simply being "less bad," We can learn to imagine designs that heal the damage and regenerate our environment. This course explores the evolvin approaches to ecological design – from neo-indigenous to eco-tech to LEED to biomimicry living buildings. Taught by a practicing archite with many years of experience designing green buildings, the course also features guest lectur ers from complementary fields - landscape architects, hydrologists, recycling contractors and materials specialists. Coursework includes in-class discussion, short essays and longer research projects.

ARCH 740 – Formal Efficiencies
Erick Carcamo – 2017A

The seminar is a discourse based in the use of multi-layered techniques and production processes that allow for control over intelligent geometries, calibration of parts, and behaviora taxonomies, normalizing an innovative field of predictability. Our goal is to explore innovative, potential architectural expressions of the current discourse around form through technique elaboration, material intelligence, formal logic efficiencies and precision assemblies as an ultimate condition of design.

The seminar will develop and investigate the notion of proficient geometric variations at a level of complexity, so that questions towards geometrical effectiveness, accuracy an performance can begin to be understood in a contemporary setting.

ARCH 741 – Architectural Design Innovation
Ali Rahim – 2016C

This seminar will explore systemic thinking and digital design techniques that yield architectura forms that have contributed to the contemporary discourse of architecture.

ARCH 742-- Function of Fashion in Architecture
Danielle Willems 2017A

The Function of Fashion in Architecture will survey the history of fashion and the architectural parallels starting from Ancient Civilization to

nt. The focus will be on the relevance of
ent design, methods and techniques and
potential to redefine current architecture
ents such as envelope, structure, seams,
nics and details. The functional, tectonic
tructural properties of garment design
e explored as generative platforms to
eptualize very specific architectural ele-
s. One of the challenges in the course is
e-invention of a means of assessment, the
opment of notations and techniques that
ocument the forces and the production of
ence in the spatial manifestations of the
rative systems.

ARCH 743 – Form and Algorithm
Cecil Balmond and Ezio Blasetti – 2016C

urse on the philosophy and generative tools
formal design, which is defined in terms
on-Cartesian, non-linear geometries and
rows algorithmic procedures from models
athematics and the physical sciences. The
rse reviews readings on the topic, introduc-
instruction in scripting and assignments
ough which students gain familiarity and skill
specific non-linear models.

ARCH 744 – Digital Fabrication
Ferda Kolatan – 2017A

s seminar course investigates the fabrication
igital structures through the use of rapid
totyping (RP) and computer-aided manufac-
ing (CAM) technologies, which offer the pro-
ction of building components directly from 3D
tal models. In contrast to the industrial-age
adigms of prefabrication and mass produc-
n in architecture, this course focuses on the
velopment of repetitive non-standardized
lding systems (mass-customization) through
itally controlled variation and serial differen-
tion. Various RP and CAM technologies are
roduced with examples of use in contempo-
y building design and construction.

Arch 748- Architecture and the New Elegance
Hina Jamelle – 2017A

e seminar will define and elaborate on the
lowing topics for the digital discourse- the
ntemporary diagram, technique, structure,
chitectural systems and aesthetic projections.
chnological innovations establish new status
os and updated platforms from which to
erate and launch further innovations. Design
search practices continually reinvent them-
lves and the techniques they use to stay ahead
such developments. Reinvention can come
rough techniques that have already been set
motion. Mastery of techniques remains impor-
nt and underpins the use of digital technolo-
es in the design and manufacturing of elegant
ildings. But, ultimately, a highly sophisticated
rmal language propels aesthetics.

ARCH 750 Parafictional Objects
Kutan Ayata – 2017A

This Representation/Design Seminar will start
with series of lectures examining the histories
of Realism in Art spanning from French Realism
of 19th Century through Hyperrealism into
Parafictional Art of the recent past with their
aesthetic provocations at the center of this inquiry. Weekly discussions of the reading material
will be followed by student presentations on as-
signed topics. The design portion of the seminar
will proceed with the generation of "Still Life
bound" objects with parafictional scenarios. The
process will carry through multiple mediums
of image patterning, line drawing, 3D modeling
and surface mapping, exploring the potentials of
cross-medium translations, evaluated through
weekly pin-ups. These objects will then be fabricated to gain physical presence in the world. The
realism of these objects as things in the world
will be further explored through a project in ren-
dering and photocomposition as each object will
be inserted into different Still Life painting.

ARCH 751 – Ecology, Technology, and Design
William Braham – 2016C

The course draws on theories of ecological
design and on the history and philosophy of
technology to examine the complex interaction
between the built and natural environments. The
energy diagramming techniques of HT Odum
are used as a common framework for projects
in the course.

ARCH 753 – Building Performance Simulation
Mostapha Sadeghipour Roudsari – 2016C

The course provides students with an understanding of building design simulation methods,
hands-on experience in using computer simulation models, and exploration of the technologies,
underlying principles, and potential applications
of simulation tools in architecture. Classroom
lectures are given each week, with a series
of analysis projects to provide students with
hands-on experience using computer models.

ARCH 765 – Project Management
Charles Capaldi – 2016C, 2017A

This course is an introduction to techniques and
tools of managing the design and construction
of large, and small, construction projects. Topics
include project delivery systems, management
tools, cost-control and budgeting systems, professional roles. Case studies serve to illustrate
applications. Cost and schedule control systems
are described. Case studies illustrate the application of techniques in the field.

EBRUARY 20TH, 2016
AROQUE TOPOLOGIES

rew Saunders Architect, principal
fessor, PennDesign Dept. of Architecture

roque Topologies" examines the potential of these new methods to redefine
enhance knowledge and understanding of the full spectrum of formal
spatial complexity of Baroque architecture. As the recipient of the
versity of Pennsylvania Research Foundation grant, Saunders traveled
taly to laser scan and amass an archive of some of the most important
an Baroque architecture. The archive includes key works from Francesco
romini, Gian Lorenzo Bernini, Girolamo and Carlo Rainaldi, Pietro da
tona, Guarino Guarini and Bernardo Vittone. The primary Baroque works
ected for analysis can be deciphered as topological variants of the cen-
ly planned church of the Renaissance. The collection demonstrates the
ssoming evolution from the early and high baroque in Rome extending
the late baroque in the Piedmont Region in Northern Italy.

New instruments from inside and outside of the discipline have a direct
uence on the way architecture is designed and realized. "Baroque
ologies" demonstrates their potential to radically redefine our under-
nding of the full spectrum of formal and spatial complexity of Baroque
hitecture. Inherent in this process is a reexamination of the value-laden
ls of contemporary representation and their impact on current
hitectural production.

onsored by Autodesk

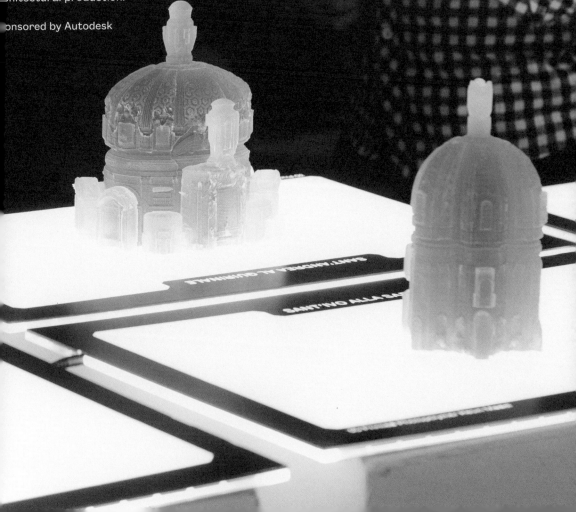

CREDITS & ACKNOWLEDGEMENTS

Publishers of Architecture, Art, and Design
Gordon Goff: Publisher

www.oroeditions.com
info@oroeditions.com

Published by ORO Editions

Design:
WSDIA | WeShouldDoItAll (wsdia.com)
Typefaces: Founders Grotesk Text and Pitch designed by Kris Sowersby of Klim Type Foundry

Editorial Team:
Winka Dubbeldam, Professor and Chair
Scott Loeffler, Department Coordinator
Maria Teicher, Graduate Publicity/Promotion Coordinator

Copy Editor:
Scott Loeffler
Sarah Iam

Project Coordinator: Kirby Anderson

10 9 8 7 6 5 4 3 2 1 First Edition

Library of Congress data available upon request. World Rights: Available

ISBN: 978-1-940743-06-6

Color Separations and Printing: ORO Group Ltd.
Printed in China.

International Distribution: www.oroeditions.com/distribution

ORO Editions makes a continuous effort to minimize the overall carbon footprint of its publications. As part of this goal, ORO Editions, in association with Global ReLeaf, arranges to plant trees to replace those used in the manufacturing of the paper produced for its books. Global ReLeaf is an international campaign run by American Forests, one of the world's oldest nonprofit conservation organizations. Global ReLeaf is America Forests' education and action program that helps individuals, organizations, agencies, and corporations improve the local and global environment by planting and caring for trees.

CREDITS